FIVE FIRES

Other books by David Wyatt

The Fall into Eden: Landscape and Imagination in California
Out of the Sixties: Storytelling and the Vietnam Generation

FIVE FIRES

RACE, CATASTROPHE, AND
THE SHAPING OF CALIFORNIA

DAVID WYATT

ADDISON-WESLEY PUBLISHING COMPANY, INC.
Reading, Massachusetts • Menlo Park, California • New York
Don Mills, Ontario • Harlow, England • Amsterdam • Bonn
Sydney • Singapore • Tokyo • Madrid • San Juan
Paris • Seoul • Milan • Mexico City • Taipei

Many of the designations used by manufacturers and sellers to distinguish their products are claimed as trademarks. Where those designations appear in this book and Addison-Wesley was aware of a trademark claim, the designations have been printed in initial capital letters.

Library of Congress Cataloging-in-Publication Data
Wyatt, David, 1948–
    Five fires : race, catastrophe, and the shaping of California /
David Wyatt.
      p.   cm.
    Includes bibliographical references and index.
    ISBN 0-201-14479-4
    1. California—Race relations.   2. California—History.
3. Culture conflict—California—History.   4. Fires—California—
History.   I. Title.
F870.A1W93   1997
979.4—dc21   96-52723
                                                     CIP

Jacket design by Evan Gaffney
Text design by Dede Cummings
Set in 11½-point Granjon by Pagesetters, Inc.

1 2 3 4 5 6 7 8 9—MA—0100999897
First printing, May 1997

Alice Joy Wyatt
1924–1971

CONTENTS

LIST OF ILLUSTRATIONS

ACKNOWLEDGMENTS

THIS BOOK IS DEDICATED to the memory of my mother, Alice Joy Wyatt. Three friends gave this project essential support. Howard Norman read and reread the manuscript with a writer's care, urging me toward the inimitable. Once I was done, he made the decisive contact with an agent. This book simply would not exist without him.

My two dear Bobs got and kept me going. Bob Schultz helped believe the story into being, when the fires were only four and the project was little more than an extended essay. As the drafts piled up, Bob Kolker firmly and gently edited the argument toward the clarity and consistency of his own good work.

The seven Maryland graduate students—Miranda Crowl, Lynn Erwin, Eric LeMay, Kumari McKie, Joseph Redington, Holly Stewart, Denise Wolitz—who worked so well together in my course on California in the spring of 1995 found a mother lode of documents unknown to me. I am indebted to the thoroughness and ingenuity of their researches. A GRB Research Award from the University of Maryland in support of this project is also gratefully acknowledged, as is the confidence of the Huntington Library and the offer of a fellowship I was obliged to decline.

An old friend—the last from high school—gave up Cape Cod days to scan the text. Thanks to Kate Van Wie for the generous appraisal of a native daughter. Over Christmas of 1995 my father sat in my living room and read through the final draft, piling up the pages neatly on the floor. "It's good," he said. I hope he got as much pleasure from the reading as I did from watching him do it.

My agent, Andrew Blauner, was suave in the approach and tenacious in the event: his confidence in the project did not waver, and his skill in negotiation yielded a happy result. Liz Maguire of Addison-Wesley had the gumption to take a chance on a cross-over book, and, as an academic looking for a new audience, I am grateful to her for taking the gamble. Editor Albert DePetrillo insisted, with intelligence and tact, on the cuts and changes that made *Five Fires* a better book.

My wife, Ann Porotti, willingly read what I gave her. A keen eye for lapses and excesses in the prose was always leavened by her faith, enthusiasm, and loving company.

December 1996
Charlottesville, Virginia

FIVE FIRES

PROLOGUE

I T WAS ROBERT HASS who gave me the idea for this book when he visited Charlottesville in the late 1970s. I knew Hass as the author of *Field Guide,* a book of surpassingly beautiful poems about living a good life on the Pacific edge of things. It turned out that he had also spent some time in the East, teaching at Virginia. In a poem written around the time of our meeting, called "Old Dominion," he remembers the *thwack* of tennis balls, the sad odor of honeysuckle, and the sense of a place where everything is easy but wrong. He makes a resolution "not to stay in the South." He got out, returned to the fog and the watery light and walking through scrub oak to the sea. Later he became poet laureate of the United States. I stayed in Charlottesville, hiked the Blue Ridge, and wrote mostly about the place both Hass and I called home.

At the College Inn, over our barbecue platters, Hass said that there was a good book to be written about California called *Four Fires.* The book would tell the story of the four events that swept—like a fire—through California to leave a dramatically altered physical and cultural landscape. The first was the inadvertent importation, in the 1770s, of the Spanish wild oat. Three fires followed: the Gold Rush, the San Francisco earthquake and fire, and World War II. The sequence of events argued for a catastrophic history of violent and consuming surprise.

As a native Californian already at work on a literary history of the state, I immediately grasped and coveted the elegance of the scheme. It provided a way of condensing California's story into a pattern as ordered and economical as a poem, a poem with a central metaphor and a pattern of recurrence. "Fire" fit because every summer California is the site of the nation's most astonishing conflagrations; as Joan Didion writes in *Slouching Towards Bethlehem,* "The city burning is Los Angeles's deepest image

1

of itself." To apply the metaphor of fire to events like the Gold Rush and
World War II was also to conceive of California as demanding and
developing a certain kind of citizen. These moments of catastrophe could
be read as moments of creation, events that call forth the sheer power of
Californians to adapt and to survive.

Hass generously bequeathed me his idea; it was a book he would never
write. In the years since we talked, it has become clear that Hass's poem
owned a built-in momentum that predicted and even required a further
rhyme. The logic of the sequence argued for a fifth fire. I think that there
was a fifth fire, and that it dramatically erupted in Watts in 1965. It is the
fire of race, and it is still burning.

The fifth fire has in fact burned from the beginning of California's
recorded history through all the others. As I read more deeply into the
literature and history of the state, I began to see that no issue has shaped
life there more powerfully than the mix of peoples. The Gold Rush
produced, for instance, the most multicultural society the United States
had ever seen. The result was collision rather than community. Writing
from the mines in 1852, Louise Clappe invoked California's past and
anticipated its future when she referred to a race riot between the
Spaniards and the Americans as "the entire catastrophe." As the world
rushed in, peopling the state with Chinese, French, Chilean, and Scan-
dinavian argonauts, the Foreign Miners' Tax, miscegenation laws, and
anticoolie labor organizations began to formalize the violent distinction
between an American self and an immigrating other.

As a student of the literature of California, I knew that the dilemmas and
conflicts arising from race have found significant and transforming expression. While the facts on the ground may be catastrophic, books like Clappe's
create a countervailing reality, a reality called storytelling, where power is
discovered and borders are crossed. The project that opened up before me
was to locate the works of imagination that not only state vividly the problem
of race in California but that propose—through their tones, forms, images,
and strategies of narrative—ways of dealing with it. The works I explore
offer us, above all, the chance to feel our way into the heart of California's
history and to exchange distance and judgment for recognition and empathy.

HISTORIES OF CALIFORNIA often position Richard Henry Dana as the lead-
off hitter, the first serious Anglo-American writer to head west and

bring back arresting news. Even the Californians of the 1850s agreed about Dana's priority: on his second visit, twenty-four years after sailing west before the mast, Dana is greeted everywhere as the author, the man who had converted the raw material of the Mexican colony into a satisfactory text. In a hotel in San Francisco—the year is 1859—Dana meets a fellow pioneer who remembers him and speaks of his book. "I found that almost—I might perhaps say quite—every American in California had read it," Dana writes, "for when California 'broke out,' as the phrase is, in 1848, and so large a portion of the Anglo-Saxon race flocked to it, there was no book upon California but mine."

In his study of American literature, D. H. Lawrence gives Dana an entire chapter. "His style is great and helpless, the style of a perfect tragic recorder," he writes. Lawrence was drawn to Dana for the accuracy of his observations and for the power of his voice. *Two Years Before the Mast* became for him a key exhibit in the construction of the American West, and its claim to be verifiable history could not be separated from its status as a work of the imagination. In the pages that follow, I also assume that the most compelling writing about California reveals its truth through and because of its *style*.

Dana's book received pride of place in my first book on California, the one I wrote *instead* of the book proposed by Bob Hass. My subject was landscape and imagination. I saw Dana as a man who was happy in the routine at sea but uneasy and haunted on land. He seemed to like solitary objects: the indigo iceberg that thundered with its cracking mass, the albatross asleep among the waves off Cape Horn, the lonely spot off San Juan Capistrano where, sitting alone, he felt his better nature return upon him. Solitude for this writer was the defining characteristic. There was little coincidence in my beginning with him; like Dana, I was drawn to the vacant spirit in empty space—to the self alone in a landscape—and shied away from the unmanageable fact that California was and is full of people.

By shifting the register only slightly, I might have seen that Dana himself depicts the California of the mid-1830s as the site of a rich cultural *"melange."* Not Mexican California: his emotions in that direction involve mostly scorn. "Lazy" is an epithet he resorts to more than once; the Californians at Santa Barbara scarcely seem to earn their sunlight. No one appears to *work:* cattle roam about freely, and when a horse is required, it is chased down and saddled. An operatic finery of dress is offset by the absence of interior design: the grandest Don occupies a small, unfurnished adobe house with a dirt floor. The women radiate a disturbing sensuality, their bare arms and dresses loose about the waist an inducement to the frequent drawing of a knife. At the big society wedding Dana attends, the young women taunt the male guests by stealthily approaching them from behind and cracking on their offered heads eggshells filled with cologne.

It is not California's settlers but her visitors that elicit Dana's positive attention. These include mostly sailors, like the "fine specimen of manly beauty," Bill Jackson, with a chest tattoo that reads "Parting moments," above a girl and a sailor lover taking their farewell; or the great calculator Tom Harris, who carries not only an entire logbook of the voyage in his head but a full inventory of the cargo as well. These were Englishmen, sharers of Dana's birth language. What he also finds on his voyage, as Ishmael would some twenty years later, is a kind of model United Nations, a floating world's fair of peoples and tongues.

During the months he spends curing hides at San Diego, Dana passes the evenings going from house to house, after the crews anchored there have come ashore, listening to "all manner of languages":

> The Spanish was the common ground upon which we all met; for every one knew more or less of that. We had now, out of forty or fifty, representatives from almost every nation under the sun: Two Englishmen, three Yankees, two Scotchmen, two Welshmen, one Irishman, three Frenchmen (two of whom were Normans, and the third from Gascony), one Dutchman, one Austrian, two or three Spaniards, (from old Spain,) half a dozen Spanish-Americans and half-breeds, two native Indians from Chili and the Island of Chiloe, one Negro, one Mulatto, about twenty Italians, from all parts of Italy, as many more Sandwich Islanders, one Otaheitan, and one Kanaka from the Marquesas Islands.

The night before the vessels sail, the European and American sailors unite for an entertainment. Through the warm California darkness echo strains of "Och! mein lieber Augustin!" "Rule Britannia," Spanish and Italian airs, "The Star-Spangled Banner," and "The Marseillaise."

Dana's favorite exotic is the Sandwich Islander, Hope. The men from Hawaii were essential to the hide trade, since only they had the skill to surf the landing boats over California's rough waves and into her nonexistent harbors. During the four months Dana lives on the beach, he and

Hope are continually together, tanning hides, hewing wood, drawing water. When the tobacco is passed, Dana learns to take the huge "Oahu puffs" that can serve the smoker for the better part of an hour. He comes to feel a strong affection for Hope and to prefer him to his own country-men. "Every Kanaka has one particular friend," Dana writes, "whom he considers himself bound to do everything for, and with whom he has a sort of contract. . . . This friend they call *aikane;* and for such, did Hope adopt me."

Dana sails north to Santa Barbara and Monterey, returning to San Diego some six months later. There he finds Hope dying, his eyes sunken, his hands like claws. Dana fights his way through the protocol surround-ing the medicine chest, has a recipe drawn up, and delivers his balm. Then he sails away again, hardly expecting that Hope will live. On a visit two months later he finds Hope decidedly better, and on the Sunday before his final sailing, Dana pays the invalid his last visit. He admits feeling for this man "such as I never before felt but for a near relation." The recovery has begun, and Hope shakes Dana by the hand and promises to be well and ready to work for him when he again comes upon the coast. Dana sails for home the following week. Taking leave of his Kanaka friends, he admits, "was the only thing connected with leaving California which was in any way unpleasant."

An astonishing exchange occurs here, although while I was writing *The Fall into Eden,* I was not prepared to notice it. Dana has been seen as holding himself apart from California, as a kind of Brahmin tourist, and I followed those who read his story as a captivity narrative rather than a romance of conversion. But Dana had in fact provided ample evidence that California did then, as it does now, solicit the "positively alone" self into forms of unlooked-for and ecstatic communion. It was and is a place where borders meet and can drop away.

"The single body corresponded well with the solitary character of everything around": this is Dana, early after his arrival in California, brooding on the remains of a lone Englishman buried at Dead Man's Island, off San Pedro. It is the "only thing in California," he maintains, "from which I could ever extract anything like poetry." Inattentive to or ill at ease about the poetry in his relationship with Hope, Dana depreciates the value of his human encounters on what he calls the "hated coast" and emphasizes instead his scorn, homesickness, and self-reliance. That he so profoundly misses the point *is* the point, since *Two Years Before the Mast* has, with its comforting and familiar melodrama of beset manhood in an alien land, drawn in so many readers. I was happy to be one of those readers. It has taken me ten years, and a lot more reading, to see that Dana's book also pays tribute to a California that permits a kind of Esperanto of the spirit, its comminglings so profound that there one can even change one's skin, as Dana realizes on sailing home into Boston Harbor, in the moment he discovers his "face burnt as black as an Indian's."

Dana was a designer immigrant; a Harvard sophomore, he voluntarily shipped out for California as a common sailor before the mast in order to cure a weakness of the eyes, then pulled rank on the captain who threatened to extend his stay by reminding him of his upper-class Boston origins. On his return to Harvard, he slipped back into the life onshore that he was to call a mistake. California had provided him with the chance to escape illness, class, sexual repression, and even the look of his body, and the book he produced about that ecstatic interval became, he was to recognize, the major achievement of his life. *Two Years Before the Mast* discovers California as the site of an unimaginable yet deeply desired act of crossing over, an experience that Dana sampled but one to which he could not, finally, surrender.

CALIFORNIA REMAINS THE PLACE where Americans draw the battle lines over difference. It is an old story; California's first professional historian, working in the 1870s, had the foresight to intuit this abiding theme. Hubert Howe Bancroft began his massive history of the Pacific states with a chapter on race, in which he concluded "that there are no absolute lines of separation between the various members of the human family." Even as Bancroft expressed this liberal hope, the lines were being drawn. The Chinese who came to California for the mines and who remained to build the railroads and the levees were rewarded, in 1882, with the Exclusion Act. The Japanese who replaced the Chinese workers in California's orchards and fields were locked out, in the first decade of the century, by the "Gentleman's Agreement." Mexican workers were imported during World War I and throughout the 1920s as a cheap source of agricultural and industrial labor. When the Depression hit, they were repatriated. Blacks poured into Los Angeles during the next war, found work, and were then barred from participation in the larger culture many of the most vivid responses to the conflicts and losses of California life.

From its beginnings, writing about California has been a deeply metaphorical enterprise, a continuing and contested act of the imagination. The fire metaphor operates throughout these chapters as a figure for consuming cultural events:

- The wild oat invaded California along with the Spanish and created the golden hills that so readily, every summer, burst into flame. It could quickly and thoroughly root itself because the native bunchgrasses it displaced grew less thickly on the ground. The human story that this botanical process parallels is the displacement of the region's native peoples—first the Indians by the Spanish after 1771, and second the Californios by invaders from the United States after 1846.

- The Gold Rush was an epoch of many actual and catastrophic fires—San Francisco burned three times between December 1849 and June 1850—as well as sudden social and environmental change. In the foothills of the Sierra, whole towns rose like exhalations and entire mountains were washed away. The real rush was less of gold out of the hills than of young men into the state— a population explosion that in its gender imbalance and unprecedented mix of peoples created an inflammable and easily romanticized frontier.

- The San Francisco earthquake produced California's most spectacular fire, one that burned the core of the city during three days in 1906. The material spectacle of the fire obscured its more profound social effects: the destruction of Chinatown; the loss of the municipal records and the consequent opening of the Angel Island immigration center; the emergence of photography as a substitute for being on the spot; and the steady eclipse of San Francisco by Los Angeles as the state's preeminent city.

- World War II compelled Los Angeles to become the nation's forge and hearth. As fire power was exported abroad, an industrial base was solidified at home. Production for war underwrote the economy, but it also unsettled the region's peace—by exploiting an immigrating black population in the Southland's aircraft hangars and shipyards, by importing millions of braceros despite their expatriation during the Depression, and by officially sanctioning an attack by a group of young men wearing uniforms on a group of young men dressed in zoot suits.

by restrictive covenants and the patterns of inner-city development
Meanwhile the Japanese, who had steadily increased their numbers sinc
the turn of the century, were sent to Manzanar.

If this is a book primarily about race, why then call it *Five Fires*
Because fire is part of the metaphor of catastrophe that controls so man
narratives about the Golden State. "It's all falling or burning," Gar
Snyder chants in his 1960 *Myths & Texts,* and the sense of this as a peculia
California sentiment—his resigned Zen proverb links earthquake an
fire—emerges from a close reading of the texts that have created the myt
of the state. As a metaphor, fire can obscure as much as it reveal
especially by distracting our attention from the sources of human confli
and shifting it toward arresting spectacles. The willful abstraction o
events from both their causes and their consequences repeats itself even i
accounts of California's natural disasters. Perhaps the single most impo:
tant political consequence of the Great Earthquake and Fire, for exampl
was the burning of the municipal records that controlled the highl
restricted flow of Chinese immigrants into San Francisco. The loss o
these records made it possible for a new generation of immigrants—o
"paper sons," as they came to be called—to construct fictional genealogi
that linked them to Chinese already living in the United States an
therefore to enter the country. "Every China Man was reborn out of th
fire a citizen," Maxine Hong Kingston writes in *China Men.* Yet ou
popular renditions of this catastrophe convert it into an operetta, th
purpose of which is to knock enough sense into Clark Gable to make hi:
realize, as he does at the end of *San Francisco,* that he really does lo
Jeanette MacDonald.

While race is the core of the California story, it is by no mea:
the whole of it. The "othering" of Californians as different because
their heritage or physical aspect is implicated with all the defensi
behaviors by which Californians establish and keep their distance. Tv
of these behaviors deserve special mention. The first is the treatment
women, or "the sex," as Bret Harte called those people who are n
male. Race often gives way to gender as a shaping and intransigent fa
in the California experience, especially within marginalized comm
nities. The second behavior is the peculiarly overdeveloped ability
Californians to frame experience as spectacle. The abstraction of so
from scene—along with the conversion of the world from a surroun
ing that might be changed into a prospect that is to be viewed—typifi

• From Watts to South Central: the words mark a sense of disturbing and amplifying repetition. The Los Angeles riots of 1965 and 1992 burned both property and hope: as these fires destroyed, they also expressed. Even the official reports treated fire as a metaphor for an internal condition as well as a label for the external event; when a black member of the investigating McCone Commission wrote of people "sweltering in ghettos," he invoked a more than physical heat. The most compelling accounts of the riots asked not why they happened but how they felt. This feeling can be most fully entered into by reading the words of participants like Stacey Koon and Luis Rodriguez, or of empathetic listeners like Anna Deavere Smith.

While this survey of California's "five fires" sketches in the outline of my project, it does not fully account for its eventual shape. As fire became, in my thinking, a metaphor for the emotions kindled by race, two additional chapters suggested themselves. The first, on the Chinese, bridges the largely anti-Mexican Gold Rush and the virulently anti-Chinese decades of the late nineteenth century. The second, on the Japanese, traces these sentiments into the twentieth century and their modification as they were transferred onto a wholly different set of immigrants whose "oriental" origin rationalized a unique suspension of their civil rights. Chapter 5, on the building of the Los Angeles Aqueduct, serves as a transition from the chapters devoted primarily to Northern California to those dealing with the emergence of the military-industrial complex in the south—a culture that had its birth not in fire but out of water.

IN TELLING A CATASTROPHIC HISTORY of California—and especially one conditioned by the trauma of race—I have endeavored to let many voices speak: this is a history mediated by literature. The brief autobiographical passages scattered throughout are meant to suggest that I see myself as not above but in the story. The model is Dana's shipboard chorus—or, a century and a half later, the echoing monologues of Anna Deavere Smith's *Twilight*. As the most populous and the most variegated state in our union, California has inspired, in its writers, artists, and audiences, a commitment to forms that are *many-voiced*. The challenge is to experience these voices as a dialogue rather than as a riot of tongues, as complex and moving testimony to the human capacity for adaptation and resistance.

CHAPTER ONE

THE WILD OAT

The Spanish and American Conquests

THE SPANISH WHO INVADED California in 1769 and the Americans who displaced them in the 1840s were both gold-seeking cultures. Only the second wave of conquest found what it was looking for. But while the Spanish dreams were certainly material, their most vivid legacy was spiritual. The two secular institutions they imported were the presidio, which housed the military, and the rancho, the key unit of the civilian economy. Neither matched, in either influence or reach, the Franciscan missions. These twenty-one sites witnessed one of the most systematic of all the European attempts to convert and order the energies of Native American peoples: for six decades the missions controlled the lives of some 90,000 souls. Christianized Indians were trained in Spanish and taught how to farm and build with adobe; more than 24,000 were joined together in Catholic marriage. Broken up and abandoned in the 1830s, after California passed from Spain to Mexico, the missions devolved into romantic ruins, sites on which writers like Bret Harte could focus a longing for the "delicious monotony" of colonial rule.

As emblem of the Spanish and Mexican period in California history, the wild oat serves to remind us that the survivals from that period have little to do with imperial designs. The oat arrived by accident, and it worked its changes quietly, enduring through all the subsequent immigrations. Installing itself as an irrepressible though undramatic presence, it marked California as no longer the province of the "native." Viewed as

11

the marker of historical change, the oat betokens the violent displacements that resulted from the arrival of the Spanish and the persistence of
the Mexican legacy after New Spain was in turn displaced by the American conquest.

This chapter deals with the years in which the wild oat took sway. In it,
I interweave the words and stories of five California writers: Juan Crespi,
the Franciscan who discovered San Francisco Bay; John Charles Frémont, the spearhead of the American conquest; Mariano Vallejo, first
citizen of Mexican California at the time of the Bear Flag Revolt; Juana
Machado, a native of San Diego who lived through and wrote about Alta
California's two "changes of flags"; and Pablo Tac, a Luiseño Indian born
near Oceanside who, in his travels and his mastery of many tongues,
defined the cultural and political borders that Native Americans who
survived the conquests were so rarely able to cross.

THE ENTRY ON PAGE 1514 of *A California Flora* reads as follows:

> A. barbata Brot. SLENDER WILD OAT . . . —Common weed in waste fields
> and on open slopes, largely replacing native grasses; native of Old
> World.

Philip Munz here condenses a drama of eighty years into a sentence
fragment. The wild oat accompanied the first post-Columbian immigration to Alta California, and its spread corresponded to the decline of the
Indian population of the region, an area that had contained more people
than any other in prehistoric North America. The oat introduced itself into a geography that was home to the continent's largest number
of microclimates and Native American language groups. The people of
Indian California spoke 113 known dialects, although these languages
did not memorialize themselves in any written record. Their final word
may have been spoken by Ishi, California's last "wild" Indian. As he lay
near death in 1916, he turned to his friends and said, in English, "You
stay, I go."

The largely uncultivated California that the Spanish invaded was to
become, in little over a hundred years, the most productive agricultural
region in the world. Tribes along the Colorado River had planted corn,
beans, and pumpkin, but agriculture entered California on a systematic

scale only with the mission fathers, who brought grapes, orchard fruits, grains, and livestock.
Beyond the small areas of mission
control lay the vast plains and
foothills of the Central Valley,
home to hundreds of species of
wildflowers and dense thickets of
chaparral; the Coast Range and
the Sierra, with their madrone,
live oak, sugar pine, and red-
wood; the Mojave and Colorado
Deserts, dotted with greasewood
or Joshua trees; and the hundreds
of microclimates that might support azalea, snake cholla, or the
Santa Cruz pine.

California's plant life has consistently mocked conventional
notions of abundance and scale.
In the 1840s Lansford Hastings
rode, he claimed, through thousands of acres covered with oats
six feet high. A wheat farmer of
his acquaintance "received one
hundred and twenty bushels to
the acre" and harvested in the
next year, from the same ground,
sixty bushels that came up sponta-
neously. Hastings's testimony is
perhaps not to be trusted; his own
Emigrant's Guide lured the Donner Party to disaster by recommending a cut-off he had never
ridden. The more sober Bayard

*Ishi on the day he was captured near Oroville,
August 29, 1911. He had lived for two years
without a human companion. Placed under
the care of Alfred and Theodora Kroeber, he
was taken to San Francisco, where he worked
as a janitor in the University of California
Museum of Anthropology. In the years he
lived with the Kroebers, he never revealed his
private name; Ishi means, simply, "man."
Courtesy of the Phoebe A. Hearst Museum of
Anthropology, University of California at
Berkeley.*

Taylor weighed in, however, with his own tale of California as "the
Brobdignag of the vegetable world," citing apples and pears weighing
three pounds apiece. At an 1859 San Francisco horticultural fair, he

wandered through piles of onions as large as his head: "Upon one table lay a huge, dark-red object, about the thickness of my body. At a distance, I took it for the trunk of some curious tree; but on approaching nearer, I saw that it was a *single beet,* weighing 115 pounds." According to Taylor, the owner of the beet had planted it in the spring of 1858. After the harvest he planted the beet again the following spring, hoping to obtain seed from the specimen. But the beet "devoted all its energies to growing bigger" and refused to go to seed.

More than two hundred commercial crops were developed in twentieth-century California. On a piece of land near Santa Rosa were "perhaps grown a greater number of varieties of plants from regions near and remote than were ever elsewhere grown on any four acres of the earth's surface." The words are those of Luther Burbank, the intrepid California Mendel. Burbank, who immigrated to California in 1875, brought with him ten tubers of the Burbank potato, a strain he had developed out of his obsession with engineered versions of fruits, flowers, and vegetables. Burbank imagined an utterly plastic botany; he would cross-graft or cross-pollinate anything. The pamphlet series he inaugurated in 1893 detailed promiscuous experiments that led to the plumcot (a cross between a plum and an apricot), the spineless cactus, and the Shasta daisy.

Luther Burbank in the 1920s among his poppies on his experimental farm at Santa Rosa. A furious hybridizer, Burbank developed more than forty new plums and prunes, as well as successful variants of berries, lilies, roses, peas, and corn. He broadcast his findings in a series of pamphlets called New Creations *(1893–1901). Courtesy of the Library of Congress.*

Burbank ambitiously imported seeds and cuttings from Japan. When it came to people, however, he recoiled from intermingling. Writing in the wake of World War I, he argued that "it becomes at least a very serious question as to whether the recent altogether unprecedented influx of immigrants of many widely divergent races are not supplying material that, blended with the existing American stock, may produce results as startling and on the whole of as doubtful value as those produced among plants indiscriminately hybridized." The man who shipped thousands of plant species into California and mingled them with such abandon could not extend the same encouragement when it came to the "human plant."

In the sequoia gigantea and the bristlecone pine, California lays claim to the world's largest and oldest living things. Its hospitality to vegetable growth was to elevate California, by the 1940s, to the position of the nation's major farming state. Agricultural dominance came quickly: for a time during the 1870s, California was the nation's largest wheat producer. In 1900 it grew 95 percent of the nation's apricots. During World War I Mexican workers were imported to harvest the cotton, which, in the 1970s, would become the state's largest cash crop. In 1923 California produced 60 percent of the world's raisins. During these years Los Angeles and Orange Counties became the richest agricultural counties in the United States, with the value of their dairy and livestock products vying with that of their citrus crops.

The status crops were oranges and grapes, and I spent my childhood among them. I was born in South Central Los Angeles in 1948 and grew up in the tinder-dry summers of San Bernardino. Located sixty miles due east of Los Angeles, the town of some 100,000 was known as the hub of the "Inland Empire." San Berdoo was a town one passed through, on the road over Cajon Pass from the Mojave Desert or on the Santa Fe railway tracks, which began in Kansas. People knew the San Bernardino Valley as the spawning ground of the Hell's Angels or as host to the row of whorehouses on D Street to which notables like Allan Sherman might drive out from L.A. Our town was also home to the first McDonald's and to the National Orange Show. The show featured huge human figures—I seem to remember one of Rita Hayworth—constructed entirely out of citrus fruit. In 1957, when my parents moved to a new development in the tablelands above the city, the yellow stucco house we bought for $11,000 had been built in a recently tractored orange grove. To the east the bright green trees still filled the view, but the houses moved steadily eastward and by the time I graduated from high school the groves were gone.

As a boy, I drove by one of the two original navel orange trees that still stood, gnarled and gigantic, behind an iron fence on Magnolia Avenue. In

1873 Luther and Eliza Tibbets had rooted California's first navels in a field near Riverside. The trees had come from Bahia, Brazil, and were of a type known as the Washington navel. A missionary in Brazil had sent the original budwood to William Saunders of the Department of Agriculture, who in turn had shipped two trees to the Tibbetses. Three years later, A. B. Chapman of San Gabriel introduced the Valencia orange to California. A seedless orange that ripened in winter and a juice orange that ripened in the fall and summer soon established California as the nation's leading supplier of citrus fruit.

California's modern viticulture dates from the arrival in 1849 of a Hungarian immigrant named Agoston Haraszthy. After a sojourn in San Diego, Haraszthy moved north to San Francisco and bought land near Mission Dolores, where he planted the muscat grape, the foundation of the state's raisin industry. He had also brought with him the cuttings of a grape named zinfandel. But the cool, foggy summers on the bay persuaded Haraszthy that he had not yet found the best site for a vineyard.

Champagne corking at the Buena Vista Winery near Sonoma in the early 1870s. Founded by Hungarian immigrant Agoston Haraszthy in 1858, Buena Vista was supported by the state's first large commercial vineyard. The baskets in the foreground were woven by Chinese workers. Photograph by Eadweard Muybridge. Courtesy of the National Archives.

After sampling the wines produced by Mariano Vallejo in Sonoma, he bought several hundred acres from him, calling his vineyard Buena Vista. When, in 1861, the state legislature appointed him commissioner of grape-growing and sent him to Europe, the future not only of California's but of Europe's wine industry was assured.

Like the wild oat, grapes were an import from Europe. But while *Avena barbata* simply colonized the New World hills and valleys, the root stock brought by Haraszthy would recolonize its continent of origin. In *Grape Culture,* published in 1862 after his return to California, Haraszthy claims to have "purchased in different parts of Europe over 100,000 vines." Sacramento refused to finance the distribution of these vines, and most were lost or scattered. But the techniques Haraszthy developed, along with his insistence on going beyond the mission grape, ensured that California would develop a stable and complex wine industry. When in the 1870s the grapevines of France were destroyed by phylloxera, a plant louse, it was the immune California root stock that helped replant the vineyards of Burgundy and Bordeaux. This cross-fertilization was anticipated by the double wedding, in 1862, of Haraszthy's two sons to Vallejo's twin daughters.

By the time I arrived on the scene, the vineyards in our part of the state had long since entered into decline. Hot southern California weather grew a grape too sweet, and the industry had moved north to Napa, Sonoma, and Modesto. On the drive from San Bernardino to Los Angeles, we often followed Highland Avenue or Foothill Boulevard through the dips and rises of a vast drainage filled with stream boulders, along the eucalyptus windbreaks that paralleled the high mountains to the north, past fields of dried-up grapevines writhing in the sun. Most of the wineries were melting back into the earth; it was as close as we came to ruins. My mother was killed on one of those roads, when I was twenty-two, and on the way back from inspecting the scene of the accident on a sunny October day, my father spotted a winery that looked open. "Let's get some wine," he said. He pulled into a ramshackle courtyard; in the center of it stood a sinister purple cone. As a man made his way to the car I watched the cone billow with reflected light; it was a pile of grape skins, ten feet high. My father asked for some wine. "Sorry, mister," the man said, "all we make is vinegar."

LIKE SO MANY IMMIGRATIONS to California, that of the wild oat was neither advertant nor licit. In *An Island Called California,* Elna Bakker likens the arrival of this opportunistic annual grass to an "invasion" and a "catastrophe." Before the Spanish, California had been host to shoulder-high native grasses that covered foothill and valley in a striking but delicate pattern, punctuated in spring and summer by an eruption of wildflowers: the yellow mustard, the purple gilia, the white sage. In the wake of the white man's arrival, immigrating species radically and quickly altered this plant community. Chaparral and forests resisted the invasion, and in some places they have held their own even against fire and development. But California's grasslands underwent a vast, unheralded reseeding. "No other plant community in Western North America," Bakker writes, "has changed so much, over such large areas, and in so short a period of time."

So began the chain of displacements that would mark California's postconquest history. The wild oat came to dominate native and imported weeds and grasses and changed the look of the place. "When mother nature started sowing her ancient Mediterranean wild oats over coastal California," Edgar Anderson writes, "she set the landscape pattern for years to come. It is the wild oats which grow so quickly after the rains have come. . . . It is these little oat glumes (the chaff around the grains) which, by the million of millions, make the coastal hills glisten in the sun. . . . it is these delicate and graceful grasses, ripened to tinder, which are one of the chief California fire hazards."

It can be argued that *Avena barbata* is the most opportunistic and successful immigrant ever to have entered California. It is a "wild oat" seed that Steinbeck's famous turtle catches under his shell, drags a distance, and deposits under a scraping of earth in the third chapter of *The Grapes of Wrath,* thus prefiguring the Joads' transplantation from Oklahoma to California. But long before that jalopy set out on Route 66, the wild oat had done its landscape-altering work.

When and how did the wild oat arrive? Most likely with the Spanish, in the 1770s. Anderson speculates that the oat entered California in the hay that the Spaniards brought for their stock animals, or in the seeds of field crops. Perhaps a few panicles slipped in with mud that was caked on cargo or in piles of discarded ballast. Once it had arrived, however, the movement of horses and cattle into the small interior valleys sped the oat's progress. By the time Joseph Walker and Zenas Leonard came across the Sierra in 1833, the oat had largely replaced the native perennial bunchgrasses in the San Joaquin Valley and so allowed newcomers to envision the "entire Central Valley as a great grassland." As invaders from the United States began to rove the valley, they helped complete the oat's conquest. In *The Resources of California* (1863), John Hittell observed that "the wild oat, in the year 1835, was found only south of the bay of San Francisco; but about that time, when the white men crossed frequently from the southern to the northern side of the bay, the oat was sown in a natural way by horses and cattle, and it spread rapidly over the Sacramento Valley and the coast region." The Spanish had unknowingly planted the oat, and the arrivals from the United States harvested it. The pattern thus set by the first "fire" was that each "catastrophe" made way for the next.

IF THIS BOTANICAL PROCESS has a human voice, it is that of Father Juan Crespi, the Spanish explorer who was to sow but not to reap. For more than two hundred years the Spanish "discovery" of Alta California—Cabrillo had entered San Diego and Monterey Bays in 1542—lay fallow. The expulsion of the Jesuits from New Spain in 1767 and the appointment of José de Gálvez as *visitador-general* opened the way for the Franciscans to move north from Mexico. In 1769 the Sacred Expedition entered California by land and founded Mission San Diego. Some fifty years of Spanish rule followed, to be ended by the Mexican revolution of 1821. In 1846 the burgeoning American presence culminated in the Bear Flag Revolt; in 1850 California was admitted to the Union.

Crespi was one of the most diligent recorders of the Spanish arrival in California. He marched with Captain Fernando Rivera and twenty-six soldiers in leather jackets in the first overland party to reach San Diego. They arrived on May 14, 1769. Meanwhile, the first Spanish ship had entered the port on April 11, under the command of Lieutenant Pedro Fages. Gaspar de Portolá, the overall commander of the Sacred Expedition, arrived in San Diego by land in late June. Two weeks later Portolá, Fages, and Crespi struck north for Monterey. A century and a half earlier, in 1602, Sebastián Vizcaíno had surveyed the bay but had, in Herbert Bolton's words, "over-advertised" it. So the later explorers, on their arrival at the much-praised bay, therefore failed to recognize it. Heading north, they stumbled on an even more impressive body of water, at a place they were to call San Francisco.

Crespi's letters to Mexico transform the first expedition to Monterey— and by extension, the Spanish experience of California—into a fable of missed opportunity. San Francisco never became a port that mattered to the Spanish, as Dana later made clear in "Twenty-Four Years After." In 1859 he observed that it had taken only a few years to transform the emptiness of Yerba Buena, the original settlement in the bay, into a "city of one hundred thousand inhabitants." Twenty-three years earlier, in the winter of 1835–36, during his first voyage to California, Dana's ship had floated into the Bay of San Francisco. It was a vast solitude. "Some five or six miles beyond the landing-place, to the right, was a ruinous Presidio, and some three or four miles to the left was the Mission of Dolores, as ruinous as the Presidio, almost deserted, with but four Indians attached to it, and but little property in cattle. Over a region far beyond our sight there were no other human habitations, except that an enterprising Yankee, years in advance of his time, had put up, on the rising ground above the landing, a shanty of rough boards, where he carried on a very small retail trade between the hide ships and the Indians." The Spanish had discovered San Francisco Bay, but as Dana's empty panorama makes clear, they did not develop it. A year after Crespi discovered the bay in 1769, a second expedition did locate Monterey and founded the Mission of San Carlos there. The prize had been won, and the capital of California was situated on a harbor far inferior to the one farther north, which sat in sleepy anonymity for eighty years more.

Crespi's letter to Francisco Palóu, the president of Baja California, gives a swift summary, in Bolton's translation, of the discovery of San Francisco Bay:

> Now I will tell your Reverence how on the 14th of July of last year, '69, we left this port of San Diego, traveling by land with faces toward the north, to go in search of the much praised port of Monterey. On the 14th of January of the present year we all arrived again on our return, having gone to the parallel of thirty-eight degrees, where lies the port of San Francisco. However, that of Monterey has become invisible to us, and we did not find it anywhere throughout the journey. And judging from what we saw all along the coast, using the greatest care that it was possible to observe and that your Reverence can think of, we did not find the port of Monterey before we came upon that of

San Francisco, which is a very noble and very large harbor and is on the
parallel of thirty-eight degrees, as I said. We were at that port about seven
days, and I will go on explaining with all detail what we saw and explored up
to that place. Unless the port of Monterey is beyond thirty-eight degrees (and
then all the accounts and Cabrera would be proved wrong, which can hardly
be believed, since we saw very clearly all that Cabrera in particular says of the
coast, with as much exactitude as if he had been with us and told it to us) that is
the place. Therefore, the best and most careful conclusion that we could come
to is that Monterey has been lost or the land swallowed up.

Monterey has been lost or the land swallowed up. For a writer so given to
precise and modest notation ("I am greatly in need of some handkerchiefs
for the dust; four or six might be sent, since they are so far away—thick
ones from La Puebla"), this surmise expresses a nearly intolerable embar-
rassment. We did not miss Monterey; it must have been "swallowed up."

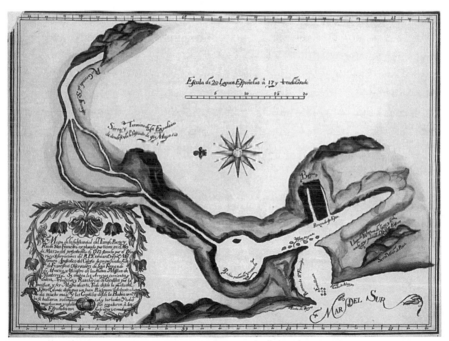

*Father Juan Crespi's map of the San Francisco Bay, 1772. Crespi entered California with
the Sacred Expedition of 1769 and accidentally discovered the bay—he was looking for
Monterey—with Portolá later that year. The map gives a fairly accurate picture of the
opening of the bay at the Golden Gate, as well as its extension south toward San Jose
and north toward Vallejo. Courtesy of the Bancroft Library.*

Some sixty years later, Zenas Leonard would also find himself overcome by California plenitude. As his party made the first east-west
crossing of the Sierra Nevada in 1833, it encountered "deep chasms" and
"incredibly large" trees. "We spent no time in idleness," Leonard assures
his reader, "scarcely stopping in our journey to view an occasional specimen of nature's handy-work." These mountain men had stumbled on
Yosemite Valley and the *Sequoia gigantea*. Leonard's goal, like Crespi's,
was also Monterey—rather than something he might find along the
way—and he too refused to allow himself to be sidetracked. His lack of
digressive vision ensured that the Yosemite would have to be redis-
covered, as it was in 1851 by a so-called "battalion" of white men who
wandered into the defile while trying to remove some recalcitrant
Indians.

For Crespi, getting lost in natural space led to a moment of chagrin
followed by an act of substitution. To displace the seeming failure of his
journey, he offered up San Francisco as a substitute for Monterey: "if the
ships do not find the port of Monterey after a time, a thing I doubt
completely since it was sought by so many eyes and with so much care,
inasmuch as the whole undertaking depended on it, we have in place of
it this fine bay of San Francisco." Conquest by metonymy; Crespi has
asked his superior to accept as token of success not the thing sought but
the thing next to it. He had in fact found what he ought to have been
looking for in the first place. But Crespi's culture proved unable to
overcome its fascination with "over-advertised" Monterey, and a disin-
clination to capitalize on the potential worth of this and other dis-
coveries—Francisco Lopez did, after all, discover gold in Placerita
Canyon in 1842—was to mark the Spanish and Mexican occupation of
California, in the minds of many invading Yankees, as a period of
charming underdevelopment.

THE AMERICAN CONQUEST of 1846 is so shrouded in a myth of neccesity or
"manifest destiny" that it is difficult to recover the pain and violence it
involved. For most Californians, the event survives in memory only by
way of the Bear Flag, the official banner of the state of California and one
that represents a highly abstract version of the strip of white cotton cloth
smudged with berry juice that a band of half-drunk men managed to
elevate over the plaza at Sonoma. In order to gain some perspective on the

event, I begin with the account of a latter-day spectator, Josiah Royce. In 1849 Royce's mother Sarah had crossed the plains in a covered wagon and settled in Grass Valley, where Josiah was born in 1855. Raised on the brutal mining frontier, Royce, blessed with a kind of counterphobic imagination, became a patron of the idea of community. The less he experienced of it in Grass Valley, the more he valued it from his desk in Boston. He began teaching philosophy at Harvard in 1882 and lived out his life as an eastern intellectual. It was Royce, not his good friend William James, who invented the phrase "the will to believe." His first book, however, was not about the idealist philosophy that later made him famous; it was about the ten years of California history

Josiah Royce in 1902. Born in Grass Valley in 1855, Royce attended the fledgling University of California and later became a professor of philosophy at Harvard. His 1886 history of California gives pride of place to the conquest of 1846 and portrays Captain John Charles Frémont as its essential villain. Courtesy of the Harvard University Archives.

that had preceded the year of his birth. Based on his archival work in Bancroft's holdings, on newspaper accounts, and on interviews with the participants, Royce's *California; from the Conquest in 1846 to the Second Vigilance Committee in San Francisco,* published in 1886, provides an early model of how the history of a place can be written by native sons and daughters with a standpoint, even an ax to grind.

Royce, who preferred Spanish and Mexican California to the American culture that followed it, focused on *how* the United States had taken California in 1846. His account portrays the American invasion as an unfortunate fall. And that fall is precipitated by a single man, John Charles Frémont. An Eden of "humane tenderheartedness" was corrupted by this ambitious invader; according to Royce, California before Frémont had known only wars of "bloodless playfulness": "Civilized warfare was, in fact, introduced into California through the undertakings of our own gallant Captain Frémont. For in civilized warfare, as is well known, somebody always gets badly hurt."

Royce's chapter on "The Secret Mission and the Bear Flag" does not at first promise to provide a dramatic and focused reading of the American conquest. "The condition of our knowledge on the subject forbids," he allows, "a purely narrative procedure." The events in California of the spring and summer of 1846 were too comic and chaotic to organize into a pattern; moreover, the official United States policy on the conquest remained shrouded by a secret. That secret involved a single unanswered question: What did Lieutenant Gillespie say to Captain Frémont? Answering that question became the focus of Royce's inquiry. It may seem moot given that the Polk administration clearly intended to gain possession of California from Mexico and given that the conquest merged with the larger rhythms of the Mexican War. On May 9, 1846—the very day that Lieutenant Gillespie reached Frémont and delivered his famous dispatch—U.S. forces met Mexican troops at the battle of Resaca de la Palma. Regardless of Royce's portrayal of Frémont as the snake in the garden, California would soon have become a territory of the United States, with or without him. It was already full of people—Americans and Californios—who favored such an outcome.

So why did Royce focus so relentlessly on the gallant captain? Because Frémont supplied his story with both the heroic villain and with the dramatic "narrative" forbidden by the condition of Royce's knowledge on the subject. Frémont is perhaps the most colorful yet elusive participant in the American conquest of California. Kit Carson rode with him as a guide, and whenever he entered Fort Laramie or Sacramento, he was surrounded by his retinue of bodyguards—a band of fully costumed Delaware Indians. It was Frémont who had named the Nevada-Utah desert "the Great Basin" and who called the opening of San Francisco Bay "the Golden Gate." These names stuck because he had been the official topographer of the U.S. government; as an army captain he had been sent West in the mid-1840s to map out routes for the immigration to come. The self-dramatizing *Report* (1845) that he published about his first two expeditions became a best-seller that many pioneers used as a guide to the Overland Trail. He eventually parlayed his role as "conqueror" into a California Senate seat, a huge gold-producing tract near Yosemite, and, in 1856, the first Republican nomination for the U.S. presidency.

In 1845 Frémont found himself, for the second time, in California. His mission, he would later aver, was wholly scientific. He had crossed the Sierra by way of a route that was to be named Donner Pass, and he had lingered in the Central Valley until the Mexican authorities ordered him to be on his way. In the early spring of 1846, after taunting California's military commander José Castro with a show of force in the Gabilan Mountains, Frémont marched his party of sixty men slowly northward and set up camp in Oregon Territory, which is where Royce picked up his story forty years later.

Royce claimed that "we must understand the conquest if we are to understand what followed." By defining the conquest as the origin story, and then by portraying it as illegitimate, Royce took a considerable risk. The Gold Rush would have happened with or without the conquest— the discovery of gold, given its ubiquity in the foothills of the Sierra, was inevitable—and both the scale and the character of the Gold Rush may be argued as more definitive of California "character" than the conquest. Yet the Gold Rush presented to its chronicler no unsolved "mystery," as Royce put it, a mystery that compelled him into producing, in his tracking of Frémont's dubious role, one of the first accomplished pieces of California detective fiction.

Royce was looking for clues. "It is a curious fact in this matter," he wrote, "that, the clew once found, absolutely all the disinterested evidence is seen to point in the same direction; while until the clew is found, the evidence looks like a mass of confusion." Chronology could deliver only a partial answer. In May 1846 Frémont marched back south to California. A month later Ezekiel Merritt and a band of some thirty men captured Mariano Vallejo at Sonoma, the pueblo he had founded in 1835, and declared the "California Republic." On June 25 Frémont entered Sonoma and took control of their Bear Flag Revolt, the unruly uprising that had begun the process of making California a territory of the United States.

As the army and the navy became officially involved in the conquest of California, the major fighting shifted to the the south. U.S. forces took control of Los Angeles in August but were expelled by the Californios a month later. In December, Andrés Pico and his long lances defeated General Stephen Kearney and Kit Carson at the Battle of San Pasqual, near the present town of Escondido. A month later Kearney retook Los Angeles; on January 13 Pico surrendered to Frémont in the Cahuenga

Capitulation, near the present intersection of the Hollywood and Ventura freeways, and the conquest was complete.

The issue for Royce—as it became for Kearney, the man who charged Frémont with mutiny after his freewheeling exercise of power as California's military governor—was the issue of following orders. While he deplored the conquest either as covert action or official policy, Royce deplored even more the conviction that Frémont acted throughout as a free and uninstructed agent. This was, of course, precisely the quality that endeared Frémont to the readers of his *Report*. He was the imperial self, manifesting the national destiny by filling in the white spaces on the map of the West and by equating the written history of a private desire—a history written in part by his wife, Jessie Benton—with a collective act of discovery and nation-building. Royce was less impressed by Frémont's aggressive self-fashioning, and held him accountable to a soldier's code of obedience.

After interviewing the general in the 1880s, Royce wrote that "The whole interview tended to this one result, that the instructions were the decisive element in determining the conduct of the captain." Gillespie, sent west by President Polk and Secretary of State Buchanan as a secret agent, undoubtedly carried an official dispatch from them. In fact, the contents of the dispatch are known, since a copy of it exists in the Bancroft Library, in papers consulted by Royce. The question that has never been settled and that Royce attempted to settle is whether Gillespie was entrusted with an additional message that he was to share solely with Frémont.

Later, before an investigating Claims Committee, Gillespie testified that "I was bearer of the duplicate of a dispatch to the United States consul at Monterey, as well also a packet for J. C. Frémont, Esq., and a letter of introduction to the latter gentleman from the Honorable James Buchanan. The former I destroyed before entering the port of Vera Cruz, having committed it to memory. The packet and letter of introduction I delivered to Captain Frémont, upon the 9th of May, 1846, in the mountains of Oregon." The U.S. consul whom he mentioned was Thomas Larkin, the father of the first child born of U.S. citizens in California. Larkin, operating from his base in Monterey, had long worked quietly to help assimilate the Mexican territory into the expanding American nation. The "packet" that Gillespie mentioned was a set of letters from Frémont's father-in-law, Thomas Hart Benton, the most vocal advocate of manifest destiny in the U.S. Senate. These letters were written in code, what Benton called a "family cipher." In his conversations with Royce, Frémont claimed that, in addition to the messages listed before the Claims Committee, Gillespie also "brought a dispatch to him from Buchanan in oral form, having destroyed the original before he passed through Mexico, to prevent its possible capture." The "substance . . . of letters and dispatch together," Frémont maintained, "was *that it was the desire of the President that Captain Frémont should not let the English get possession of California, but should use any means in his power, or any occasion that offered, to prevent such a thing.*" In response to these purported communications, Frémont marched south into California. The legitimacy of his action, then, depends upon whether Gillespie did in fact deliver a special oral dispatch. Despite Senator Benton's power, his letters, however detailed and however coded, could not have been construed by Frémont as official orders from the government.

"How fate pursues a man!" Frémont wrote in his *Memoirs*, about the night of Gillespie's arrival. It was a night on which he had been reviewing his plans for exploring the Cascades. "Thinking and ruminating over these things, I was standing alone by my camp-fire, enjoying its warmth, for the night air of early spring is chill under the shadows of the high mountains. Suddenly my ear caught the faint sound of horses' feet." Gillespie arrives, messages are exchanged, and the captain forgets, for only the second time in his career, to post sentries. His guide Kit Carson awakens to the sound of an ax slicing through a man's skull. A bloody struggle with the Klamath Indians follows in the light of the smoldering fires. As he pushes south in the following days, Frémont pauses for a search-and-destroy mission that leaves twenty Indians dead and a village destroyed. The greenhorn Gillespie is led to expostulate, "By heaven, this is rough work."

Frémont so constructs his account of the meeting with Gillespie that its content can only be verified by the two participants. Royce undermines the claims of memory and hearsay by presenting documentary evidence; namely, a copy of the dispatch sent to Larkin that had come into the possession of the indefatigable Hubert Howe Bancroft.

Royce's "clew," then, is the actual text of the dispatch. Quoting from it liberally, he made it clear that the Larkin dispatch was the only official dispatch brought to California by Gillespie. A letter from Frémont t

Senator Benton supports this claim. Royce presents the text of the letter as follows: "Your letter," said the captain to the Senator, "led me to expect some communication from him [Buchanan is the antecedent of him] *but I received nothing.*" Internal evidence derived from the dispatch itself provides, however, the primary solution of the mystery. The dispatch refers to California as a "sister republic" and to the Californios as "brethren." Whatever can be done, Buchanan writes, must "be done without giving Mexico just cause of complaint." Larkin is to work toward the voluntary separation of California from Mexico. Frémont's name is not mentioned. Perhaps, Royce speculated, the government instructed Larkin to do one thing on paper and gave Frémont oral instructions, via Gillespie, to do another? But such a policy would make no strategic sense, he argued, except to "exasperate beyond endurance a friendly people" and "to ensure all the possible causes that could combine to make their chief men hate us forever and the people fight us as savagely as they could." For Washington to ordain two separate policies in one cabinet—"no reader," he concluded, "can even dream that it was done."

The secret that Royce discovered, then, is that there was no secret. He concluded that Gillespie brought no secret official commission to Frémont. Gillespie's rendezvous with Frémont occurred after his meeting with Larkin in Monterey and proved, finally, an "afterthought." Royce bolstered this claim by producing a cover letter from Buchanan, discovered in the files of the State Department, that had been meant to accompany Gillespie on his trip to California. The letter, dated October 27, 1845, reads as follows:

Thomas O. Larkin, Esq, *U.S. Consul, Monterey*

Sir,—I enclose herewith a package for Captain Frémont, of whose movements you may be enabled to obtain some information, and request that it may be transmitted to him by the first safe opportunity which presents itself, or retained by you for delivery, according as the state of your information may suggest.

I am sir, etc.,
James Buchanan

On the basis of this letter, Royce constructed the following scenario: Gillespie was given a secret dispatch to deliver to Larkin. Before leaving

Washington, he was also entrusted with some letters from Benton and was asked to get them to Frémont. No official connection existed between the two tasks. Buchanan's cover letter assumes that Gillespie will get to Larkin first and that there is no particular hurry in getting to Frémont. And as it turned out, after visiting Monterey, Gillespie did travel north and share with Frémont the content of the dispatch to Larkin; then he delivered the letters from Benton. Frémont construed what he had read and heard for his own purposes.

Royce's detective work finally solved very little. The language of diplomacy can cloak a multitude of intentions, and the federal government may have been guilty of a deliberate vagueness meant to prompt someone to act. No third party has provided an account of the meeting between Frémont and Gillespie, so it remains possible that the captain was encouraged to take something the lieutenant said as fuel for his ambitions. Royce did establish that Frémont acted like a man with a secret, and that the single most valuable territorial acquisition made by the United States was indeed accomplished in a bathetic confusion of policies, motives, and rhetorics. Frémont provided a compelling subject for Royce's history lesson because, like Conrad's Kurtz or Faulkner's Sutpen, he consisted largely of what was said by him and especially about him. But the values of the historian collided with those of a vastly popular media figure, and Royce seems to have resigned himself to the defeat or irrelevance of his views. As he wrapped up his argument, he also conceded that "I have meanwhile the perfect consolation of knowing that the personal reputation of a distinguished public man such as is General Frémont, who has been a household name in our nation for a generation, is quite independent for good as well as for evil of what I may happen to choose to write here." The first strong history of California by a nonprofessional historian succeeded, in the end, in uncovering a past that was not so much illegitimate as indeterminate.

MEXICAN RULE HAD BEEN CHAOTIC—since 1822 California had had thirteen governors and its own independence movement. But even those Californios who favored an end to Mexican rule were aroused to oppose absorption by the United States because of the actions of Frémont, Merritt, Ide, and the other participants in the Bear Flag Revolt. The most detailed record of this response was left by a Californio named Mariano Vallejo.

In 1846 Vallejo's Casa Grande faced the plaza of the pueblo of Sonoma, which he had founded eleven years earlier. In his late thirties at the time of the Bear Flag Revolt, he had, through military service, a strategic marriage, and the steady acquisition of property, become the leading citizen in the northern portion of Alta California. After a falling out with the independence movement of the 1830s, which he briefly supported, Vallejo withdrew into the life of a grandee. He built up an estate of over 175,000 acres, planted the first grapevines at Sonoma, amassed a vast library, fathered sixteen children, and imported a carriage from Paris. He formed extensive ties with American settlers in the region and was believed to favor American annexation. Although at the time of the conquest he did hold the rank of general, he was no longer active in either the army or the government of Mexican California.

Vallejo's capture by the Bear Flaggers and his subsequent imprisonment at Sutter's Fort was thus a pointless humiliation. The small band of men who took it upon themselves to seize Sonoma and its leading citizen in June 1846 acted upon a host of motives, many inchoate, and Vallejo provided perhaps a convenient symbol of a California they meant to appropriate. The immigration that followed the conquest slowly stripped

Mariano Guadalupe Vallejo outside his Sonoma home, Lachryma Montis, in the 1870s. Born in Spanish California in 1808, Vallejo was a leading figure in Mexican California at the time of the conquest. Despite the rumor that he favored annexation, Vallejo was imprisoned by the Bear Flaggers for two months at Sutter's Fort. He later wrote and dictated extensive memoirs about his life under many flags. Courtesy of the Bancroft Library.

Vallejo of his land and wealth. Thirty years later he had become dependent on borrowing from friends.

In the 1860s Vallejo wrote more than nine hundred pages of a memoir, only to have the work destroyed when his house was consumed by fire. But he continued to do historical work. In the 1870s, at Bancroft's urging, he traveled the state eliciting memoirs or *testimonios* from the surviving Californios. At the same time he worked to recover his own lost story with Enrique Cerruti, one of Bancroft's scribes. Finally he produced the five-volume *Recuerdos historicos y personales tocante a la alta California,* which later became the backbone of Bancroft's history and still provides the most expansive personal record of life in Spanish and Mexican California. (Unfortunately, this and the majority of the sixty-two narratives that he gathered from the Californios, which are held in the Bancroft Library at the University of California, remain unpublished, even untranslated.)

The *testimonios* Bancroft elicited were necessarily a collaborative project: the result of a Californio's memories, a transcriber's capacity to listen, and Bancroft's professional ambitions. Bancroft called the resulting artifacts "dictations"; most were the product of an interview between a Spanish-speaking informant and an English-writing scribe. Cerruti and Thomas Savage gathered the bulk of the *testimonios* and transmitted them, in written form, to Bancroft's history "factory." By the time a *testimonio* entered one of Bancroft's published volumes, it had been thoroughly mediated by the circumstances of its acquisition, translation, and quotation. Rosaura Sanchez argues that the *testimonios* thus eloquently transmit the "split voice" of an occupying and an occupied people. Their assimilation into Bancroft's official history has given them a kind of ghostly life, but their full force subsists in a kind of historical unconscious, awaiting the recovery work of the present.

Genaro Padilla edited a portion of the *Recuerdos* dealing with the Bear Flag Revolt for the 1990 *Heath Anthology of American Literature.* Vallejo is to Padilla as Frémont is to Royce: "he and California were coterminous." Vallejo has generally been remembered as a conciliator; a standard history maintains that he "was known to favor American acquisition of California." Kevin Starr reports that "a legend grew up that Vallejo argued brilliantly before the junta in Monterey in favor of joining the American Union." In 1860 Vallejo even shared a stage with Frémont in San Francisco during an oration by Edward Randolph about the splendid, idle 1840s. Yet in his *Recuerdos*—a document that has seen print in occasional excerpts and that has been available in full only to scholars traveling to the Bancroft Library—Vallejo described Frémont as "a soldier who belies his glorious mission and becomes a leader of thieves."

Lost in the shuffle of history has been Vallejo's tone. As he admitted in a letter to his son, he wrote his memoirs in order "to regain a loss." Outwardly he did accommodate himself to the American invasion, although, like all Californios, he lost his lands in the end. But the story told has been of his successful accommodation to the American conquest. Kevin Starr's account (in the first volume of his history) omits to mention, for example, the decline in Vallejo's fortunes. Writing the *Recuerdos* was his revenge, an antithetical account of the conquest by a man who was as angry as Josiah Royce but for far more immediate reasons. Vallejo told the intimate story of the degradation that Royce had deplored only from the outside.

He did not do so by claiming for himself the status of a victim. Instead, he subjected the behavior of the conquerors to an amiable irony. Skillfully using bathos, he emptied the story of any heroic dimensions and converted it into farce. By focusing less on the issues underlying the struggle than on the style of the Bear Flaggers—especially their manners, clothing, speech patterns, and symbolic gestures—Vallejo outdid Royce in belittling them. He was aided in this effort by the pliability of his captors, who, after entering his home on the morning of June 14, came into the possession of some brandy and got wildly drunk.

That morning, when Vallejo had first heard a shout of alarm, he looked out his window and saw a motley crew: "The recent arrivals were not in uniform, but were all armed and presented a fierce aspect. Some of them wore on their heads a visorless cap of coyote skin, some a low-crowned plush hat, and some a red cotton handkerchief. As for the balance of the clothing of the assaulters of my residence, I shall not attempt to describe it, for I acknowledge that I am incapable of doing the task justice." His attackers were beneath his notice, and their attire conveyed their ungoverned emotions, if not their ungovernable selves. Vallejo's first act was therefore to put on his uniform. He then threw open the vestibule door. "The house was immediately filled with armed men," he wrote, in a sentence that conveys not only the sudden menace of the moment but an almost cartoonish and unsoldierly haste. In a bitter joke about the liability of a democratic body to collapse into a headless mob, he continued: "I asked them what the trouble was and who was heading the party, but had to repeat that question a second time, because almost all of those who were in the parlor replied at once, 'Here we are all heads.' " *In the parlor:* Could any phrase more simply convey the bad taste of abusing a man's hospitality while also enjoying it? More powerful is the metaphor of the many-headed hydra, one supplied by the Bear Flaggers themselves: "When I again asked with whom I should take the matter up, they pointed out William B. Ide who was the eldest of all. I then addressed that gentleman and informed him that I wanted to know to what happy circumstance *I owed the visit of so many individuals.*"

Ide was the poor man's Patrick Henry of the revolt, a speaker so taken by his own oratory that once he had gathered some forty of the Spanish-speaking citizens of the town in a jail, or what he called the "calaboose," he saw fit to harangue them on the virtues of democracy and "the common rights of man" in an English "not the twentieth part translated." It was Ide who claimed that Vallejo produced the brandy on which the men negotiating the articles of capitulation got so drunk, and it was Ide who, once the party had broken up and the heroes hesitated at the thought of marching the hospitable Vallejo as a prisoner to Sutter's Fort, uttered the immortal line, "We are robbers, *or we must be conquerors.*" The result was Vallejo's imprisonment in the home of a former companion-in-arms, a humiliation Sutter compounded by providing the prisoners, for their first meal, "a jar filled with broth and pieces of meat": "He did not send us," Vallejo added, "a spoon, knives, or forks."

In his own account Vallejo maintains that the barrel full of brandy had been provided by a neighboring Canadian, and that the tumult arose not within the room where negotiations were going on but outside it, where Merritt and Ide were enjoying the liquor. Ide's major contribution to the affair has been taken to be a long-winded proclamation, but Vallejo suggests rather that it was a flag. This is his description of it:

> The flag was nothing more nor less than a strip of white cotton stuff with a red edge and upon the white part, almost in the center, there was painted a bear with lowered head. The bear was so badly painted, however, that it looked more like a pig than a bear.

He adds, charitably, that "the bear and the star were very badly drawn, but that should not be wondered at, if one takes into consideration the fact that they lacked brushes and suitable colors."

Vallejo concludes his account with the argument that Ide and his men raised the wrong flag: "If the men who hoisted the 'Bear Flag' had raised the flag that Washington sanctified by his abnegation and patriotism there would have been no war on the Sonoma frontier." Certainly capitulation to the American flag might have offered the consolation of being overcome by a respectable adversary, even by a power with which one could imagine a profitable alliance. But the flag that was actually raised was not so much wrong as ugly—a "queer flag," as Vallejo calls it. The awkward symbol of the piglike bear bespoke the "true character" of the men who fashioned it.

Vallejo desired a formal transition of power, one with symbols and decorum adequate to preserve the dignity of both sides. The missing decorum is exemplified best by the restrained expressiveness of his own literary style. Vallejo finally converged with Royce in his concern with the legitimacy of the conquest and in his conviction that the founders of California as a state had betrayed the founding of the nation they would have it join. The carelessly improvised revolt was a parody of the revolution that George Washington had so skillfully managed; it was a failure of imagination as much as a violation of law. The enterprising spirit of the American Revolution "had filled us," Vallejo concluded, "with admiration." "Ill-advisedly, however, as some say, or dominated by a desire to rule without let or hindrance, as others say, they placed themselves under the shelter of a flag that pictured a bear, an animal that we took as the emblem of rapine and force. This mistake was the cause of all the trouble, for when the Californians saw parties of men running over the plains and forests under the 'Bear Flag,' they thought that they were dealing with robbers and took the steps they thought most effective for the protection of their lives and property."

THE BEAR FLAG REVOLT put an end to seventy-seven years of Spanish and Mexican rule in California. But the now-displaced Californios had themselves displaced, and in the not-so-distant past, the native dwellers in the state—the immigrants from Asia who moved down into California perhaps thirty thousand years before the arrival of the Spanish. Estimated by James D. Hart to have numbered as many as 300,000 in the year of the founding of Mission San Diego, their population had been reduced to about 150,000 by the time the missions were secularized in 1834. For Juana Machado, a surviving Californio who dictated her memoir to one of Bancroft's scribes in 1878 and who also lived through what she called the "change of flags," the memory of Indian resistance in the years leading up to the conquest provided a way of refiguring the liminal status history had also accorded her and her people.

The Spanish in California, unlike the Americans who would displace them, adhered to a policy of "domestic unity" that encouraged the immigration of intact families. In 1505 the Spanish throne ruled that married men living in the colonies of New Spain without wives or families had to either return to their wives or bring them to the colonies. Spain met the threat of undomesticated single men on the frontier with edicts giving married men with families priority in land assignments, as well as larger holdings. In March of 1774 the first eight women were brought by ship to San Diego. Recruited from the artisan and professional classes, this group did not stay. Spanish California was to be settled by kinswomen of the leather-jacketed soldiers who derived from the lower classes of New Spain. These women came into a culture where, according to Junípero Serra, Spanish soldiers went about routinely killing Indian men to take their wives. Serra described soldiers who "catch an Indian woman with their lassos to become prey for their unbridled lust." In order to discourage these depredations, Serra recommended a policy of intermarriage between soldiers and converted "daughters of the land." When Juana Machado was born in San Diego in 1814, she thus entered a world in which women had, for over four decades, served as the central element in cultural stability and exchange.

Señora Doña Juana Machado Alipaz de Ridington (Wrightington) was the daughter of Maria Serafina Valdéz and José Manuel Machado, a member of the presidial force at San Diego. Alipaz and Wrightington were her two husbands. In introducing her twenty-page narrative, titled *Times Gone by in Alta California,* transcriber Thomas Savage began by identifying Machado as a wife: "This lady is the widow of the late Thomas Wrightington." He went on to enumerate her sons, daughters, grandchildren—even a cousin. But Machado, able to speak English quite fluently, showed little interest in talking about matrimony and filiation. In the paragraph devoted to her first wedding, she gave over only one sentence to describing her husband: "All the weddings in those times," she concluded, after naming the guests and the extent of the dancing, "were generally celebrated in the same way." And she gave no account at all of her wedding to her second husband, although the event fell well within the chronological bounds of her narrative, which culminates with the Battle of San Pasqual and the Pauma Massacre of 1846.

Instead, Machado reserved her narrative energy for a "celebration of Indian wrong-doing." Or as she put it in the first story that takes place after her baptism: "When I was eight or ten years old, my father left in command of an expedition of twenty-five men. At the time he was taking care of the National Ranch belonging to the presidio of San Diego. The object was to go in pursuit of Indian horse thieves. There were at that time three bad Indians, celebrated for their wrong-doing." For Machado, violence generates narrative; it is such bad deeds—rather than the conventional events of baptism and marriage—that truly deserve to be "celebrated."

Machado did not "celebrate" in any literal sense: she maintained a solidarity with her own Spanish culture throughout by applying adjectives like "bad" to Indian uprisings. But her narrative acquires its greatest complexity and most ironic shadings when dealing with these violent events. Her father tracks the horse thieves to a narrow canyon:

> My father and his soldiers had a very stubborn fight with the Indians. Agustin grasped my father by his braided hair and pulled him off his horse. Fortunately one of the soldiers . . . hurried to his aid, and my father was able to draw his knife and plunge it into the belly of the Indian, scattering his intestines and leaving him dead.
>
> My father cut off his ears and tore out his hair (it was the custom then) and these he presented to the Commandante of San Diego on his return.

The prowess of the father is asserted, along with his customary and casual violence.

Machado's most detailed memory is of the Indian revolt of 1837. "A very sad California episode," she calls it. Her sorrowful tone here contrasts sharply with her harsh dismissal of the repressive governor Victoria, who delayed the secularization of the missions. He was a "hated" man, she says. By all accounts a despotic administrator, Victoria had tried to hold the mission system together during his brief tenure as governor in the early 1830s. Secularization officially began in 1834. Under the plan, the missions were to become parish churches and the neophytes were to be released from mission jurisdiction. The property of the missions was to form pueblos, while the Indians connected with the missions were to receive land and livestock.

In its results, secularization bore an unhappy resemblance to Reconstruction in the American South. It liberated the Indians from their dependency on the paternalistic slave economy, yet it quickly revoked the promises of land and privilege that it had made them. Mission land did not pass into the hands of the newly freed Indians but simply expanded the size of the ranchos. The missions quickly fell into disrepair. The "sad episode" of the Indian revolt, described by Machado, took place during this time of loss and uncertainty, in the year after secularization was officially complete. Her sadness issued, perhaps, from her mixed feelings about an attack on her culture by the Indians for whom secularization had meant the exchange of servitude for chaos.

The 1837 raid on Rancho Jamul was perhaps the most famous Indian

Juana Machado in the cactus hedge in Old Town, San Diego. Machado's life (1814–1901) intersected major events in the early history of Southern California: the Indian uprisings of the 1830s, the secularization of the missions, the Pauma Massacre, and the Battle of San Pasqual. Fluent in English as well as Spanish and local Indian dialects, in 1878 she dictated her recollections to Thomas Savage, an agent of historian Hubert Howe Bancroft. Courtesy of the San Diego Historical Society.

uprising of California's Mexican period. It produced a compelling captivity narrative in which two daughters of the *gente de razón* were forever lost to their community. The Mexican institution of the rancho, a large and loosely defined landholding, replaced the pueblo and the mission in the 1830s as the dominant arrangement of California space. The raid tested its efficacy; as Rosaura Sanchez argues, "The Jamul episode is also the Californio's story of the *rancho*-nation under attack by hostile forces."

Rancho Jamul was a large rancho located nineteen miles east of present-day San Diego; before secularization it had belonged to the San Diego Mission. In 1829 it passed to the Pico family, members of which had entered California with the Anza expedition in 1776. Living at the rancho at the time of the revolt was the widowed Doña Eustaquia Lopéz, who was the mother of two of California's most prominent figures: Andrés Pico, the commander at San Pasqual, and Pio Pico, last Mexican governor of California.

In Machado's account the uprising begins when an Indian woman named Cesarea approaches Doña Eustaquia and asks her for some salt. The widow orders that salt be brought. But Cesarea motions for Doña Eustaquia to get the salt herself. As the widow departs to retrieve it, Cesarea follows her and, in a secluded spot, tells her that the Indians are going to rise. The widow sends her daughters out for a walk along the edge of the cornfield and alerts the ranch foreman, Juan Leiva. He refuses to place her family in safety but agrees to send a wooden cart to carry the mother and her daughters to the neighboring Rancho Jamacha. The Indians attack Rancho Jamul on the following night.

Leiva, while fighting in the cornfields, sees that his own family is in danger and breaks away toward the ranch to protect them. "When he went towards the gun room an Indian cleaning woman of the house who had locked that room and put the key in her pocket, mockingly showed him the key; saying that there were no hopes in that direction." The Indians kill Leiva, burn the rancho, and carry off his twelve- and fifteen-year-old daughters, Tomasa and Ramona. "Until this day what was the fate of those unhappy creatures is unknown."

The story appears to end here, but Machado adds a coda about a failed rescue mission in which a "celebrated" Indian fighter and uncle of the captives locates the girls' abductors on Jacumba Mountain: "He said that actually he saw these two girls, apparently with white bodies painted and with hair cut in Indian fashion." He holds fire for fear of killing his nieces, but then the Indians disappear and he loses the trail. "It was not possible for him to climb with his horses to that height." Machado concludes this portion of her *testimonio* by adding, "The authors of these misfortunes were the Indians Cartucho and Martin I have spoken of before. Other Indians afterwards said that Cartucho had Tomasa for his wife and Martin had Ramona for his wife." Machado makes no more of these "marriages" than she does of her own; in both cultures the event is something arranged by a man.

THE WILY AND PERSISTENT Indian guerrillas who evaded capture in Machado's account scarcely accord with the textbook image of California's "Digger" Indians to which grade schoolers were exposed in the social studies classes in the 1950s and 1960s. Even Anglo students of the state's history were meant to feel a slight shame at the unwarlike and barely clad Diggers who lived in holes in the earth or harvested flies by some sullen lake. Their warmaking technologies were nearly nonexistent—a fact that made them and other native peoples very appealing to me. The YMCA Indian Guide troop I joined in 1954, while living in South Pasadena, elected as its tribe the pacific Hopi, even though the Hopi did roll boulders down from the tops of their mesas when attacked. At the time of the Spanish arrival only one Indian group in California, the Yuman, possessed a weapon clearly designed for making war. Despite the technology at their disposal, California Indians nevertheless engaged in a century of steady resistance to Spanish and American conquest.

The Gabrileño Indians attacked the soldiers at the Mission San Gabriel at the moment of its inception in 1771: "A great multitude of savages, armed and headed by two chiefs, appeared and with frightful yells attempted to prevent the founding of the Mission." The Gabrileños tried to destroy the mission a second time in October 1775; a month later the Yumans attacked San Diego Alcala, burned the mission, and killed the padre. Within six years of their arrival in California, the Spanish had concluded that the native peoples were "fearful creatures" and that colonization would not be easy.

San Gabriel, 1810; Santa Cruz, 1812; Santa Inez and Santa Barbara, 1824; San Bernardino, 1831—these are the places and dates of major uprisings, and for each year of the Spanish and then the Mexican occupation, one could document a herd of sheep stolen or a warehouse

in flames. Pastoral fantasies were projected on the period even by
writers as informed as Helen Hunt Jackson in *Ramona*. Yet the 1812
revolt at Santa Cruz belies those fantasies. Here the Indian neophytes set
out to avenge themselves on a notorious flogger, Father Andrés Quintana, after he had whipped an Indian named Donato. First they induced
an Indian gardener to feign death; as Qunitana was administering the
last rites, they seized him. One of his testicles was crushed, and he was
strangled. But during the ensuing bacchanal the Indians discovered that
Quintana was still alive. In the process of finishing him off, they crushed
his other testicle. Such an incident lends support to Royce's claim that
the "final outcome" of the work of the padres "was, for the cause of true
spiritual progress in California, simply nothing."

In 1916 the Indian population of California stood at 16,000, less than
one-twelfth the number estimated to have been living in the state in 1769.
By the year gold was discovered, disease and the civilizing process had
already reduced this number to some 100,000. Disease continued its work
in the 1850s and 1860s, as did enslavement and outright murder. In 1860 a
young newspaperman who had not yet changed his name to Bret Harte,
working near the present town of Eureka, ran the following headline
about the killing of some sixty Indians during a religious ceremony on
Indian Island in Humboldt Bay:

INDISCRIMINATE MASSACRE OF INDIANS
WOMEN AND CHILDREN BUTCHERED

He was forced to flee to San Francisco.

The last stand of the California Indians against the United States came
with the Modoc War. Led by a Captain Jack in the early 1870s, the Modocs
attempted to return to their ancestral lands in the northeastern corner of
the state after their removal to Klamath country in the 1860s. Some fifty
Modoc men along with 150 women and children took up a position in the
volcanic landscape that later became Lava Beds National Monument. For
over two months the Modocs held off three hundred U.S. soldiers, then
consented to a parley. There they killed the only U.S. general to die in the
Indian wars, then returned to the lava beds to continue fighting. After
howitzers and a lack of water weakened the Indian force, Captain Jack
and three others were captured and hung. The action left eighty-three U.S.
soldiers dead and cost the government close to $1 million.

A scene from the Modoc War of 1872–73, the last armed struggle of Native Americans in California against the U.S. Army. The National Archives caption reads: "San Francisco Bulletin correspondent takes notes while two Warm Springs scouts keep lookout." Courtesy of the National Archives.

In 1814 at Mission San Diego, two Franciscans undertook to answer a questionnaire about Indian life sent out by the Spanish government. Known as the *Preguntas y Respuetas,* these documents give a rosy but candid picture of Christianized Indian life. One of the thirty-six questions asks whether "any inclination toward reading and writing in their own languages [is] noted among them." This was how the Franciscans replied: "We notice that they have no inclination for reading or writing; indeed, we cannot find any inclination that might prove that they at any time made use of written characters. But if the missionaries assign one or the other to reading and writing, they learn readily. They write on our paper." While the fathers added, "They find it difficult to learn to speak Spanish at this mission," they did succeed in converting a few Indians to its use. One of these was a Luiseño named Pablo Tac.

Born in 1822 at the Mission San Luis Rey (located near the present town of Oceanside), Tac died less than twenty years later in Rome. His

"Conversion de Los San Luiseños de la Alta California"—Tac wrote in Spanish—is described by the editor of its English translation as "the first writing of a literary nature produced by a native of California." Tac wrote about the mission where he was born, the same mission where Juana Machado's father had served in the guard while she was a little girl.

Tac learned Spanish at the mission school and proved so diligent in his studies that, in 1832, mission founder Antonio Peyrí brought Tac and another neophyte with him on a voyage to San Blas, then on to Spain, and finally, in 1834, to Rome. Peyrí's voyage on the *Pocahontas* was involuntary; having built up San Luis Rey into the largest mission in Alta California, the complications of Mexican rule forced him to flee. Once in Rome, Tac registered as a student at Urban College, where he wrote the "Conversion" soon after his matriculation. Tac went on to study Latin grammar, compiled a grammatical sketch of the Luiseño language under the direction of the great linguist Guiseppe Mezzofanti, and died of illness on December 13, 1841, before he could return to California to take up work as a missionary.

The "Conversion," which fills some fifteen modern pages, begins by describing the arrival of the Spanish, the conversion of the Indians, and the building of the mission. Tac details the daily mission routines and concludes with descriptions of three kinds of Indian dances and a fractious ball game. The key words in the English translation are "strife" and "trouble." "Trouble" is in fact the last word in the text, referring to a dispute over a kind of field hockey match between two groups of Indians. "Strife" is what the Spanish put an end to by their arrival. "Always there was war," Tac wrote about the years before the conquest, "always strife day and night with those who spoke in another language."

Tac associates California Indian life with clashing tongues and warfare; the Spanish impose a kind of peace by imposing a single belief system and an official language. While Tac's narrative ostensibly argues that this displacement of many tongues by one—a kind of permanent linguistic and spiritual authority—was beneficent, the textual history of the "Conversion" reveals revisions, contradictions, and erasures that make it a palimpsest.

The Indian "captain" who confronted the first troop of Spanish invaders, Tac records, greeted them with the words "What is it that you seek here? Get out of our country!" The Spanish gave him gifts and made him their "friend." Writing from the viewpoint of one converted, Tac considers the moment lucky for the Indians rather than ominous. "It was a great mercy that the Indians did not kill the Spanish when they arrived, and very admirable, because they have never wanted another people to live with them, and until those days they were always fighting." Internecine strife gave way to grateful submission, reflected in the architecture of the mission itself, which Tac carefully describes in a list of fifty-nine numbered points. He lists spaces like "place where *posole* and *atole* are made" and architectural features like "a small door for the missionary to get out easily in case of earthquakes." The importance of walls and entrances is emphasized by Tac's drawing of the mission's turnstile gate: the sign of civilization is the control and measurement of property and space.

Pablo Tac's drawing of two Luiseño dancers. Born at Mission San Luis Rey in 1822, Tac was the 3,896th neophyte to be baptized there. At the age of ten he departed the mission with Father Antonio Peyrí; in 1834 they arrived in Rome. Tac's "Conversion," written in Spanish shortly after his arrival in Italy, stands as the only surviving account of California mission life written by a Native American. Courtesy of the library of the Santa Barbara Mission.

The Indians may have built the mission, but "none of the neophytes can go to the garden or enter to gather the fruit," Tac says. Inevitably, the prohibition was transgressed:

Once a neophyte entered the garden without knowing the gardener was there, and as he was very hungry, he climbed a fig tree. Here he began to eat with all haste a large ripe fig. Not by bits but whole he let it go down his throat, and the fig choked him. He then began to be frightened, until he cried out like a crow and swallowed it. The gardener, hearing the voice of the crow, with his Indian eyes then found the crow that from fear was not eating more. He said to him,

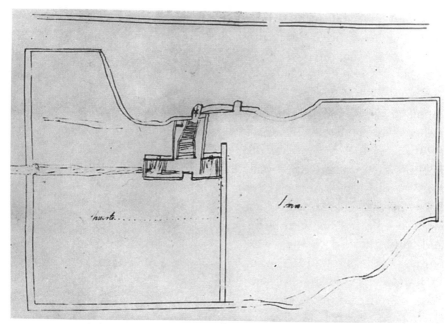

Tac's line drawing of the turnstile and mission gardens at San Luis Rey. Peyrí oversaw construction of this, the largest of the missions, in 1811–15. The church could accommodate a thousand worshippers. The mission's extensive gardens contained trees of pear, apple, peach, quince, fig, and pomegranate, as well as plots of melon, cabbage, lettuce, radish, mint, and parsley. Neophytes ate from the produce of the garden but were not allowed to enter it. Courtesy of the library of the Santa Barbara Mission.

"I see you, a crow without wings. Now I will wound you with my arrows."
Then the neophyte with all haste fled far from the garden.

So is the ancient script played out. In this little parable of the fall, the expulsion of the Indian from the garden of California, initiated by the Spanish arrival, is reenacted on a tiny scale. Tac's point of view is that of the "Indian eyes" of the gardener, the outsider who has been initiated into the rules and privileges of the game and consents to police its borders, even against other Indians. Yet it is difficult to believe that he savors the outcome. The metamorphosis of neophyte into crow certainly makes the expulsion more charming and therefore more palatable; perhaps it also registers Tac's uneasiness with this story.

Like Vallejo and Machado, Tac reveals that in the experience of conquest many of the most adept and culturally adaptive "native" people become Malinche figures and end up living betwixt and between. In *The Labyrinth of Solitude* (1950), Octavio Paz fixed this figure as a cultural icon. La Malinche was the Aztec woman who mediated between Cortez and her people during the conquest of Mexico. The stories about her render her variously as victim, betrayer, seducer, and translator. She is, at best, a figure of compromise, and many will resist the precedent of her role, just as any Native American will object to contemporary appropriations of Pocahontas and Sacajawea. Still, such figures recur with enough frequency in the history of the Americas to warrant considering them a type. As Richard Rodriguez writes in *Days of Obligation:* "In the annals of the famous European discoverers there is invariably an Indian guide, a translator—willing or not—to facilitate, to preserve Europe's stride. These seem to have become fluent in pallor before Europe learned anything of them." Pablo Tac, fluent in at least two European languages besides his own, nonetheless found a way to convey, in passages like the story about the forbidden fig, the harsh realities faced by the excluded and the unassimilated.

For all his understanding of such realities, however, Tac imagines that only an external force like the Spanish could have created solidarity among the Native Americans of California. This view comes out in his account of a ball game at Mission San Juan Capistrano between the Luiseños and the Sanjuaneños, a neighboring people who spoke a dialect closely related to the Luiseño. In the game, which resembles field hockey, teams of thirty to forty men use arched sticks to move a wooden ball the size of a turkey egg toward a goal. The ball is not to be carried by hand for long but must be moved on the ground with a stick. In the contest that Tac describes, the Sanjuaneños have secured a change of rule that bans any hand-carrying of the ball at all. After the Luiseños gain a quick advantage, however, a Sanjuaneño picks up the ball. A fight ensues over hand-carrying the ball, in which one player is trampled by a horse and another is pelted with stones.

The chasm between the two groups seems at least as great—and as trivial—as that between Europe's modern-day soccer fans; it is a fight, in Tac's words, between "countryman" and countryman:

The Sanjuaneños fled with their split heads. The Luiseños remain alone. One wanted to give a blow to another, believing he was a Sanjuaneño. Such was their rage they did not recognize each other, and they were afraid of

nothing. The Spanish soldiers arrive, although the uproar was ended, because
they too were trembling, and they wished to end the tumult with words. The
chief of the thirty Luiseños was an Indian and spoke like the Spanish. The
Indian said to him, "Raise your saber, and then I will eat you," but in his
language, and afterwards there was no trouble.

The "trouble" in the ball game evokes the state of war that obtained,
according to Tac, between Native American language groups, even
closely related ones, before the invasion of the Spanish. Even after the
Sanjuaneños were gone, the Luiseños in their rage failed to recognize
each other. Local mayhem is prevented, as it was in the conquest on a
much broader level, only by the timely arrival of the Spanish. In Tac's
thinking the authority of a master language embodies the hope for ending
the tumult.

Yet what saves the day is not negotiation but incomprehension. The
chief of the Luiseños threatens the Spanish not in their own tongue—a
tongue that he knows—but "in his language," which the Spanish do not
know. What saves the day, then, is also what ruins the day: difference. By
not knowing the Luiseño language, the Spanish soldiers cannot take
offense at what the chief says to them.

Still, the Indians have indulged in what Freud called, in *Civilization
and Its Discontents,* "the narcissism of minor differences"; the two Indian
groups are, after all, closely linked by language and geography. By doing
so they have jettisoned a solidarity that could have united them against the
invader alien to them both. Pablo Tac may have sailed to Rome and died
in the arms of the church, but in his memory he registered the divisions
within himself and among his people, a tumult that could not be ended by
the imposition of a single European tongue.

IN 1846 MEXICAN CALIFORNIA found itself fighting off both the colonized
and the colonizers. The colonized Indians continued their resistance to
Mexico up until the Battle of San Pasqual, which was itself the biggest
battle of the conquest and a defeat for the American colonizers. Machado's account enmeshes the two struggles: "A few days before this San
Pasqual battle," she dictated, "eleven Californians were murdered by
the Indians on this side of Agua Caliente in the Arroyo de los Alamos," at
the Pauma ranch, not far from Mission San Luis Rey. The Indians who

rose up were Luiseños, Pablo Tac's people. Machado maintains that the men killed in this massacre had retired "with their few belongings, in order not to take part in the war between the Americans and the inhabitants of the country." In fact, the Pauma Massacre occurred a few days *after* the Battle of San Pasqual, and the murdered men were Mexican rangers retreating from it. In this battle, which took place on December 6, 1846, the Mexican cavalry under Andrés Pico routed General Stephen Kearney's one hundred dragoons. The Mexican victory marked a temporary delay in the inevitable American conquest, which was completed less than two months later, when Pico surrendered to Frémont at Cahuenga Pass.

In the closing words of her *testimonio,* Machado spoke of "a brother of mine named Raphael Machado," who "was also with his little belongings at Pauma, with others, [and] likewise managed to escape from the Indians." She thus positioned her brother with the group of retreating Californios who were captured and killed at Pauma. Raphael's position in this group of Californios would have been a compromised one. In the chaos following the battle, the Indian massacre at Pauma may have provided a cover for his activities at San Pasqual, which involved working as a scout and a spy for General Kearney. The night before the battle, Raphael had even managed to obtain valuable intelligence for the Americans after making his way into Pico's camp.

Machado repressed this fact or was ignorant of it. She represented Raphael as strangely neutral, someone on the scene but not on a side. Thus when the Americans finally entered San Diego, Raphael's mother had to intercede on his behalf. "My brother succeeded in reaching here some days before Kearney's entry. When he presented himself my mother went to the Commodore to obtain a safe-conduct for him. He gave this without objections." A son here is apparently saved by a mother. Yet Raphael needed no such intercession; he was already hard at work for the invaders. Instead of describing Raphael's role, Machado invented the need for a mediating woman, a wish-fulfilling figure who reconciles an excruciating conflict between cultures.

Machado's stories about Indians express the central issues in her Mexican-American life. If she used the Mexican displacement of the Indian as a metaphor for the American displacement of the Mexican, her stories of Indian revolts are organized around examples of male incompetence and disloyalty that contrast starkly with female resistance and self-reliance. The two key figures in her accounts are Cesarea, the Indian woman who warns Doña Eustaquia of the coming attack, and the female keeper of the keys, who mocks her former master. Both are figures caught betwixt and between, either compromised or radicalized by virtue of being women within a culture.

Yet Machado was not only a woman but a Californio. This is why she ended her *testimonio* with the vexed and contradictory figure of her brother, with his dual status as both victim and collaborator. During the American conquest political loyalty necessarily meant something different for a Californio man than it did for a Californio woman. The very compression of Machado's narrative conveys the sense that governments change arbitrarily while patriarchy persists. Vallejo directed his anger at the clumsy flag of the revolters, deploying it as a metaphor for the displacement of a genteel world by a loutish one. Machado cared less about the shifting symbols of political authority. She had lived through one "change of flag in 1822," when California passed from the control of Spain to that of Mexico. Pico's capitulation to Frémont twenty-five years later provoked in her only this dry summation: "Since then this country has been under the flag of the United States." Yet by ending her *testimonio* with her brother, Machado linked the surviving women and men of her culture, however disparate their experiences, as participants in a common ordeal. For the Californio, male or female, the conquest opened up a breach in identity, a breach later expressed through acts of discreet but "oppositional" storytelling, as Genaro Padilla calls them. In the carefully coded reminiscences of a Mariano Vallejo or a Juana Machado, the breach was acknowledged and, to some extent, overcome.

A FEW MONTHS BEFORE the Battle of San Pasqual, a thoughtful Edwin Bryant was riding south to join Frémont near San Juan Bautista. Upon arriving at the mission, he found himself in an elegiac mood:

> During the twilight, I strayed accidentally through a half-opened gate into a cemetery, enclosed by a high wall in the rear of the church. The spectacle was ghastly enough. The exhumed skeletons of those who had been deposited here, lay thickly strewn around, showing but little respect for the sanctity of the grave or the rights of the dead, from the living. The cool, damp night-

breeze sighed and moaned through the shrubbery and ruinous arches and corridors, planted and reared by those whose bones were now exposed to the rude insults of man and beast. I could not but imagine that the voices of complaining spirits mingled with these dismal and mournful tones; and plucking a cluster of roses, the fragrance of which was delicious, I left the spot, to drive away the sadness and melancholy of the scene.

The remains Bryant had strayed upon were probably those of California Indians, killed by European diseases. Juan Crespi's northward marches had set in motion not only the accidental reseeding of California's grasslands but a catastrophic cycle of decimation and exhumation. The Spanish brought not only seeds but also infection. The *Personal Narrative* of mountain man James Ohio Pattie—he entered California by the Gila River route in 1826—reckoned that its hero was forced by a hostile Mexican governor to vaccinate some 22,000 souls against smallpox. A few years later the missions were secularized. Each Indian family was to receive a small private plot of land, but the plan was never carried out. The missions crumbled, to be revived much later by the automobile associations. Spanish became merely a "second" language, causing Bret Harte to lament the shift to English as a diminishment of speech, with harsh gutturals replacing more musical linguals and sibilants. In 1910 only 51,000 persons of Mexican descent were living in the state.

But their ancestors had changed the face of California earth. As Bryant rode toward San Juan, he traveled through late November rains. "The hills and valleys are becoming verdant with fresh grass and wild oats," he recorded, "the latter being, in places, two or three inches high. So tender is it, however, that it affords but little nourishment to our horses."

CHAPTER TWO

THE GOLD RUSH

Men Without Women

Aꜰᴛᴇʀ ᴛʜᴇ Cɪᴠɪʟ Wᴀʀ, the Gold Rush was nineteenth-century America's most diligently recorded public event. The writing about the
Gold Rush, along with thousands of diaries that were generated over the
twenty years of movement on the Overland Trail, established runaway
immigration as one of California's dominant cultural themes. Some writers
came to look rather than to settle, like Bayard Taylor, J. D. Borthwick,
Goldsborough Bruff, Walter Colton, Frank Maryatt, Alonzo Delano, and
J. Ross Browne. But two-thirds of those who went to "see the elephant"
stayed on and in so doing produced, at least temporarily, the most eclectic
mix of peoples the United States had yet seen.

The wild oat entered California slowly and silently and created a
tinderbox, but the Gold Rush was the first full California blaze. Fire here
becomes a metaphor for the suddenness of the event. President Polk's
announcement of the discovery of gold on December 5, 1848, provoked a
massive redirection of the westward migration, as well as a crush of
immigrants from the four corners of the earth. In one year the foothills of
the Sierra acquired names like Italian Gulch, Kanaka Bar, Spanish
Diggings, Norwegian Mine, and Chinee Camp. The population explosion transformed California into an unmanaged experiment in inter-
ethnic comity, while the absence of a substantial number of women
encouraged a culture of acting out.

In the first eighty years of its European development, from 1769 to
1849, the state that would eventually become the nation's largest was

dramatically underpopulated. In the year of the United States occupation it contained only a handful of U.S. citizens, 100,000 Indians, and some 14,000 *gente de razón*. In 1848 only 400 people emigrated on the Overland Trail to California. Before James Marshall found nuggets of gold in the tailrace of Sutter's mill on January 24, 1848, most emigrants to the West set their sights on Oregon as their destination. But in 1849 25,000 people set out on the five-month trip. At the time of the first statewide census, in 1860, the state boasted a population of 308,000; half of them lived in the Sacramento Valley or in nearby mining regions, and about a quarter lived in the vicinity of San Francisco.

While overland travel on the California or Santa Fe Trails suited the majority of citizens from the eastern United States, some avoided the five-month journey by taking the much faster route across Central America. A steamer from New York to Chagres, a trek across the isthmus, and a ship north from the city of Panama brought a forty-niner to San Francisco as early as February, after a trip of only two or three weeks. An ocean voyage around Cape Horn risked the perils of storm and iceberg, but it appealed to argonauts with a seafaring tradition; some 6,000 from Massachusetts chose the Horn route in 1849. From across the Pacific men and women of Canton, usually traveling as indentured servants or as outright slaves, sailed east on clipper ships; Sandwich Islanders, famed for their skills at maneuvering California's rough and undeveloped seacoast, could hitch a ride from Oahu. And from Sonoma men rode or walked north to work the mines of the southern Sierra.

The Gold Rush overwhelmed California's physical as well as its human ecology. Bret Harte used the word "commotion" to describe the rhythm of life in a mining camp, but the term is perhaps too sanguine. Any miner deemed "foreign" could quickly become an object of assault, claim-jumping, or a lynch mob—even an official tax. Casual and accepted violence against "foreigners" found a disturbing parallel in the epic abuse of mother "Nature" herself, to use one of Harte's euphemisms. Excavating the Sierra foothills by spade, sluice box, and hydraulic nozzle appeared as merely the cost of doing business, but in its lasting effects it would become California's first tragedy of development.

Bayard Taylor's 1850 *El Dorado* quickly became the authoritative account of the Gold Rush years. In his first pass through California, the popular journalist saw life in the mines as a triumph in both economics and politics. "Ages will not exhaust the supply" of gold, he wrote after visiting the diggings on the Mokelumne River. In a mining district of 100,000, Taylor argued, "there was as much security to life and property as in any part of the Union, and as small a proportion of crime. The capacity of a people for self-government was never so triumphantly illustrated." Josiah Royce was to fault Taylor for noticing only the prime parts of the elephant: "He saw, for instance, but one drunken man in all the mines."

In "San Francisco After Ten Years," the first chapter of his 1862 *New Pictures from California,* Taylor detailed the more abiding and disastrous results of the Gold Rush. Upon his arrival in San Francisco in 1849, he had found a city of 5,000. He took "quarters in the loft of an adobe building—a rude bed, and three meals of beefsteak, bread, and coffee, at thirty-five dollars a week." He returned ten years later to a city ten times as large, with "spacious and well-built streets" and with "fifteen massive piers out into the bay." "There was nothing which I recognized. Four great fires had swept away the temporary structures, which had cost almost their weight in silver, and stately houses of brick or granite stood in their places." As for the inexhaustible supply of gold, 1852 had marked the peak for gold production, and thereafter only large companies could realize significant profits from its extraction—a fact that Taylor repressed.

Taylor saw a "grandeur" in the new technology of hydraulic mining. In hydraulic mining a sixteen-foot nozzle directs water at a hillside at 120 pounds of pressure per square inch. "Like a giant bleeding to death from a single vein—the mountain washed itself away," wrote Taylor. In *Assembling California* John McPhee notes that within the space of only a year and a half, hydraulic mining had washed "enough material into the Yuba River to fill the Erie Canal." Other forms of mining—the huge pit mines, the diversions of streams and even rivers—accomplished an equally considerable damage. Between Columbia and Sonora, Taylor found a vast excavation where "the earth seemed to have been madly *clawed into.*" Although Taylor attempted to celebrate California as "a land where life seems to be most plastic," his metaphors of clawing and bleeding reveal it as a site of abuse as well.

The Gold Rush flooded the U.S. economy with liquid capital just at a moment of dire need. John Bidwell, the man who led the first wagon train to California in 1841, made this point in his 1890 *Echoes of the Past:*

Hydraulic mining, Nevada County, 1866. After the early years of the Gold Rush, placer mining gave way to large-scale open-pit and hydraulic operations. The hoses pictured here could direct a stream of water at a hillside at pressures of more than a hundred pounds per square inch. Invented in 1853 by Edward E. Matteson, hydraulic mining was prohibited in 1884 after washing enough earth out of the Sierra to silt up many of its rivers and damage vast areas of Central Valley farmland. Courtesy of the Library of Congress.

It is a question whether the United States could have stood the shock of the great rebellion of 1861 had the California gold discovery not been made. . . . California gold averted a total collapse and enabled a preserved Union to come forth from the great conflict with only four billions of debt instead of a hundred billions.

By Bidwell's calculation, the Gold Rush was a piece of national good luck, and "luck" became the dominant metaphor for agency during the Gold Rush years. In "How I Went to the Mines," Bret Harte relates how he passed from tenderfoot to veteran pioneer by learning a lesson about luck. "Gold miners were very superstitious," he writes. "It was one of their firm beliefs that 'luck' would inevitably follow the first essay of the neophyte or 'greenhorn.' " On his own first day of digging, Harte confides, he found a nugget worth twelve dollars. He dutifully worked the claim for three hard weeks—and found nothing more. Thereupon he quit mining and turned to another sort of "essay," the kind that made him a fortune and left him, in the early 1870s, the highest-paid writer in the United States. The lesson here is ambiguous, and a reader can take the sketch as recommending either abandon or wise prudence.

The pace of social and material change so accelerated during California's 1850s that standard notions of the value of work and effort gave way to a belief—celebratory or rueful, depending on whether the day's luck was good or bad—in fortune as something beyond human control. The condition or even the existence of a man or a town became dependent on sudden and ineluctable processes, with "luck" often serving as a jaunty synonym for catastrophe. Almost a century later Carey McWilliams was to argue that any understanding of life in California has to be founded on a "sociology of good luck."

To many Gold Rush observers, the supreme signal of luck was surviving a fire. "Do you know what constitutes a legal incorporation in California?" writes Alonzo Delano, the most acute satirist of the Gold Rush years. "Why, it's being burnt down and built up again in a month, more fair and beautiful than ever by the purification." J. D. Borthwick, another traveler in the mines, remarked on the speed with which Californians recovered from their conflagrations. In Sonora, after the fire of 1852, "in the afternoon the Phoenix began to rise"—that is, rebuilding was immediate.

Less fortunate witnesses of the Gold Rush saw only the losses it caused. In Baltimore in 1855 Hinton Rowland Helper, fresh from a long tour of California, published his notoriously grouchy *The Land of Gold: Reality Versus Fiction*. A gold-seeker from North Carolina, Helper had reason to feel disgruntled; after three months of digging in the mines, he calculated, he had realized a profit of 93 and ¾ cents. His book exhaustively chronicles misfortune in page after page of lists of "bad things" that can be found in California. California's "bad things" are so compellingly and distinctively bad, in fact, that Helper sums them up with his most memorable phrase: "California can and does furnish the best bad things that are obtainable anywhere in America." Yet the net result of his pages of lists is to create a curious abundance-effect.

San Francisco affords, for instance, seventy separate intoxicating liqueurs—and Helper provides a list of them. Since the opening of the mines, Californians have "invested upwards of six million dollars in bowie-knives and pistols." Helper furnishes a list of floods and another of wrecked ships, subdividing the latter into steamers and sailing vessels. A table of "lives lost by violent measures" includes a line for "Insanity, (produced by disappointment and misfortune) . . . 1,700." Helper's hates are catholic, but of all the adversities in this "country of unparalleled casualties and catastrophes," the one that clearly commands his attention is fire.

"A California conflagration is a scene of the most awful grandeur that the mind is capable of conceiving," Helper maintains. He quantifies his fascination by estimating that the "sundry fires in different parts of the state" number 4.4 million. His big moment of verbal rapture, a moment when he stops counting and starts looking, occurs as he witnesses the burning of a city:

One of the most beautiful sights I ever beheld was during a large fire in San Francisco. It was a moonless night, and there was nothing visible in the dark concave of heaven, save a few twinkling stars. Others were concealed by the detached masses of floating vapor which obscured them. Soon after the conflagration commenced, the brilliant illumination attracted large flocks of brant from the neighboring marshes; and as they flew hither and thither, high over the flaming element, they shone and glistened as if they had been winged balls of fire darting through the air.

Helper's is not simply the awe of Lot before Sodom, but wonder at a culture that builds a future through self-immolation. In the logic of these phoenixlike recoveries, California releases her seeds like the cone of the Douglas fir, after they have been touched by fire.

Arrested by the spectacle of catastrophe suffered or overcome, eastern visitors had neither the time nor the inclination to analyze the social conditions that gave rise to so many of these conflagrations. Borthwick omits to mention, for instance, that fires like the one that burned down Sonora were often set by those determined to drive Mexican workers out of the mines. Writing about the Gold Rush was meant to produce awe rather than analysis. Constructed by sojourners who were white and also male, these "see the elephant" texts fulfilled their contract with the reader by providing an image of a world ruled by forces rather than by men. Like the full-blown Naturalism of California's 1890s, this view transposed the human drama into a realm where those with "morals" need not apply, where the gentility that insists on character as the guarantor of prosperity and progress is irrelevant. Women were, conveniently, the thing left out.

The Gold Rush that secured the future of the Union was paid for, by the gold seekers, with a radical experience of separation. In *The World Rushed In,* J. S. Holliday likens the rush westward to "a national tragedy, much like a war, with families separated not only by distance but equally by fear and silence." The culture that developed in the California of the 1850s was "a society of lonely men." And most of the men were young, of marrying age. In post-1849 San Francisco, Peter Burnett recalled, "It was difficult to find a man with grey hair." An 1850 editorial in the Marysville *Herald* maintained that "unlike any other country in the world's history, California has not been drawn together by the gradual aggregation of families and persons bound together by ties of kindred and relationship." "You see no women here," James Pratt wrote from California in 1849. Of the 41,000 pioneers who sailed into San Francisco Bay before the end of that year, fewer than eight hundred were women, and fewer still were wives. Those few married women who arrived tended to travel overland. At Fort Laramie in 1850 the count for the year stood at 39,560 men and 2,431 women. In Nevada City a young man not long on the frontier wrote: "Got nearer to a female this evening than I have been for six months. Came near fainting." Julie Ray Jeffrey estimates that prostitutes "may have constituted 20 percent of the female population in California in 1850 and outnumbered respectable women in early mining camps by 25 to 1." A prostitute who worked the mines in men's clothing and on horseback was said to have cleared upward of $50,000.

California's gender crisis did not fail to attract women willing to meet it. "At that period in the history of San Francisco," a '49er wrote, "it was so rare to see a female, that those whose misfortune it was to be obliged to be abroad felt themselves uncomfortably stared at. Doorways filled instantly, and little islands in the streets were thronged with men who seemed to gather in a moment, and who remained immovable till the spectacle passed from their incredulous gaze." The words are those of Eliza Farnham, author of *California, In-doors and Out* (1856). Commodity or spectacle; these were the emerging options for women that Farnham sailed west to confront. Her husband had died in California in 1849, while Farnham worked on prison reform as the matron of Sing-Sing. She undertook the voyage both to settle her husband's affairs and to import a "company of females" into California. Her goal was to help the new territory overcome the "privations" attendant upon "the absence of women."

Two hundred women answered Farnham's advertisements in the East, but only three eventually sailed with her. Two of these turned back; "the third is at this time," she wrote from her California homestead, "a member of my family." The voyage meant to resolve a crisis of separation seemed instead only to promote one. At Valparaiso Farnham's ship sailed without her. On board were her two children. Unable to leave Chile until a month later, she was reunited with her children on board their original ship, docked in San Francisco Bay. Moving her party south to Santa Cruz, she took up farming there. Her cohort in this enterprise were her two sons, a male hired hand, and "a female friend." In the middle of June her first crop was attacked by hordes of grasshoppers; later, immense herds of cattle wandered into the fields and feasted on the remains.

"There is little in the condition of California society . . . to engage," Farnham wrote, "the higher orders of female intelligence." Among earnest women, "there is a universal feeling of being sadly out of place." Such a woman "will feel herself in an enemy's country." Within this "theatre of unrest," as she called it, Farnham nevertheless found the means to adapt. Although her plan to import earnest and intelligent women failed, she did learn how to work the land. The gentility that had formerly limited her perspective on California and on the capacities of women slowly gave way to a pleasure in competence. Over the course of the year, Farnham learned how to shingle a roof, wear bloomers, and repair a fence. She was assisted by Geordie, "a woman of genius" who turned up one day and pointed out that Farnham's "theory and practice" on the question of the rights of women "were at war." The real issues, as Geordie framed them, were women's morale and self-sufficiency. Encouraged by her new friend, Farnham resolved to stick with farming and to plant a crop again the following spring.

Farnham saw California not as an ordeal by hunger but as a trial by opinion. Earnest women suffered there "a universal sense of discomfort, amounting, in many cases, to wretchedness, from distrust and reserve in their own sex, and insulting suspicions in the other." Men in California assumed there was not "an honest one in the country," while the female gender was divided against itself as a result of incorporating these suspicions: "The true worth and real integrity of men and women was never more severely tried, on a broad scale, than it has been in California." Farnham cites the Donner Party of 1846 in support of her case, nominating Mrs. Breen, rather than Tamsen Donner, as its heroine. For Farnham, the choice seems a strange one: Tamsen Donner stood by her man, eventually dying at the cabins in the snow while sending her children out with relief parties. Mrs. Breen held her family together and sheltered Virginia Reed while refusing food and water to others. Her primary achievement was to endure and to survive.

Not being separated from husband and children—that was one of Mrs. Breen's accomplishments. She and her family came out of the mountains and eventually became the first non-Spanish-speaking residents of San Juan Bautista. Perhaps it was her stubborn refusal to see her family broken up that made Mrs. Breen appealing to Farnham. The Gold Rush had certainly flooded California with single men, thus promoting both prostitution and the resulting projection of male distrust endemic to any mining frontier. It also divided loyal wives and husbands. Given the distances and the risks involved, as well as the sheer number of husbands who went west alone, the Gold Rush was bound to have an immense effect on the lives of ordinary married people. The book that best captures this effect is Holliday's *The World Rushed In,* in which a faithful Penelope awaits the return, across an emotionally incalculable distance, of her nostalgic Odysseus.

PART OF THE CREDIT for this achievement goes to Holliday; most of it to William Swain, his wife Sabrina, and his brother George. Holliday's book is a carefully annotated edition of the letters and diaries written by husband, wife, and brother between April 11, 1849, the day William left his farm in Niagara County, and January 28, 1851, the day of his arrival in New York City and ten days before his return to "the family circle at home." Unlike most editions of letters from the California frontier, both sides of this correspondence have been preserved. Where William or his correspondents do remain sketchy or silent on an important topic or where much time passes, Holliday interpolates excerpts from the writings of other participants in the migration, creating a polyphony.

To write letters across such a distance involved taking substantial emotional and imaginative risks. This was not writing that could count on the reinforcement of a response. The most reliable mail service to California was by sea: The clipper ship *The Flying Cloud* set a westbound record of eighty-nine days from New York to San Francisco—but it did so in the summer of 1851, nine months after William had left the mines. On August 26, 1849, the ocean steamer *Panama* delivered 25,000 letters to the San Francisco post office. By Halloween more than 45,000 letters had piled up. People coming to the post office to pick up their mail had to wait up to six hours. Some men made a living by selling their places in line. Expressmen carried mail from the mines to Sacramento and San Francisco, charging one or two dollars for each letter delivered and fifty cents for each one picked up. After William received his first letters from home, on May 7, 1849, he heard nothing more for almost a year. George and Sabrina waited seven months after William's April 10 letter from Fort Laramie before receiving another. After eleven months of diligent correspondence, George wrote that "I have written to you every month

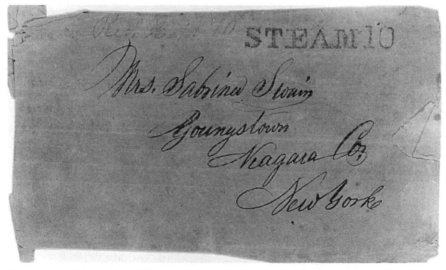

An envelope addressed by William to Sabrina Swain. Swain left Niagara County for the gold fields in April 1849 and returned to his home in New York twenty-two months later. Traveling to California on the Overland Trail, he kept a daily diary and wrote frequent letters home. His wife Sabrina and brother George wrote to William as well. The three-way correspondence generated one of the richest records of the Gold Rush as well as a powerful story of married love. Yale Collections of Western Americana and American Literature, Beinecke Rare Book and Manuscript Library, Yale University.

since you left, as per agreement, and sent your regular files of the New
York *Express* and some other scattering ones; I have directed all to Sutter's
Fort. And I only write this to keep my word good, for it seems like
writing to the wind."

Howard Lamar has portrayed the Gold Rush, for young men, as a
transforming rite of passage, but William does not romanticize what he
has gained. "Stay at home" is his most powerful refrain. He does affirm
that "I should ever be glad that I have taken the trip to California. It has
learnt me to have confidence in myself, has disciplined my impetuous
disposition and has learnt me to think and act for myself and to look upon
men and things in a true light." Yet three months earlier, in the first of the
letters to reach New York, William had written to discourage George
from following him:

> There was some talk between us of your coming to this country. For God's
> sake think not of it. Stay at home. Tell all whom you know that are thinking of
> coming that they have to sacrifice everything and face danger in all its forms,
> for George, thousands have laid and will lay their bones along the routes to
> and in this country. Tell all that "death is in the pot" if they attempt to cross the
> plains and hellish mountains.

William had not gone to the mines in order to mature; he had gone to
make money. In over ten months of prospecting, he amassed $500 in gold
dust, as well as a profit of $279 for work on a claim at Taylor's Bar. This
profit was offset by the $250 he had spent on the journey out and back.
What California did give him and Sabrina was something more intimate:
a chance to "realize our attachments." The phrase is Sabrina's. "We
cannot realize our attachments and fondness for one another," she wrote,
"until we are deprived of the society of those fond ones."

Unlike the grandfather in Steinbeck's 1945 story "The Leader of the
People," William Swain balanced his act of westering with an act of
eastering. Built into his trip and giving it its entire purpose was the
intention to return. The grandfather can imagine motion only in one
direction, west and away. "It wasn't getting here that mattered," he
concludes, "it was movement and westering." This appetite for endless
movement may sound like mere wanderlust, but Steinbeck reveals that it
leads inexorably to a kind of running-in-place. Once by the Pacific, the
grandfather's life freezes into the story he endlessly repeats. Steinbeck

provides an acute analysis of the national equation of the movement West with the pursuit of an endless desire, a desire valuable precisely because it cannot be fulfilled and therefore one at war with the domestic and with married love. Lived out as the grandfather has lived it, such a desire maroons the self in heroic narrative. This is why Steinbeck embeds the grandfather's story within the relentlessly family-centered routines of the Tifflin farm. In the end, Steinbeck's protagonist Jody must resolve the extremes represented by his nostalgic grandfather and his fully domesticated father, a resolution that will depend upon linking a mobility of spirit with cultivation of the hearth.

William Swain lived out the tensions that Jody only dimly apprehends. On the Overland Trail he discovered, as most unaccompanied men did, the rigors of housekeeping. As a Kentuckian in a neighboring camp wrote to his sister: "I have always been inclined to deride the vocation of ladies until now. But I must confess it is by far the most irksome I have ever tried. By way of taking lessons in sewing, I have often examined your stitches in my work bag. And then the cooking! I wish you could take supper with me, that you might judge the hardness and durability of our biscuits. I must at some time send you a recipe for making this lasting sort." The challenge of making do without the domesticating power of women was, for many men, a practical matter. For William and Sabrina, the separation opened up previously unrealized emotional worlds.

Sabrina's letters are particularly affecting in their unguarded admission of lack. This "crucifixion of feeling" she relieves with fantasies of rapture and flashes of wit or anger. The phrase "crucifixion of feeling" appears in a letter of William's from Foster's Bar, but the metaphor is lifted from Sabrina's first written words to him: "I want very much to describe my feelings as near as I can, but in doing so I hope not to crucify yours. I feel as though I was alone in the world. The night you left home I did not eat, nor could not, close my eyes to sleep." William's incorporation of the metaphor, many months later, suggests that in writing to each other husband and wife not only gave shape to their feelings but found ways to instruct each other in how to grieve.

Sabrina misses William's physical presence. "O! William, if I could see you this morning, I would hug and kiss you till you would blush." Less than a month later, the fantasy of physical reunion gives way to an astonishing reversal: "I often dream about you, but cannot have any satisfaction, for you treat me with disdain," she laments. By using the word "satisfaction," Sabrina expresses rather than represses the thought of the pleasure she is missing. Her letters make the bold claim that in attempting to fulfill one duty to his wife, William has betrayed another.

Sabrina registers this deprivation most openly through the illnesses she develops. "My anxieties for you are beyond description," she writes, a more or less permanent mood that takes its bodily toll. "Not only my back, but my stomach troubles me very much; also I have a great deal of pain in my head, particularly on the top." Her appetite is poor; "the fact is, William, I feel bad every way." She attributes this condition to missing him, surely, but also to her shock at discovering the power and depth of that emotion. "Hitherto I was a stranger to my attachment," she writes in the same letter, and seven months later she repeats the phrase. "Never, until your absence, had I learned the strength of my attachment."

The discovery of her own capacity for longing catapults Sabrina into a kind of epistolary sublime. Her typical strategy is to diminish or to deny her own powers of expression, as in sentences like "My feelings are such that I cannot describe them, and more than that, I try to conceal them as much as I can." "To describe my feelings"—this is the want Sabrina expresses in her first letter to William. But her continual suppression of this want—either in tribute to the untellability of her feelings or out of consideration for William's—converts the correspondence into one of nineteenth-century America's great minimalist love stories. Although Sabrina relentlessly curtails her own pen, her two-year-old daughter scrawls, at the bottom of one of her mother's letters, the most uncensored cry of the heart. It is appended as a postscript below her mother's name: "Poor pa. See Pa. Love Pa. See Papa. Kiss Pa."

William did not go West on an existential errand; the end of his journey was known. He left and meant to come back. Married love can be, of course, like crossing the continent, a continual experience of surprise, and the faith that William and Sabrina kept was to a living, changing thing. There was risk involved in going, and no guarantee of safe passage. But the pleasure in reading these letters and diaries provides a modest version of the pleasure Coleridge claims we feel in reading Shakespeare: "Expectation in preference to surprise." We believe that William will get home, and we wait, confident in that gathering possibility, for the emotions that can be felt in witnessing the moment of return.

For his return voyage, William sailed from San Francisco on the *Mosconome,* which arrived at Panama City on Christmas Day 1850. There had been cholera on board. He crossed the isthmus on foot and by mule, arriving at Chagres on New Year's Eve. From there a steamer took him to New York in twenty days. In his last letter, from the Lovejoy Hotel, he wrote that "I was attacked with Chagres fever the day before I left Chagres and was very sick all the passage." Upon his arrival in New York, George came down to meet him. His brother appeared much changed: "He looked pretty thin in flesh, dark in color, and shabby in dress, and taken by and large was a hard-looking customer." On a sunny January day, Sabrina's brother met William and George at the train station in Niagara Falls.

At the top of Lewiston Hill, which overlooks the gorge of the Niagara River and William's home village of Youngstown, the traveler stood up in the sleigh. "I have been many miles and seen many places," he said, "but this is the finest sight I have ever seen." At the house, Holliday reports, "Sabrina stood alone; she felt self-conscious when she looked into William's eyes; she waited for him to jump down and come to her." Once the couple were joyfully reunited, William slipped back into domestic life. In after years, with his brother George, he became the major peach farmer in Niagara County. At the celebration of their fiftieth wedding anniversary, Sabrina looked at her husband and proposed a toast to the separation that had sealed their attachment: "To my '49er."

THE MOST ENDURING firsthand account of the crisis of gender in the Gold Rush comes not from a miner but from a "*mineress*." Louise Clappe gave herself this title in her tenth letter from the mines. Known to her generation of Californians as Dame Shirley, Clappe had rounded Cape Horn with her itinerant doctor husband in 1849. In the fall of 1851, they settled in Rich Bar, on the East Fork of the Feather River, and they stayed on in the foothills through the 1852 season. The letters she sent home to her sister in Massachusetts were published in the *Pioneer,* the first magazine dedicated to the culture of California, in 1854 and 1855. Royce and Bancroft praised them, and Bret Harte and Mark Twain built their latter-day romances out of the careful notations of *The Shirley Letters.*

Throughout her letters, Clappe was searching high and low for a room of her own. Where standard accounts of these years describe the tumult of San Francisco's streets, Clappe gives her attention to California's interior spaces. "California herself might be called the Hotel State," she writes, "so completely is she inundated with taverns, boardinghouses, &c." Virtually all of these structures prove "innocent of a floor," or at least a level one; those of the Empire Hotel in Rich Bar "are so very uneven, that you are always ascending a hill or descending into a valley." "Guiltless of glass," the buildings are held together by little more than the ubiquitous construction material—red calico. Men live as if they were camping indoors, in pieces of "carpentering as a child two years old, gifted with the strength of a man, would produce, if it wanted to play at making grown-up houses." "No place for a lady": the phrase that sums up Clappe's early impressions of California.

During Clappe's second week in Rich Bar, one of the four women living in the settlement—a proprietor of the Empire Hotel—dies of peritonitis. Her body is laid out on a board supported by two butter tubs. On the way to the graveyard, a dark cloth, borrowed from a neighboring monte table, is flung over the coffin. Clappe finds herself painfully shocked "by the sound of the nails—there being no screws at any of the shops—driven with a hammer into the coffin, while closing it. It seemed as if it *must* disturb the pale sleeper within." The next day Clappe visits the "sixty-eight pounder woman" who runs the town's other hotel. On the way over, she hears a miner praise the bantamweight for having earned her husband nine hundred dollars in nine weeks of washing. Suddenly Clappe is aware of her status as mere surplus value: "I find it difficult to be utilitary," she will later admit. By comparison, she feels herself to be a "mere cumberer of the ground." But she consoles herself by concluding that "as all men cannot be Napoleon Bonapartes, so all women cannot be *manglers;* the majority of the sex must be satisfied with simply being *mangled*."

Clappe's anger erupts out of the sudden exposure, in the violent life of the mines, of the cash basis of the institution of marriage. The women around her are mangled by the demands placed on them as wives or as "those unfortunates," as Clappe calls them, "who make a trade" of their bodies. But, as the wife of a physician, she finds herself free to indulge in the "excessive egotism" of being a writer. In the very act of apologizing for this indulgence, however, Clappe reminds her sister that "you have often flattered me by saying that my epistles were only interesting when profusely illuminated, by that manuscriptal decoration represented by a great I." Clappe's fascination with interior spaces expresses her anxiety over being afforded the luxury of an inner life, while California's ramshackle material arrangements lead her to wonder whether residents of the state will themselves ever develop anything like one.

Clappe discovers a terrible freedom in the mines, a world so inattentive to convention and ceremony that it accommodates her anger and even allows her to distance herself from the underlying social "formations" that dictate a woman's work. She nevertheless maintains a careful remove from the Bloomers, as she calls self-consciously liberated women, preferring instead, when openly confronted by the matter of the rights of women, to quote such lines of poetry as "He sings to the wide world, she to her nest." Yet she follows this submissive rhetoric by saying, "Speaking of birds," then telling the story of a wild pheasant that she lets run about her cabin. But the bird dies. It dies of "home-sickness," Clappe allows; wild birds need the "beloved solitude of their congenial homes." Perhaps the moral of the story is that every bird needs her own nest. Or perhaps the story reveals that for any "free and wild" nature, being housebound is fatal.

That wildness Clappe locates in what she calls the "power of language," and nothing incites it more than the violence of mining life. "How oddly do life and death jostle each other in this strange world of ours!" she exclaims early on, and takes her greatest relish in this chronic cognitive dissonance. In twenty-four days "we have had murders, fearful accidents, bloody deaths, a mob, whippings, a hanging, an attempt at suicide, and a fatal duel." She details each incident, then, at letter's end, boasts of having cooked up such a "dish of horrors." Its primary ingredient is the stabbing of Tom Somers by Domingo, a "majestic-looking Spaniard."

A rumor spreads through Indian Bar that the Mexicans have conspired to kill all the Americans on the river. As the cry of "Down with the Spaniards" echoes through the valley, the Mexican "foreigners" barricade themselves in a saloon. The street fills up with a sea of heads, and the women of the settlement, sent to watch affairs from a distance, seat themselves above the town to witness the strange scene below.

Behind such riots lay the Anglo resentment of the success enjoyed by Mexican miners, who pioneered in the techniques of panning and dry-wash separation of gold. The Mexicans used a *batea,* a wooden bowl for washing out gold, and an *arrastra,* a device equipped with a water wheel that increased the efficiency of placer operations. Although the American miners gladly borrowed these techniques, their indebtedness to the Mexicans did not lead to gratitude. In 1849 the California Assembly even voted to prevent all "foreigners" or native Californians from working in the mines. The bill did not become law, but another bill, establishing the Foreign Miners' License Tax, did. Passed in 1850, this law required non-U.S. citizens to pay twenty dollars monthly in order to work their claims. In the early period of its administration—the law was later repealed, modified, and then reinstated—the tax fell most heavily on the Spanish-speaking immigrants who worked the southern mines. "To many foreign miners," writes Walter Noble Burns, "it was an edict of banishment." The year the tax was enacted, three thousand Anglo miners attempted to burn down the Mexican settlement of Sonora. The five thousand Sonorans who had created the town were soon gone, banished by vigilantism and by the weight of the mining tax.

From her seat above the town, Clappe watches the race riot. At the center of the fracas is a Mexican woman who was seen hanging upon "the arm" of Domingo, the man with "the long, bloody knife." A vigilance committee is elected and apprehends her.

> The first act of the Committee was to try a *Mejicana,* who had been foremost in the fray. She has always worn male attire, and on this occasion, armed with a pair of pistols, she fought like a very fury. Luckily, inexperienced in the use of fire-arms, she wounded no one. She was sentenced to leave the Bar by day-light, a perfectly just decision, for there is no doubt that she is a regular little demon. Some went so far as to say, she ought to be hung, for she was the *indirect* cause of the fight. You see always, it is the old, cowardly excuse of Adam in Paradise: "The *woman* tempted me, and I did eat."

In the Mejicana two kinds of "foreigners"—women and people of color—converge to threaten the cozy instability of a culture built on the exclusion or suppression of both. In addition, the Mejicana also cross-dresses. For Clappe herself, she embodies the uncanny knowledge that continually undermines her attempts to remain a mere *"wife."* In the mines Clappe has discovered a culture that projects its own violence onto the absent female yet is so sentimental about the actual women in its midst that either indoors or outdoors there is for them no safe place.

Somehow a life will have to be built for women and for men outside their given roles. For Clappe, it will be a life "stained" not by blood but by ink; she chooses to dwell within the liberating egotism of her letters and to address all twenty-three of them to her sister. In an ending worthy of

Marilynne Robinson, she gives up housekeeping. Cooking only with an iron dipper, a brass kettle, and a grid-iron, made out of an old shovel, the "invalid" from the East finds herself gaining "unwonted strength" in California's "barren soil." At the close of this final letter, she describes herself not as a wife but as "your *now* perfectly healthy sister."

In her letters Clappe proved more alert to the status of women than to that of "foreigners." For her, life in the mines became a romance of gender rather than a tragedy of race. Sisterhood was the variable that counted. For the Mejicana, however, it may well have been otherwise. She was more likely to feel that mining life led to a collision of immigrants rather than their integration.

The 1840s were the years, as Reginald Horsman reminds us, when "the use of Anglo-Saxon in the racial sense . . . became commonplace" in the United States. The model provided by the fate of blacks and Indians argued that as the nation expanded into a new territory, like California, non-"Anglo-Saxon" peoples would either be subordinated or would disappear. As a "foreigner" with brown skin, the Mejicana was threatened far more seriously than was Clappe. In 1851 in Downieville, a woman named Juanita had been hanged after stabbing a miner who broke into her cabin on the Fourth of July. The Chinese later suffered the most overt and prolonged discrimination, but the miners from Mexico and Chile, along with native Californians of Spanish heritage, bore the first brunt of California's stubbornly exclusionary politics. While the Sonorans were being harried from the southern mines, in San Francisco the Hounds, a group of Mexican War veterans, set about harassing or "hounding" the tent community of Little Chile. It was mob violence against the city's Spanish-speaking communities, as much as anything, that spurred the creation in 1851 of San Francisco's first vigilance committee.

DURING THE 1850s the persecution of immigrants from Mexico and points south generated a powerful myth of reaction. In the figure of the bandit Joaquín Murieta, Californians of all races joined together to create a fable of payback. The founding version of the Murieta story, published in 1854, was written by John Rollin Ridge. On the title page, under *The Life and Adventures of Joaquín Murieta, the Celebrated California Bandit,* the publisher printed the author's name: *Yellow Bird*. Ridge, half-white and half-Cherokee, had been given the name Yellow Bird before emigrating in 1850 to California from his native Georgia; his novel was the first written in English by a person of Native American ancestry.

As Ridge tells it, the Murieta story begins in justifiable revenge. Within the first few pages the immigrant from Sonora is subjected to intolerable humiliations. Ridge presents the actions against Murieta as race-based—that is, as gratuitous. They are precipitated by "the lawless and desperate men" who profess "contempt for any and all Mexicans." The catastrophe they inflict is threefold. First, a band of men order Murieta to leave his claim. They beat him and ravish his mistress "before his eyes." Second, a "company of unprincipled Americans" drives him from his little farm. Third, Joaquín, accused of stealing a horse that has actually been lent him by his brother, is publicly whipped; his brother is hanged. "Then it was that he declared to a friend that he would henceforth live for revenge." Joaquín organizes his band and begins his three-year career as the most efficient bandit ever to terrorize California.

Ridge's Joaquín is a double hero. "There were two Joaquíns," his second paragraph begins, "bearing the various surnames of Murieta, O'Comorenia, Valenzuela, Botellier, and Carillo." The confusion of names reinforces the rumor that "no less than five sanguinary devils" ranged the country at the same time. But, Ridge asserts, "it is now fully ascertained that there were only two," and that the second Murieta was "a distinguished subordinate to the first." Still, the duality of the hero is retained when Ridge pairs Joaquín with a sidekick, Three Fingered Jack. Jack proves as bloodthirsty as Joaquín is restrained. He preys with special fury on the Chinese, exterminating them with a casual if inventive violence. "I can't help it," Jack allows. "Somehow or other, I love to smell the blood of a Chinaman."

Ridge's Joaquín begins as a bounded soul, "mild and peaceable." No less than three blows are necessary to open him up. After the first, Joaquín's reaction is relatively moderate: "the soul of the young man was from that moment darkened." After the second, "his blood boiled in his veins." But only after the third does he seek revenge: "His soul swelled beyond its former boundaries, and the barriers of honor, rocked into atoms by the strong passion which shook his heart like an earthquake, crumbled about him." Trauma darkens and kindles, and Ridge's language swells his hero into a kind of avenging sublime.

Why construct a hero so multiple, so spread out, so fugitive? Ridge

attempted to construct an adequate symbol for the rage that
existed in his historical moment,
a rage both personal and collective. The Sonorans who were
driven from their settlement in
the southern mines were only one
instance, albeit the most vivid, of
the institutionalized persecution
of "dark" Californians. During
the 1850s, as Leonard Pitt has
shown, "a war of the races" between the Spanish- and English-
speaking residents of Los Angeles
was a near-constant condition.
Competing vigilante committees
sprang up there in order to
"equalize" the treatment of ban-
dits like Joaquín—and plenty of
them did speak Spanish—before
the law. But Ridge himself was
not of Mexican descent, and his
fascination with what he called "a
deep-seated principle of Revenge"

*A photograph of John Rollin Ridge from the
1850s. Son of a Cherokee and a white
woman, the Georgia-born Ridge arrived in
San Francisco in 1850 at the age of twenty-
three. His 1854 pamphlet,* The Life and
Adventures of Joaquín Murieta, *invented
the most enduring myth about Mexican life
during the Gold Rush and allowed him to
avenge, if only in fiction, the murders of his
father and grandfather. Courtesy of the
Society of California Pioneers.*

probably had more to do with the events of his childhood in Georgia.

In 1839 John Ridge Senior, a Cherokee, was stabbed to death before the
eyes of his twelve-year-old son. On the same night the boy's paternal
grandfather was also murdered. The two men had been leaders of a
Cherokee faction that had reluctantly come to support the removal of
their people to Indian Territory beyond the Mississippi; they were killed
for their politics. Living in the style of a prosperous Georgia planter,
Grandfather Ridge had provided his son with a white man's education
but had objected to his marriage to a white man's daughter. John Ridge
had provided a similar education for his son, and after the murders, John
Rollin Ridge continued his schooling in Arkansas and in New England.
He also joined a guerrilla movement against the faction that perpetrated
the murders. After he moved to California, he invented a fictional hero
who wrought mayhem with a knife and who "*wiped out* the most of those

prominently engaged in whipping him." To a gathering of fellow editors in San Francisco, Ridge recalled the "thirty-six men who had driven knives into his father's body," and added that by 1861 only four of them remained alive.

Like Juana Machado, John Rollin Ridge projected his own personal and tribal losses onto the story of another oppressed people. "Only his wiry, jet-black hair indicated his racial heritage," Franklin Walker writes of Ridge; and "long, glossy black hair" became Joaquín's major signature as well, the visual link between author and character. Yet the actual merges powerfully with the imagined in Ridge's story. Beginning with the uncertainty of names and the irony of motivations, it ends with evidence so confused that Ridge seems to have taken the advice a newspaper editor delivers at the end of John Ford's *The Man Who Shot Liberty Valance:* "When the legend becomes fact, print the legend."

The facts are that in 1853 the California legislature offered $5,000 for the capture of a bandit called "Joaquín." An ex–Texas Ranger named Harry Love organized a posse that scoured the state. On July 25, 1853, Love and his men came upon a group of Mexicans camped somewhere in Fresno County. State Historical Marker 344 identifies the Arroyo Cantua, near Coalinga, as the spot. A shoot-out ensued. Three days later Love arrived in Stockton carrying the head of one man and the hand of another. The head was said to be Joaquín's; the hand, Three Fingered Jack's. Pickled in alcohol and displayed in San Francisco, the head generated a number of positive IDs, even one from a prostitute named Salome.

The first known poster advertising the exhibition, in Stockton, California, August 12, 1853, of the remains of Joaquín Murieta and his sidekick, Three Fingered Jack. Courtesy of the Bancroft Library.

Ridge narrates all this pretty much as it happened; the acts performed and exhibits provided by Love converge with his story. "He caused the head of the renowned Murieta to be cut off," Ridge writes, and "that terrible, three-fingered hand" to be preserved. "Three-Fingered Jack's head was also cut off, but being shot through, soon became offensive, and was thrown away." The fragility of the evidence anticipates the eclipse of fact by legend. The story of Murieta began to displace the events that had given it meaning; in the 1980s it even sent writer Richard Rodriguez on a strange journey, which he recounts in *Days of Obligation*.

In the mid-1980s a Jesuit priest named Alberto Huerta has written of his wish to find and bury the severed head of Joaquín Murieta. After reading one of Huerta's essays, Rodriguez gives him a call. They meet and talk about Murieta, and Huerta convinces Rodriguez to accompany him on his search for the head. They discover that the marker commemorating the shoot-out was destroyed by an earthquake in 1983. Seventy-seven years earlier another earthquake had also destroyed a number of exhibits in Dr. Jordan's Pacific Museum of Anatomy and Science on Market Street in San Francisco. "The jar with the head and all the other jars moved on their shelves, then crashed to the ground," writes Rodriguez. "It was the Great San Francisco Earthquake. A hideous stew bubbled on the floor for several days as the city burned. Dr. Jordan's Museum did not burn down, but it never reopened. A janitor mopped up the gore and it all got thrown away or was buried somewhere. So they say."

But Father Huerta's search for the head wouldn't die. He calls Rodriguez again. "He has found the head. It is in Santa Rosa. It belongs to a man named Walter Johnson, an ornamental-rock salesman who paid twenty-five hundred dollars for it several years ago." They drive to see the head. At first, Rodriguez will not look at it: "I look away." He notices the disorder in the house around it. Then he looks a little. "The dark hair floats like sea grass." The eyes are open. Father Huerta offers to buy the head and to bury it, but the owner says nothing, and they leave.

Another legend concerns Murieta's last words. Walter Noble Burns, the most successful of the many retoolers of the original story, gave him four sentences in Spanish. According to Burns, after Love trapped him, Murieta fled on foot but was felled by three shots. " *'Es bastante,'* he said in a clear voice. *'No tire más. El trabajo se acabo. Ya estoy muerto.'* " In his account Ridge condensed the last words into one sentence: "Don't shoot any more—the work is done." But Burns's version has something over Ridge's; knowing that he was writing for a readership with little or no Spanish, Burns provided an English translation of the valediction. The bandit's words not only sum up his legend but chasten any fascination with it: "It is enough. Shoot no more. The job is finished. I am dead."

A SINGLE WHITE MALE living in California during the 1850s, then, would very likely have detected a shortage of women and an abundance of "foreigners." The immigration of the one was as welcome as the other was not. During these years race became the cultural flashpoint, and most political careers were founded on a rhetoric of purity and exclusion. In 1854, for instance, in the People *v.* Hall, the California Supreme Court ruled that a white man charged with murder could not be convicted on the testimony of a Chinese witness. "We are of the opinion," the court wrote, "that the words 'White,' 'Negro,' 'Mulatto,' 'Indian,' and 'Black person,' wherever they occur in our Constitution and laws, must be taken in their generic sense, and that, even admitting the Indian of this continent is not of the Mongolian type, that the words 'Black person,' in the 14th section must be taken as contradistinguished from White, and necessarily excludes all races other than the Caucasian." So did California warm itself up for the Civil War.

Politicians did not publicly apply such exclusionary rhetoric to women, but the virtual absence of a female presence during the Gold Rush years allowed a culture to grow up in which women, except as members of the sex trade, were largely omitted. The original myth of California, laid out in Montalvo's *Las Sergas de Esplandían* (1510), imagined it as an island populated by women and ruled by a queen named Calafia. In the 1850s California could not have been further from that myth.

When Bret Harte wrote in an 1868 short story that "no encouragement was given to immigration," he was referring to the invitation of women into a blessedly all-male valley. One of the most profound clichés of American studies holds that when men light out for a new territory, it is to flee women. A scathing contemporary version is Raymond Carver's "So Much Water So Close to Home," the story that became the center of *Short Cuts,* Robert Altman's 1992 film about life in southern California. In the story, the men go fishing in order to get away, but what they catch is a woman—the corpse of a drowned female. They find her in the river, tie her to a tree, and go on fishing. The drowned body that refuses to stay submerged can be taken as a metaphor for the repressed but irrepressible female. This female power haunts narratives from which she is absent, but by the 1980s it had come fully to the surface in novels like Robinson's *Housekeeping* (1980), where women choose willingly to go West and to go into water.

A woman surfacing: this image can serve as a metaphor for the history of the West. Harte's mining stories register the continual pressure created by the imminent return of the repressed female. Attitudes between the sexes are notoriously difficult to gauge, but it is possible to read Harte's mining stories as expressing a male hysteria over the prospect of having to modify the fundamentally adolescent and comfortably homoerotic society of the mines by a significant influx of women. In *The Ordeal of Mark Twain*, Van Wyck Brooks reached a similar conclusion about the emotional lives of men living on the mining frontier. "There were so few women among them . . . that their sexual lives were either stunted or debased; and children were as rare as the 'Luck' of Roaring Camp, a story that shows how hysterical, in consequence of these and similar conditions, the mining population was."

Harte mined *The Shirley Letters* with more profit than any prospector did the Mother Lode, and he would have followed Louise Clappe, as well as William Swain, in defining the mines as a site of men without women. He quarried his breakthrough story, "The Luck of Roaring Camp," from an incident in Clappe's seventeenth letter. The fame that that story accrued made him, in the early 1870s, the country's most widely read author. His first volume of short stories, published in 1870, not only generated a contract for $10,000 from the *Atlantic Monthly* and *Every Saturday* but established a warm-hearted Gold Rush as the originating myth of Anglo California.

As the editor of the *Overland Monthly*, Harte proved remarkably open not only to talents like Mark Twain and Ambrose Bierce but to myriad subjects. The articles he published during the inaugural year, 1868, represent California as host to a choir of voices and boast titles like "Chinese in California: Their Sign-Board Literature," "The Apache Race," "The French in Mexico," "Hawaiian Civilization," "Japanese Holy Places," and a study of Mexico called "High Noon of Empire." Harte and his stable of writers saw California as a nexus, with San Francisco as its central bazaar.

Yet Harte's own fiction, written for the magazine, displays sure signs of "Imperialist nostalgia," a term Renato Rosaldo applies to a dominant culture's yearning for the "primitive" forms of cultural life that it has

Bret Harte in the 1860s. The cravat and pin testify to the "good taste in clothes" that Mark Twain mercilessly belittled in his recollections of Harte; the two men met in San Francisco in 1864. While editor of the Overland Monthly, *Harte published Twain and achieved national acclaim with his 1868 Gold Rush story "The Luck of Roaring Camp." After departing for the East and a lucrative contract with the* Atlantic Monthly *in 1871, Harte never returned to California. Courtesy of the University of Virginia.*

intentionally destroyed. Harte's "The Right Eye of the Commander," set in the year 1797, establishes the nostalgic tone: "It was that glorious Indian summer of California history, around which so much poetical haze still lingers,—that bland, indolent autumn of Spanish rule, so soon to be followed by the wintry storms of Mexican independence and the reviving spring of American conquest." Summer, autumn, winter, spring: Harte converts the changes of flags, with their attendant violence, into mere changes of season. So adept did he prove at these compressions and idealizations that, for over a century, his writing established an autumnal Indian summer as the dominant myth of Spanish California.

Harte cannot be dismissed, however, as a mere tourist in California's turbulent reality. His stories and sketches conduct a sly exposé of the costs, to everyone, of California's period of Americanization. He wrote with particular fervor about the fate of the Californios and the Chinese. Even before he broke into print as a writer of fiction, Harte the newspaperman had deplored the massacre of Indians in Humboldt County and had established himself as a staunch abolitionist. To be sure, the cultural struggle over gender issues was the most persistent focus of Harte's attention—in *The Education* Henry Adams maintained that except for Harte and Whitman, the writers of his day "used sex for sentiment, never for force." But Harte also registered, beneath his nostalgias, an insistent racial sorrow.

Earlier than most, Harte saw that the emerging myth of the California frontier—a myth of freedom and the purity of the national character—

veiled a struggle over race and gender. Although the myth served to invite everyone in, the politics on the ground proceeded with relocations, exclusions, and scapegoatings. Harte's foundational story begins, after all, with a fantasy of assimilation: the birth of a mixed-race baby in an all-male valley. But the Indian mother, the camp's sole prostitute, is punished for her womanhood by dying in childbirth, and the baby, who creates as much commotion as comity, is finally eliminated as well, in the flood that washes away Roaring Camp's experiment in utopian child-raising.

This is a California of broken contracts and sudden carnage but also of small victories. "Notes by Flood and Field" reenacts the appropriation of the Mexican ranchos by the invading Americans but predicts, through its flood imagery, the eventual engulfment of the invaders. "The Mission Dolores" imagines the "last Greaser" giving way to the bustling Yankee. In a sketch called "John Chinaman"—Harte used the epithets of the day in order to expose their careless shorthand and to acknowledge his complicity in the impure dialect of his tribe—he condemns the "vulgar clamor about servile and degraded races," while in "Wan Lee, the Pagan," the narrator draws us into a bemused tour of the exotic, then abruptly exposes us to the jingoism that "set upon and killed unarmed, defenseless foreigners." In "The Argonauts of '49," Harte celebrates the acts of resistance displayed by the "Spaniard" and the "Heathen Chinee," both of which represent what he calls "available memory." Deprived of a sphere in which they can distend their manhood, they become heroes instead of "inner consciousness." Harte also shows how they "get even," as does the Chinese citizen who opens a "doctor's office" in San Francisco.

Harte arrived in California at the age of eighteen, in 1854. He may have traveled, a year later, to the mines. By then the Gold Rush was over; his knowledge of it, unlike Clappe's, was therefore not firsthand. When Harte began to write fiction, he adapted Clappe's materials to express a post–Civil War social situation anxious about the presence of many "races" and especially about the growing cultural presence and power of women. The overt hostility toward the "sex" in Clappe's world submerged itself, in Harte, into the category of the "sentimental."

"The Luck of Roaring Camp" is typically read as a charming if shallow tale about an all-male family romance. Its one female character, Cherokee Sal, is an Indian and a prostitute who dies in childbirth and leaves the miners to raise the child. They are transformed by the task, planting vines and flowers around their houses and learning to wash themselves twice a day, for the sake of the baby, whom they name "The Luck." The sentimental and defensive assumption here, one to which Harte's readers appear to have so powerfully responded, is that men can domesticate a world without significant assistance from women.

But Harte's prose in fact submits this fantasy to withering scrutiny. He summons a rhetoric of turgid solemnity and violent inarticulateness: Sal is described by the narrator as "dissolute, abandoned, and irreclaimable," while the miners can only opine that the birth and death must be "rough on Sal." The effect is to reveal that this world lacks a language or a set of social practices that can give Sal or any other mother a place. Harte also interrogates the sentimental by assigning Kentuck the role of camp spokesman. The gambler's belief that everything signifies and can be read as predictive is projected onto both "Nature" and "the d—d little cuss." Thus the baby does not simply respond reflexively to Kentuck's probing hand; "He rastled with my finger." Thus the trees do not merely move in the breeze; toward the Luck, "The tall red-woods nodded familiarly and sleepily." Through Kentuck and through the language of personification, Harte explores the superstition, verging on paranoia, with which the all-male camp interprets the world, especially the world inhabited by women.

Harte offers up the ending of "The Luck of Roaring Camp" as a result that satisfies a desperate kind of male wishing. The miners are debating whether to open the valley to the immigration of families:

> With the prosperity of the camp came a desire for further improvement. It was proposed to build a hotel in the following spring, and to invite one or two decent families to reside there for the sake of "The Luck,"—who might perhaps profit by female companionship. The sacrifice that this concession to the sex cost these men, who were fiercely skeptical in regard to its general virtue and usefulness, can only be accounted for by their affection for Tommy. A few still held out. But the resolve could not be carried into effect for three months, and the minority meekly yielded in the hope that something might turn up to prevent it. And it did.

What turns up is a flood, one that washes away most of the camp along with the Luck, who is found dead in the dying Kentuck's arms. The threatened immigration of "the sex" will not prove necessary after all. In the sentence "And it did," the sentence preceding the paragraph that delivers the flood, Harte admits that plot manages and allays male anxiety. The purpose of the flood is to strand them where they want to be—in a world of men without women.

In "A Protegee of Jack Hamlin's," Harte alludes to an "evasion of emotion peculiar to all brothers." In Harte's miners, emotion is replaced by continual low-grade hysteria. He does not celebrate this easily mystified complex of behaviors but analyzes it—although he permits readers to overlook the analysis. A love of understatement, an obsession with order and cleanliness, humor bordering on cruelty, a homoerotic bonding that cloaks itself in violence and expertise—Harte casts these behaviors as originating in a fear of female sexuality and power. Feelings are equated with women and actions with men, a split that not only opposes the sexes but forces individuals to deny a part of their human selves. Wise enough to anticipate the inevitable return of the repressed, Harte's Gold Rush stories are thus haunted by the whole realm of emotion that has been banished and with which women are culturally associated. The stories necessarily turn upon a moment when exiled feeling comes surging back in distorted and melodramatic forms, when a man like Kentuck acts like a woman—when he *feels*.

So Harte's Gold Rush stories get at a profoundly disturbing truth: that the "sentimental," a category traditionally associated with women, actually flourishes in their absence. Among writers who took up the subject of the Gold Rush, it was men who romanticized it; the women, like Farnham and Clappe, saw less its color than its costs. Like any other frontier, California was born out of a society of men. Whether most of them liked it that way or were lonely for women remains an open question. A fierce skepticism "in regard to the general virtue and usefulness of women" was certainly not shared by William Swain; it was, in part, Harte's literary invention. But the immense popularity of his fiction, a phenomenon that persisted well into the 1870s, argues that twenty years after the Gold Rush, Americans felt a need to repress its actual tensions and costs and to see instead a fantasy Gold Rush, one in which men were redeemable and self-sufficient and women were conveniently unnecessary.

CHAPTER THREE

EXCLUSION, THE CHINESE, AND THE DAUGHTER'S ARRIVAL

THE IMMIGRATION HARTE IMAGINED the miners resisting was of "the sex." In post–Gold Rush California the hottest political issue had to do, rather, with the immigration of the Chinese. And that immigration was defined and demonized, in turn, as a male ordeal. Much more than for Harte's miners, the Chinese proved a group for whom women were radically absent. Of the 11,794 Chinese who were living in California in 1852, only seven were women. By 1870, some 3,500 Chinese women had immigrated to California—and 61 percent of those were listed as "prostitute." Called "one hundred men's wife," these Chinese sex workers were brought to California largely by trickery or force to serve the entire male population of the state. The China Men who came to the Golden Mountain to work the mines stayed on to build the levees, roads, and railroads, and at low wages. Very few were able to marry; as Maxine Hong Kingston writes of one male immigrant, who entered California as late as 1924: "He did not know that he had come to a country with no women." Chinese immigration to California took on enormous symbolic weight in the politics of the state because it foregrounded, in visible and exotic ways, the abiding issues of racial difference, the continuing struggle between capital and labor, and above all, given the

stunning imbalance between the male and female populations, the rights
and status of women.

IN 1951 JOHN STEINBECK RETOLD "The Luck of Roaring Camp" through
the voice of a Chinese narrator. In Chapter 28 of *East of Eden,* when Lee
tells the story of his immigrant mother and father, he borrows the
ingredient that makes Harte's story work: one woman alone and pregnant in a world of men. What Steinbeck added, some eighty years later,
was a violent male anger.

Lee's Cantonese father is forced to leave China in order to pay a bad
debt. Dressed like a man, his wife stows herself on board the ship carrying
him to America. They end up building the railroad across the Sierra.
"Only males were brought—no females," Lee says. "The country did not
want them breeding." The two manage to stay together by claiming that
the wife is the husband's nephew. They begin to make preparations for
the birth of a baby, hoarding food and saving matches:

> A little boulder jumped down a hill and broke my father's leg. They set the leg
> and gave him cripples' work, straightening used nails with a hammer on a
> rock. And whether with worry or work—it doesn't matter—my mother
> went into early labor. And then the half-mad men knew and they went all
> mad. One hunger sharpened another hunger, and one crime blotted out the
> one before it, and the little crimes committed against those starving men flared
> into one gigantic maniac crime.
>
> My father heard the shout "Woman" and he knew. He tried to run and his
> leg rebroke under him and he crawled up the ragged slope to the roadbed
> where it was happening.
>
> When he got there a kind of sorrow had come over the sky, and the Canton
> men were creeping away to hide and to forget that men can be like this. My
> father came to her on the pile of shale. She had not even eyes to see out of, but
> her mouth still moved and she gave him his instructions. My father clawed me
> out of the tattered meat of my mother with his fingernails. She died on the
> shale in the afternoon.

So Lee becomes "the Luck" of another all-male camp. "No child ever had
such care as I. The whole camp became my mother."

Steinbeck's tale melodramatically expresses not only the persistence of
certain plots in the California imagination but the specific pertinence of

the "Luck" plot to the situation of the Chinese. The Chinese immigration
to California, precipitated by the discovery of gold, created a crisis of labor
that was inseparable from a crisis of gender. One reason the China Men
were able to work so hard for so little and to survive was that they did not
have the freedom to maintain families. According to Benson Tong,
"Family development in Chinese America almost completely disap-
peared." In 1900 only five percent of the 89,863 Chinese living on the
United States mainland were female. Not until the 1950s, after the 1943
repeal of the Exclusion Act and the 1945 passage of the War Brides Act,
did the numbers begin to come into balance. The terrible disproportion
between Chinese men and women in the Far West allowed for the
sublimation of male energy into an unsurpassed act of region-building.
This is the energy that erupts in Lee's story—an energy that is also a
hunger, the hunger of men without women, the anger of a life of work
without love. The story of the Chinese in California is the story of the
daughter's arrival, the slow and painful restoration to this immigrant
culture not only of the woman's presence but of her untrammeled voice.

Few Chinese voices from nineteenth-century California survive. One
of the most impressive testimonies is the 1868 "Remonstrance from the
Chinese in California to the Congress of the United States." Translated by
William Speer and published in his *The Oldest and the Newest Empire*
(1870), the "Remonstrance" speaks in a collective and powerful voice
from a Chinese standpoint. For the most part, however, the Chinese were
the objects of a uniquely paranoid discourse rather than its generating
subjects, a discourse that culminated in the 1882 Exclusion Act. The act,
which prohibited Chinese "laborers" from entering the United States,
effectively halted immigration from China.

In the years leading up to and following the Civil War, the Chinese
came to stand in for blacks in writings about race. Even *Frederick Douglass's Paper* enacted this synecdoche. In an 1855 letter from "Nubia" that
dismisses Chinese habits as "filthy" and argues that their "unmention-
ables resemble a couple of potato sacks sewed together," the writer also
admits that "the Chinese have taken the places of the colored people, as
victims of oppression."

Bret Harte, Frank Norris, Jack London, and Dashiell Hammett all
wrote stories about the "Heathen Chinese." Even if Harte's astonishingly
popular poem by that name, published in 1870, was one he later repudi-
ated, the suspicions it expressed prospered. A significant body of late

nineteenth-century fiction was devoted to fantasies of a Chinese takeover of the United States. An 1880 story published in the *Overland Monthly* imagines that, in the administration of oaths at City Hall, the new Chinese rulers of San Francisco have replaced the hand on the Bible with the decapitation of a chicken. These fantasies crested in London's 1907 "The Unparalleled Invasion," an utterly deadpan account of the Western response to a "China rampant." In an imagined 1976 tubes of fragile glass containing microbes and mosquitoes bombard China, wipe out the population, and clear the way for "a vast and happy intermingling of nationalities that settled down in China in 1982 and the years that followed."

Pierton W. Dooner's *The Last Days of the Republic,* published two years before passage of the Exclusion Act, gave these anxieties a full novelistic treatment.

Dooner's book scarcely reads like a novel. Like our late twentieth-century conspiracy theorists, Dooner starts with a few facts, disguising his fiction as straight social history. He admits early on, for instance, that the Chinese have a reason to hate Anglos. "The local prejudice entertained by the Chinese immigrants to California, against its Caucasian population, was nurtured by the abuses to which their pioneers were subjected." Having conceded this, however, Dooner proceeds to elaborate on the hate until it becomes a threat to American California. The Chinese anger, combined with their "consuming avarice" and "incredible cunning," "laid the foundations of a scheme of conquest unparalleled in the history of the

THE GOVERNOR OF CALIFORNIA.

An illustration from Pierton W. Dooner's 1880 The Last Days of the Republic. *Published at the height of the anti-Chinese agitation in California, the novel imagines a scheme in which "the Chinese Empire" succeeds in the military conquest of the United States. Courtesy of the University of Virginia.*

human race," nothing more than the third conquest—counting the arrival of the Spanish and the Americans—of California.

In the mid-1850s, according to the novel, the Chinese Empire sent out "a corps of observation." "I have not been able to find that any reference to this Commission has ever been made," Dooner admits, "in the correspondence between the two governments." He bases his claim on the activist role played by the Six Companies during the early years of the Chinese immigration. Also called Tongs, the Six Companies were formed in the 1850s in San Francisco to represent and organize Chinese interests. Dooner maintains that "a scheme of immigration was fixed upon by which every immigrant was assured a support"—meaning the loans and payback programs by which most immigrants, with the help of the Six Companies, financed their trips to California. Dooner then quickly sketches the decades in which the Chinese became pawns in a class war that spawned the San Francisco riots of 1864, the birth of the Workingman's Party, and the general cry of "the Chinese must go."

Like Hinton Rowland Helper, who devoted a chapter in his *The Land of Gold* to "The Chinese in California," Dooner emigrated to California from the American South. But Helper had gone West in the decade before the Civil War; Dooner, in the years afterward. He was deeply affected by the defeat as well as by the redistribution of power between the races that Reconstruction at least temporarily promised. But his history shifts into an openly fictional mode when it prophesies a turn-of-the-century replay of the War Between the States. South Carolina proves the heroine of the struggle—"she saw that eleven states of the Union had passed over to Mongolian citizens"—and so promptly takes action. The state's supreme court declares null and void an election that the Chinese have rigged precisely in order to provoke federal troops to march into her territory. Rebellion is thus redefined as an act of patriotism—or racial solidarity. The war culminates in a siege of Washington, D.C., in which federal troops are surrounded by the Imperial Chinese Army. "The very name of the United States of America was thus blotted from the record of nations and peoples" and was replaced by "the barbaric splendor known as the Western Empire of his August Majesty of the Emperor of China and Ruler of all lands."

Dooner notes in passing one "peculiarity" of the Chinese immigration, "of which no plausible explanation was ever made. . . . the fact that less than five per centum of the Chinese immigrants to our shores were

THE WAR OF THE RACES.

This illustration from Dooner's novel shows the Imperial Chinese Army laying seige to Washington, D.C. Courtesy of the University of Virginia.

women. . . . The immigrants, consisting chiefly of men, lived in communities, and established a species of family circle without the presence of their women. This fact, if noticed at all, was simply regarded as a national eccentricity, and elicited no further study or comment. Time, however, was destined to explain its great significance, and to establish, as well, that no peculiar feature of this movement was the work of chance." The same fantasy expressed by Harte in "The Luck of Roaring Camp" is here attributed to the Chinese. These men, he implies, have *chosen* to live without women. And they have done so, in Dooner's logic, because they must maintain the ascetic discipline of an invading army.

It was a period of extreme racialist imaginings, and the rapidly growing anti-Chinese sentiment soon resulted in the imposition of the Foreign Miners' Tax, a tax that was collected largely from the Chinese and which, by 1870, represented between 25 and 50 percent of all state revenue. The Chinese voices that did see print were often drawn into a racialist discourse. In 1855 Lai Chun-chuen, writing on behalf of the Chinese merchants of San Francisco, issued a pamphlet in response to an anti-Chinese speech by California governor John Bigler. Lai Chun-chuen's depiction wavered between a view of Chinese culture as a natural set of givens and a play of constructed and varying differences. He began by taking up the issue of women:

> We have read the message of the Governor.
>
>   First. It is stated that "too large a number of the men of the Flowery Kingdom have emigrated to this country, and that they have come here alone, without their families." Among the reasons for this course we may mention the following: That the wives of the better families of China have generally compressed feet. They are accustomed to live in the utmost privacy. They are unused to wind and waves. And it is exceedingly difficult to bring families upon distant voyages over great oceans.

In this paragraph Lai Chun-chuen treats cultural practices as if they were natural facts, part of the weather. He lists foot-binding—a custom likely to arrest an outsider—first in a series of facts about women over which no human agency appears to have control. The reasons that few Chinese women willingly emigrated to California were many, and the immobility brought on by foot-binding was certainly one of them. But foot-binding was also an exotic symptom of the vulnerability of women in a culture where daughters could be sold for two bags of seed, as in Ruthanne McCunn's *Thousand Pieces of Gold*. The power to send women off to California as sex workers was the ironic corollary of the widely enforced cultural attempt to immobilize them.

Having appealed to culture as necessity, Lai Chun-chuen argues (omitted in Speer's translation) that culture is unified and universal: "Now, the natives of China, or any strange country, have one nature. All consider that good and evil cannot be in unison. All nations are really the same." If American rulers declare that "the people of the Flowery land are altogether without good," then these rulers clearly "defer their own knowledge of right to a undue desire to please men"—that is, to gain public approval. But if the natives of a country, like China, have "one nature," and if all nations are "the same," then it logically follows that all people, including the Chinese, deserve the same treatment. A differential treatment can only originate from a political strategy to gain public approval at the expense of the Chinese. Lai Chun-chuen thus makes the classic liberal argument for tolerance, one based on a view of culture as given, unchanging, monolithic, and universal.

Yet Chinese behavior was different in obvious ways from that of other groups of immigrants. "Some have remarked that emigrants from other countries bring their families," Lai Chun-chuen continues. But to those who would have the Chinese do as others do, he advances a remarkably postmodern rejoinder:

> The manners and customs of China and of foreign countries are not alike. This is an ancient principle, and is prevalent now. What if other countries do differ somewhat from your honorable nation in hats, clothes, and letters, and other things, while there is much that is common? In China itself, the people differ.... Their dialects, their manners, their sentiments, do not wholly accord. Their articles of use are not all made by one rule. Their customs all differ. One line cannot be drawn for all.

The borders between cultures turn out to be no more significant than the borders within cultures, his earlier protestations of Chinese cultural unity notwithstanding. By discarding the vocabulary of unity and sameness, Lai Chun-chuen opens a space in which not only California but China itself can acknowledge and value difference.

The condition of Chinese women remained at the center of racialist debates because it revealed the contradictions within a venerable culture that suddenly found itself oppressed by an upstart one. The 1868 "Remonstrance," sponsored by the Chinese merchants of San Francisco, treated prostitutes, or what it called "abandoned women," as a problem to be dealt with by the authorities of the United States. Lai Chun-chuen's letter and the "Remonstrance" both display an evasiveness about the condition of Chinese women—in both documents women are spoken for by men. Indeed, Chinese prostitution in California depended upon a cross-cultural alliance between men that relegated Chinese women to a status even more degraded than that of China Men.

Chinese prostitution was a form of chattel slavery. "Almost all Chinese prostitutes," Benson Tong argues, "travelled unwillingly to the American West." Some were sold by destitute families to a procurer, shipped to California under a promise of marriage, then sent straight to a brothel. A Ch'ing dynasty official calculated that many families in the Canton region subsisted on the earnings of a daughter working as a prostitute. In the 1850s and 1860s the sale of female children to procurers reflected the political and economic hard times that had provoked Chinese immigration to California in the first place. Even for those women who came willingly to the Golden Mountain, prostitution remained their likely future.

Xin Jin, who went into debt for her passage to San Francisco, consented to work as a prostitute for four and a half years. Her working conditions were arduous: She could be returned to her "master/mistress" for contracting one of the "four loathsome diseases"; for "menstruation disorder" she was "limited to one month's rest only." Despite Tong's portrayal of them as unsubmissive women, few prostitutes survived the sex trade or were able to escape it. In 1870, of the 3,536 Chinese women in California, 2,157 were listed by the census as "prostitute." Like Chinese men in the United States, Chinese women lacked the fundamental civil rights that might have furthered resistance. They could not become citizens, vote, testify at trial, or marry "a white person"; nor, after 1882, could Chinese "laborers"—a designation that covered virtually all potential immigrants—enter the country.

The Tongs began importing women for prostitution in late 1853. On their arrival the women, most of them in their twenties, might be auctioned openly on the San Francisco docks, in full view of the police. Wong Ah Sing, sold for twenty dollars at the age of ten, went for $750 at the age of twenty. Most prostitutes serviced their clients at night and worked by day in San Francisco's sweatshops; these combined labors could bring the owner $850 a year, while costing less than a hundred dollars. Some prostitutes operated out of fancy pleasure houses; the less marketable worked in dank cubicles below street level, from which they could attract passing customers by running a stick across the bars of a grate.

Chinese prostitution boomed in San Francisco in the 1860s, as Chinese men returned to the city after being expelled from the mines. The city's Chinese population increased from 3,000 in 1860 to 12,000 in 1870. San Francisco contained the greatest concentration of Chinese women: statewide, the ratio of Chinese men to women was fourteen to one. During the 1870s a few men brought their wives over from China, and the number of prostitutes as a proportion of the total Chinese population in California began to decline. In the 1880 California census only twenty-four percent of the Chinese women counted were listed as prostitutes. But attitudes adjusted less swiftly than did the numbers. In 1876 the state printing office issued a publication called

Chinese Immigration. One of its index entries read: "Innocent men ruined."

Wong Ah So, tricked into prostitution in 1922, left two documents recording her experience. The first has been given the title "Story of Wong Ah So—Experiences as a Prostitute." It is a typed double-spaced letter of two and a half pages. The second is labeled "Letter from Wong Ah So to Her Mother Found in Suitcase After Arrest in Fresno, February 7, 1924." Both documents appear in a typed manuscript called "Orientals and Their Cultural Adjustment," papers assembled by Dr. Robert E. Park between the years 1924 and 1929, as part of his study of race relations on the West Coast. Wong Ah So's story and letter eloquently attest to the imbalance of power between women and men in nineteenth-century Chinese America.

In her "story" Wong Ah So represents her parents as unwitting participants in her prostitution. In Canton a man tells her mother that in America there is a "great deal of gold." He offers to take Wong Ah So to San Francisco as his wife. Two weeks after her arrival, a woman comes to Wong Ah So and tells her that she had sent the man to China "to buy her a slave." Wong Ah So will be set free in two years if she agrees not to "make a fuss."

After some months working as a prostitute, Wong Ah So sees a friend of her father's at a Tong banquet. She refuses to admit that she is the daughter for fear of disgracing her parents. She wants to "shield her mother"; her father, she believes, is "absolutely innocent." Ten days after the banquet Wong Ah So is rescued and taken to the Chinese mission. "I don't know just how it happened," she writes, and resolves to send her mother money whenever she can. Nowhere in the story does Wong Ah So mention that the procurer had given her mother a bride price of 450 Mexican dollars, money supplied him by the madam. The madam made good on her investment: after working Wong Ah So in a number of small towns for over a year, she had sold her to a madam in Fresno, where Wong Ah So had been arrested.

Wong Ah So's one-page single-spaced typed "letter" was actually written before the "story," during her months as a prostitute. Whereas the story delivers a pious and mystified account of Wong Ah So's experience, the letter is an angry and penetrating analysis of the status of Chinese daughters. Yet the sequence in which they were written—angry letter followed by mild story—reveals a process in which a tonic and political anger was absorbed back into a rhetoric of repression and obedience.

From all indications, the letter is Wong Ah So's first communication to her mother since her arrival in California. "I have left you for several months," the letter begins. "Your daughter has come to America." It goes on to allude to an "illness"; then, as if impatient with evasions and small talk, the letter shifts gears: "Your daughter's condition is very tragic, even when she is sick she must practice prostitution (literally do business with her own flesh and skin). Daughter is not angry with you. It seems to be just my fate." Wong Ah So's sudden and yet offhand mention of prostitution indicates that she knows that her mother knows about the bondage into which she has been sold. The knowledge is so punishing that, in the sentences that follow, she comforts herself by invoking two Chinese heroes of filial piety. She proposes to become one of these, to earn "money for my mother," to expiate what she calls her "sin."

Her anger breaks out brutally, however, in the conclusion to the letter:

> A son is a human being, and so is a daughter. At home, everybody looks down upon a daughter. How is it now? When I was at home, Mother, you looked down upon me as a daughter. Since daughter came to California by right she should forsake you. But in thinking it over, the greatest virtue in life is reverence to parents so I am keeping a filial heart. My present misfortune is due to the sins of a previous incarnation. Now I may be somebody's daughter, but some day I may be somebody's mother.

It is difficult to imagine a more compelling analysis of the gender inequities that conditioned not only nineteenth-century Chinese culture but its transplantation to California. Wong Ah So recognizes that the oppression of women is due in part to the collaboration of women and to their internalization of a discourse that her own letter, angry as it is, cannot entirely renounce. In the chilling but unassailable prophecy of her last line, she admits that the reproduction of motherhood afflicts her culture of origin as surely as it does her culture of adoption. As I have been cared

Wong Ah So, husband Louie Kwong, and family in 1933. Arriving in San Francisco at the age of nineteen, Wong Ah So discovered that she had been sold into prostitution before leaving her native Canton. After escaping to the Presbyterian mission, she learned to speak English and agreed to marry a merchant from Boise, Idaho. Her written accounts of her experiences reveal the complex pressures that maintained Chinese prostitution in California. Courtesy of Judy Yung and Missionary Review of the World.

for, so I may learn to care. The mother-daughter bond is broken less by patriarchy than by the internalization of its values by women. But because the liberation of daughters depends so clearly upon the liberation of mothers, and because this is a process that can occur largely between women, there resides, in Wong Ah So's bitter conclusion, some cause for hope. It would rest with her Chinese-American sisters to find a way through this dilemma and clear a cultural space not only for their gender but for their "race."

The story does have a kind of happy ending. Wong Ah So escaped prostitution and took refuge in Donaldina Cameron's Presbyterian Mission. There she learned to read Chinese and to speak English. A year after her escape, she agreed to marry a Chinese merchant from Boise, Idaho. In the following decades she raised a blended family of five daughters and three sons. She even managed to return to China, where she discovered that her mother had died and left four younger siblings in her care. In 1935 Wong Ah So testified for the prosecution in the last trial involving a Chinese prostitution ring held in San Francisco.

IN THE LATE 1870s the man who would later write *Quo Vadis* summed up the labor situation on the Pacific slope: "Let us now look at the kind of work the Chinese perform in California. A simple word describes it accurately: everything." While some of this work was performed by women—by 1872 in San Francisco Chinese males and females constituted nearly half of the workforce in the four major industries of boots and shoes, woolens, cigars, and tobacco—most of it was carried out in regions far beyond the city by the people Maxine Hong Kingston calls "China Men." By splitting the invidious "Chinaman" into two independent nouns, Kingston converts an epithet into two words of praise. Her book of that title is the most powerful account of how these men came to build the Central Pacific Railroad.

In 1866 the Union Pacific was putting out eight miles of track to the Central Pacific's one. The Central Pacific had contracted with the federal government to build a railroad from Sacramento eastward. The Union Pacific was to build westward from Omaha, across the plains of Nebraska and the mountain passes in Wyoming. The two lines were to meet somewhere in the Great Basin. Speed meant profit, since each corporation was granted a section of land in an alternating checkerboard pattern along every mile of track laid. U.S. bonds were issued to each concern at the rate of $16,000 per mile of track on level ground, $32,000 in semi-mountainous land, and $48,000 in the mountains.

Within sixty miles of Sacramento and some three years after beginning construction, the Central Pacific hit the greatest mountain wall in the continental United States. The road aimed to surmount the seven-thousand-foot Donner Pass and curve within a few hundred feet of the spot where Tamsen Donner, after placing her three youngest daughters in the hands of a rescue party, turned and, without looking back, walked to the cabin that held the dying husband for whom the pass would be named. The next rescue party would find no trace of Tamsen Donner,

The High Secrettown Trestle in the Sierra Nevada, 1867. Chinese workers for the Central Pacific fill the trestle with dirt. Especially skilled at blasting and tunneling, the Chinese played the key role in the Central Pacific's race against the Union Pacific in the building of the transcontinental railroad. Their progress over the highest mountain wall in the continental United States was speeded by the invention of dynamite. Courtesy of the California History Room, California State Library, Sacramento, California.

although it did find a pan full of organs freshly taken from a human body. Twenty years later the winter snows that had marooned the Donner Party on Halloween of 1846 had not lessened in the central Sierra. Frustrated by delays and determined to keep pace with the Union Pacific, company superintendent Charles Crocker resolved to force his laborers to work through the winter of 1866. Virtually all the men who remained in the mountains for the task were China Men.

Crocker had hired his first fifty China Men in February 1865, in answer to white workers threatening a strike. They worked so well and so cheaply that he sent out a general call for more. Within two years ninety percent of the workforce on the Central Pacific was Chinese. The China Men were particularly skilled at blasting. Kingston's protagonist, modeled after her own grandfather, spends three years tunneling through Sierra granite. In the last year of Ah Goong's work on the tunnel, dynamite is invented: "The dynamite added more accidents and ways of dying, but if it was not used, the railroad would take fifty more years to finish. Nitroglycerine exploded when it was jounced on a horse or dropped. A man who fell with it in his pocket blew himself up into red pieces." Ah Goong's world is so hard, impenetrable, and lonely, so empty of solace or pleasure, that he comes to wonder "what a man was for, what he had to have a penis for."

He wonders this on the seventh day of a strike that begins on Tuesday morning, June 25, 1867, and that proves emblematic of the race and class divisions faced by China Men. The Central Pacific has offered the workers a four-dollar raise per month. " 'What's the catch?' said the smarter men. 'You'll have the opportunity to put in more time,' said the railroad demons. 'Two more hours per shift.' " Two more hours a day meant sixty more hours a month for four extra dollars. The China Men decide to strike. " 'Eight hours a day good for the white man, all the same good for China Man.' " The China Men deliver messages to each other by hiding them in their summer solstice cakes.

On the fourth day comes news of the company's response: no food. Some of the foresighted China Men have food of their own—cured jerky, fermented wine, dried and strung orange and grapefruit peels, pickled and preserved leftovers. Ah Goong shares some of his cache, hides the rest, and spends the time having a reader read again the letters from home. The strike ends on the ninth day. "The Central Pacific announced that in its benevolence it was giving workers a four-dollar raise, not the fourteen they had asked for. And that the shifts in the tunnels would remain eight hours long. 'We were planning to give you the four-dollar raise all along,' the demons said to diminish the victory." The non-Chinese workers had not joined in the strike.

IN THE 1860s and 1870s the Chinese came to play a central role in the fight between capital and labor in California. In 1869, the year the golden spike was driven, the state's Democratic Party platform opposed the Fourteenth Amendment, predicting that its passage would bring "untold hordes of pagan slaves" into competition with white workers. In San Francisco two years earlier, a gang of four hundred men had attacked a group of Chinese excavating an alley. The Chinese had been stoned, some maimed, their shanties burned. At least fifteen Chinese men were hanged during the 1871 anti-Chinese riots in Los Angeles. An 1886 account of these riots located their origin in "a dispute concerning the ownership and possession of a Chinese woman."

In an 1869 New York *Tribune* article, Henry George, the author of *Progress and Poverty* (1879), argued the following: "It is obvious that Chinese competition must reduce wages, and it would seem just as obvious that, to the extent which it does this, its introduction is to the interest of capital and opposed to the interests of labor." George proved the high-toned equivalent of the violent Denis Kearney, who founded the Workingmen's Party of California in 1877. In the same year, at an open-air meeting in San Francisco, Kearney "bade the man who put the Chinese above the American working men beware or they would import a tree from Oregon and set it up in the plaza where every morning it would be found bearing fruit." The anti-Chinese riots of that year lasted for three days and burned down the Chinese quarter of the city. Bret Harte had anticipated the carnage in his 1874 story, "Wan Lee, the Pagan."

The China Men did often work for lower wages, for longer hours, and in more demanding conditions than those tolerated by other groups of workers. Writing in the 1860s, William Speer gave a sympathetic reading of a disturbingly efficient Chinese work culture. "They work cheerfully eleven hours a day. They are never drunk one day and good for nothing the next. There is no fighting." Writing in 1869, one California farmer put it bluntly: "I must employ Chinamen or give up."

The demonization of this work culture by members of the same class resembles Sutpen's conviction in Faulkner's *Absalom, Absalom!* that his enemy is not the owner class but the black butler who turns him away from the mansion front door. The Chinese were used in California, as were African Americans in the South, to convert a class struggle into a race war. The natural solidarity that the Irish and other working groups might have felt with the Chinese got lost in the language of "The Chinese Must Go" and in an oversimplified argument that identified Chinese workers with the very owners that exploited them. In the Workingmen's Party resolution of 1878, "cheap Chinese labor" is directly associated with "the schemes of individuals and corporations" to control "vast tracts" of California land. During the 1870s San Francisco experienced record unemployment that had its sources in eastern speculation, the panic of 1873, widespread monopolies on water and land, and the damage done to

Sacramento Valley farmland by hydraulic mining. While the Chinese were a target of labor unrest, California's working groups remained, in fact, interdependent; despite the rhetoric of racial division, they often labored side by side.

At Utah's Promontory Point, Robert L. Harris witnessed the laying of the last rail. Executives of the two railroads were presented a laurel wood tie and four spikes: two of gold, one of Nevada silver, and one of Arizona iron, silver, and gold. They tried to hit the symbolic spikes with a sledgehammer wired to telegraph the event of the blow, but they failed. Fifty-six feet of rail remained to be laid. The Union Pacific crew, made up of Caucasians, positioned their rails and drove their spikes. "The Central Pacific people then laid their pair of rails," Harris wrote, "the labor being performed by Mongolians."

In *CHINA MEN* a woman author gives the working Chinese of California's nineteenth century a voice. Kingston published her history-as-novel in 1980; nine years later Amy Tan published *The Joy Luck Club*. Near the end of Tan's book, Jing-Mei Woo listens to her father tell her mother's story on the balcony of a hotel in Shanghai. *The Joy Luck Club* deals with the recovery of women's stories as an activity that will and must be conducted largely by women, and it does so, in part, by having the generosity to imagine that a portion of that story can be told by a man. Not only do Kingston and Tan's narratives signal the arrival of two powerful female voices; but in their willingness to allow one gender to speak on behalf of another, they figure in fiction the gradual reunion between Chinese men and women made possible by the changing legal and political climate in twentieth-century California.

Three books written by Edith Eaton, Jade Snow Wong, and Amy Tan can be read as forming a sequence that measures the costs and pleasures of what I have called the "daughter's arrival." These are writers with "too much fire," as Jing-Mei Woo's mother puts it. Jade Snow Wong is told by her herb doctor that "you have fire all through your body." Edith Eaton imagines a Chinese-American woman whose "element of Fire" has "raged so fiercely within her that it had almost shriveled up the childish frame." In each case, the fire signals an internalization of rage, the unfulfillable female desire that has been driven back upon the self as anger. Creative activity—writing—the acquisition and deployment of *"perfect American English,"* proves the adaptive response. While only one of these books qualifies as straight autobiography, the subject of each becomes storytelling as self-composition, an endeavor in which each writer becomes a "heroine," in Kingston's words, by virtue of her role as "maker of a book."

Straight description of racial and gender conflict cannot alone provide an adequate understanding of the Chinese experience in twentieth-century California. We need to move to the interior, to the writer's text, if we are to comprehend the text of history. The memories recorded in these three books are the product of long and lonely periods of incubation, decades in which losses were consolidated and incidents acquired weight. The power of these stories lies in their willingness to risk the reach back, an act in which the remembering daughter acknowledges the gaps and suppressions in the record, her marginality within the culture of origin, and her present sense of connection with and reservations about the community of past time.

EDITH EATON WAS BORN in England in 1865 to a Chinese mother and an English father. Sixteen children would be born to the Eaton parents. After the arrival of the first six, the Eatons emigrated to New York and finally, in 1874, to Montreal. Edith Eaton spent the years 1898–1900 in San Francisco; it was the place, she later wrote, where all the old ache in her bones fell away. Charles Lummis, California booster and founder of the Southwest Museum, encouraged her to continue writing about Chinese life, and she did so, while moving on to settle for fourteen years in Seattle. Eaton published her first article in 1888 and adopted the pen name Sui Sin Far, which means "water fragrant flower," in 1895. During her writing life her stories appeared in such major periodicals as *The Century, Good Housekeeping, Overland Monthly, Sunset,* and *Western.* In 1912 thirty of these stories were gathered into *Mrs. Spring Fragrance,* published two years before her death. Amy Ling describes this volume as "the first collection of short stories about Chinese American life at the turn of the century by a Chinese Eurasian."

Eaton begins her book by writing that "when Mrs. Spring Fragrance first arrived in Seattle, she was unacquainted with one word of the American language." This claim is followed by a sudden and compressed reversal: "Five years later her husband, speaking of her, said: 'There are

Edith Maud Eaton emigrated from England to New York in 1874 with her Chinese mother and her English father. Writing under the pseudonym Sui Sin Far, Eaton published Mrs. Spring Fragrance *in 1912, the first work of fiction by a Chinese Eurasian about Chinese-American life. Courtesy of Amy Ling.*

no more American words for her learning.' " Effortlessness here bespeaks anxiety; as Richard Rodriguez makes plain on the first page of his *Education,* while Mrs. Spring Fragrance may have been taught the master's language, her profit on it may be to know how to curse. Not that her anger expresses itself directly; she remains committed to a ceremonious engagement with "the common uses of women." While she does work through the master's language—she resolves to become a writer—Mrs. Spring Fragrance also sets out to change her world by engaging and exploiting the illusion, one entertained by her husband, that she confines her verbal prowess to "the secret talk of women."

In the volume's title story, we encounter a woman who successfully deploys the American language on behalf of another woman's happiness. Her primary target is the arranged or loveless marriage. Her goal is to convert the passive daughter into an active woman and thereby to destabilize the gender arrangements which racism enlists in its support. So she travels to San Francisco and unarranges the neighbor daughter's arranged marriage.

During her visit, she sends two letters to Seattle. The first goes next door to Laura, the girl whose marriage she has unarranged. "May the bamboo ever wave," she begins. Then she tells Laura a little story. "Next week I accompany Ah Oi to the beauteous town of San Jose. There we will be met by the son of the Illustrious Teacher, and in a little Mission . . . the little Ah Oi and the son of the Illustrious Teacher will be joined together in love and harmony." This is a way of saying that she has engineered a match for the boy who was to be the unwilling Laura's mate. The flood of adjectives here only serves to heighten the swift conveyance of the message: You are free to marry as you like. In its offhand brevity the opening salvo about the bamboo humorously signals that the letter, however indirectly, will be all about business.

In the second letter, written to her husband, Mrs. Spring Fragrance invents a wholly fictional reason for prolonging her visit to San Francisco. A cousin, she writes, has asked her to stay and make fudge. She opens the letter with "from your little plum blossom," and closes with "your ever loving and obedient woman, JADE." While the husband may fasten his attention upon these terms of endearment, the wife embeds in the letter a protest about a lecture she has recently attended called "America, the Protector of China." There she was told, in effect, that anti-Chinese policies are really instances of federal government efforts on behalf of the Chinese. Mrs. Spring Fragrance, so enlightened, counsels her husband to "murmur no more because your elder brother, on a visit to this country, is detained under the roof-tree of this great Government instead of under your own roof." The reference here is to the federal government's policy of detaining Chinese immigrants, often for months at a time, on Angel Island in San Francisco Bay. By deploying irony against the arguments of the lecture and the policies of the government—policies that have struck at her husband's family—Mrs. Spring Fragrance not only steals the master's language but uses its conventions to mock the cultural contradictions it would rationalize.

In the second story in the volume, Mrs. Spring Fragrance convinces a class-bound socialite to allow her son to marry a working girl. Marriage, as Eaton's two opening stories attest, is something that can be arranged— or rearranged—by women. This story, like the ones that follow, becomes an allegory of its own creation by demonstrating that the power to so arrange depends upon the power to narrate. The remaining stories treat all that stands in the way of the fulfillment of female desire: divorce, murder, suicide, accidental death. In an ironic tribute to what had been the most common fate of China Women in California, Eaton even invents a prostitute who steals from her Chinese brother the money he has saved to set her free. In imagining such a story, Eaton not only invokes a major passage in the Chinese translation to California but acknowledges that the barriers to full arrival lie, to some extent, within. "It was there between us: that strange, invisible—what? Was it the barrier of race—that consciousness?" Her Chinese and Chinese-American characters prove in some degree self-wounded, veterans of a struggle in which consciousness has not been fully raised on any side. While this view often subjects Eaton's characters to the punishment of a heroic masochism, it also confers upon them responsibility and therefore the capacity to change. Eaton thus establishes the link between storytelling and power in the world central to Jade Snow Wong and Amy Tan.

JADE SNOW WONG was born in San Francisco in 1922. Her autobiography, *Fifth Chinese Daughter* (1950) recounts her upbringing in Chinatown, her college education at Mills, the beginning of her career in ceramics, and her wartime work in the Marin shipyards. *No Chinese Stranger* (1975) extends the account through the years of Wong's marriage, motherhood, and visits to Asia. Despite the reservations expressed about *Fifth Chinese Daughter* by Elaine Kim and Frank Chin, in *The Big AIIIEEEEEEE!* (by Jeffrey Chan, et al.), Kingston credits her reading of it as the inspiration for *The Woman Warrior* (1976) and nominates Wong as "the Mother of Chinese American literature."

Autobiographical writing is itself a central subject in *Fifth Chinese Daughter*. The climactic sentence in the story turns on the verb "to write." While Wong's central critical act is her assumption that her story is worth telling, she balances this assertion of self with a strategic withdrawal. "Although a 'first person singular' book, this story is written in the third person from Chinese habit," she explains in her author's note. "The submergence of the individual is literally practiced. In written Chinese, prose or poetry, the word 'I' almost never appears, but is understood." Yet one "I" does soon surface in the book. Before the narrator submerges her voice into the third person, she maintains that "I tell the story of their fifth Chinese daughter, Jade Snow, born to them in San Francisco." The very grammar of this sentence, with its reference to the self in both the first and the third person, argues that her book will be one "centered around Jade Snow's desire for recognition as an individual."

Jade Snow has her epiphany of independence while listening to a lecture in sociology. The instructor refers to a historical period when parents had children for economic reasons, then says: "Today we recognize that children are individuals, and that parents can no longer demand their unquestioning obedience." On the streetcar home, Jade Snow inwardly responds, "I am an individual besides being a Chinese daughter. I have rights too."

The flatness of this insight reveals Wong's strategy of distancing herself throughout. She speaks of herself not only in the third person, but in generic terms. After the birth of her brother, for instance, she grasps the "full meaning" of the gender hierarchy in a nuclear family. She realizes "that she herself was a girl and, like her younger sister, unalterably less significant than the new son in their family." Such a belated recognition is likely to strike a reader as old news. By portraying herself as a slow learner, Wong affords her reader a superior and even a smug position. On the other hand, her understandings, when they do arrive, are so obvious as to be indisputable. If ideology is what goes without saying, Jade Snow's insistence on saying it results in a surprisingly pungent critique.

Jade Snow recognizes more fully that she is an individual after her father refuses to pay for her college education. "Sons must have priority over the daughters," he tells her, "when parental provisions for advantages must be limited by economic necessity." The family money must be saved for the brother's medical training. Jade Snow answers that she wants to be more than an average Chinese or American girl. "If you have the talent," her father answers, "you can provide for your own college education." Jade Snow recognizes that "Daddy had spoken." Trained to make inquiries by asking only one question and to accept the answer, she says nothing more. But her

Jade Snow Wong at the Greek Theater, Mills College, mid-1940s. Wong published Fifth Chinese Daughter *in 1945, at the age of twenty-three. The autobiography describes her childhood in San Francisco's Chinatown, her undergraduate years at Mills, work in the Marin shipyards during World War II, and the beginning of her career as a ceramicist and writer. Courtesy of Jade Snow Wong.*

inward reaction is not the customary "Daddy knows better." "No, his answer tonight left Jade Snow with a new and sudden bitterness against the one person whom she had always trusted as fair to her." While *Fifth Chinese Daughter* may advertise itself as a Bildungsroman, its core story, as revealed by this conversation, is less the education of the narrator than the education of the father.

Jade Snow settles for junior college, has her epiphany in the sociology lecture, and confronts her father with her "unfilial theory" that "I am an individual besides being your fifth daughter." Admitted to Mills College on a full scholarship, she graduates Phi Beta Kappa without a penny of help from her parents. She finds work in the war production department at the Marin shipyards and wins a coastwide essay contest on absenteeism. Her parents try to arrange a marriage for her but fail; her mother sighs that her daughter was born too tall. Informed of the obvious by her boss at the shipyard—"You can't compete for an equal salary in a man's world"—and reluctant to submerge herself in a life of social service, she hits upon a life plan. "The answer which came to her . . . was that she should try to write."

Having studied pottery at Mills, Jade Snow resolves to finance her writing career by setting up a wheel in a Chinatown shop window. From the first time she throws down a ball of clay, the street is packed with customers lining up to buy her ceramic wares. But they are all Caucasians; the "Chinese did not come to buy one piece." She sells all the pottery she can make, and the newspaper carries her picture. Soon she is driving the first postwar automobile in Chinatown. "Chinatown was agog," she writes. She has learned, happily, how to brag.

In response to these unignorable public successes, Jade Snow's father is forced into a stunningly belated confession. Shortly after he arrived in America, he tells Jade Snow, he had written to a cousin in China: "You do not realize the shameful and degraded position into which the Chinese culture has pushed its women. Here in America, the Christian concept allows women their freedom and individuality. I wish my daughters to have this Christian opportunity. I am hoping that some day I may be able to claim that by my stand I have washed away the former disgraces suffered by the women of our family."

The shock of this admission lies less in its content than in its timing. It comes on the last page of the book, after Jade Snow has had to prove to her father the very thing it turns out that he already knows. He has all along possessed the knowledge that would lead to taking a stand on the position of Chinese women, but of course it is Jade Snow, largely unassisted, who has taken the stand. She has had to explicate the father's unremembered "wish." The word "wish" connects Wong's narrative with Amy Tan's, since Jing-Mei Woo will realize her mother's "long-cherished wish" on the novel's last page.

The timing of Wong's father's admission reinforces the conviction, available to the reader from the autobiography's first page, that people carry within them a saving knowledge that hard experience can compel them to express. Jade Snow states the obvious in order to suggest how it might feel if one proceeded from this already-known rather than from its repression. She is not a slow learner; rather, she is so fully in command of the received knowledge of her culture that she can demonstrate that it is both arbitrary and clichéd. Within any culture lies the means of its own critique, her narrative reveals, and education occurs in the tension between the accepting "third person" and the questioning "first person." *Fifth Chinese Daughter* proves a romance of "education" by returning to the root meaning of the word—*to lead out*. Growth, recognition, education—all this depends less on filling one's mind with the new than on listening to the "I" of the self as it returns upon the cultural heritage it already possesses and tests it against its emergent wishes and desires. Such an education proves indistinguishable from life in an immigrant culture because the illuminating conflict between cultures adds this inner dialectic. The result in Jade Snow Wong's case is a work of polite transgression, one in which the act of leading out results in the arrival of her own "immodest" voice.

THE JOY LUCK CLUB recounts, in sixteen sections, the story of four Chinese mothers and four Chinese-American daughters while also accommodating the salient facts of its author's life story. The frame tale about the lost Woo sisters is a version of Amy Tan's own. Tan was born in Oakland in 1952 to parents who had emigrated from China in 1949. The parents left three young daughters behind. Tan learned of their existence at the age of twelve. In the mid-1980s Tan located her sisters and visited them in China. "They wrote to me in Chinese," she said in 1989, "and my mother read the letters to me."

"My father has asked me to be the fourth corner at the Joy Luck Club. I am to replace my mother, whose seat at the mah jong table has been empty since she died two months ago." Amy Tan's novel begins with these sentences; they are spoken by Jing-Mei Woo, the framing narrator, who lives as a young woman in 1980s San Francisco. The novel ends with her return to China in order to fulfill her mother's long-cherished wish— the recovery of the two infant girls she was forced to abandon on the road from Kweilin. The loss of these two daughters forms the overarching story of *The Joy Luck Club,* one that must be told four times before it is fully told.

To privilege any one of the novel's stories is perhaps to read against the careful symmetries that Tan maintains by way of her fourfold structure. For the triangle of father, mother, and daughter, Tan substitutes the dyad of mother/daughter, then multiplies that dyad by four. Four mothers born in China, four daughters born in California. Four sections divided into four chapters, with one woman's story per chapter. Each of the sections traces a developmental stage in a cross-generational sequence. The first section deals with the mothers as children in China; the second, with the daughters as children in America; the third, with the daughters as wives; the fourth, with the mothers as daughters of *their mothers,* back in China. We move from the distant past, to the past, to the present, to an even earlier past. All mothers were daughters once, this sequence argues; mothers are not so much replaced by daughters as they replace with a mother's role the daughter in themselves. Daughterhood remains the fundamental female condition because it proves so incomplete; not only do the mothers in the novel all lose their own mothers, but the action, once it shifts to the relatively stable political climate of the United States, works to reveal all that still stands in the way of being able to receive or to deliver a mother's love.

Despite Tan's fourfold symmetries, the single figure of Jing-Mei Woo is central. She is the only character with a named chapter in each of the four sections. She is the only daughter without a living mother. The three living mothers each tell their own stories, but Jing-Mei must speak for her mother. "I have a story," Auntie Ying says, and the sure sign of the eclipse of self is the loss of the power to tell one. Jing-Mei, her voice narrating on the first page of the first chapter, has already replaced that mother, and at more than mah jong.

Within three pages of Jing-Mei's opening words, her mother, Suyuan Woo, reclaims the chapter that by rights should be hers. She tells Jing-Mei the first version of the Kweilin story. Her husband brings Suyuan and their two babies to Kweilin because there, he hopes, they will be safe. He is an officer with the Kuomintang, and the Japanese are on the advance. Out of her fear and her boredom, Suyuan sets up her first Joy Luck Club.

This first version of "the Kweilin story" unfolds as "a Chinese fairy tale." Despite the famine in the streets, the members of the club treat themselves to special foods on their meager allowances. They eat dumplings shaped like silver ingots, long rice noodles for long life, and boiled peanuts for conceiving sons. They eat, play sixteen rounds, feast again, then tell stories. They choose their own happiness and refuse despair. Suyuan wins thousands of yuan. During the first years of retelling this story to Jing-Mei, the "endings always changed," but they also always concluded on a "happy note."

Then one evening, Jing-Mei says, Suyuan "told me a completely different ending to the story." This is the second version of the Kweilin story. An army officer tells Suyuan to flee the city. She packs her things and her two babies into a wheelbarrow and begins pushing their way to Chungking four days before the Japanese march into Kweilin. The wheelbarrow breaks, so she ties scarves into slings and puts a baby on each shoulder: "I carried these things until deep grooves grew in my hands." She passes treasures that others have abandoned along the way. This version of the story then comes to an abrupt end: "By the time I arrived in Chungking I had lost everything except for three fancy silk dresses which I wore one on top of the other."

The third version is the version that the surviving mothers tell Jing-Mei after her mother's death: "We have something important to tell you, from your mother." Before Suyuan died, they reveal, she wanted to find her daughters in China. After searching for years, she found an address, but she died before making the connection. "So your aunties and I, we wrote to this address. . . . We say that a certain party, your mother, want to meet another certain party. And this party write back to us. They are your sisters, Jing-Mei." The aunties hand Jing-Mei a check so that she can go to Hong Kong, take a train to Shanghai, and see her sisters. She must tell her sisters about their mother, the three aunties insist. "What can I tell them about my mother?" Jing-Mei replies. "I don't know anything. She was my mother." Seeing the fright in their eyes, realizing the fear that "their own daughters" are just as ignorant of the truths and hopes that they brought to America, Jing-Mei consents to go to China and to "tell them everything."

Jing-Mei's father tells the fourth version of the Kweilin story when she is in Shanghai. He does not set out to tell it to Jing-Mei directly; she overhears it as her father begins to tell it to her great-aunt. "Suyuan didn't tell me she was trying all these years to find her daughters," he begins. The great-aunt soon falls asleep, and from the bed Jing-Mei whispers an enabling question to him. He continues with the story, now speaking directly to her. Her name "Jing" means "good leftover stuff," he explains. The name evokes "the younger sister who was supposed to be the essence of the others." Jing-Mei asks the big question: "So why did she abandon those babies on the road?" The father, having long wondered this himself, proceeds to answer her in Chinese.

The mother sets the babies down by the side of the road, the father tells his daughter, and she stuffs jewelry into the shirt of the one and money into the shirt of the other. On the back of photographs she writes names and a Shanghai address. She goes down the road to find food, then faints and is placed in a truck. In Chungking she learns that her husband has died. She meets her second husband—the man now telling the story—in a hospital. An old peasant woman finds the babies, cares for them, and begins searching for the true parents. Meanwhile the mother and her new husband search for the babies. In 1949 Suyuan and her husband finally leave China for the United States. Suyuan stops speaking of the babies, and the father comes to believe that "they have died in her heart."

But the mother has not given up; she has just gone quiet. When letters can again be openly exchanged between China and the United States, she resumes the search. A Shanghai schoolmate sees the grown sisters on the street, and together they remember the names written on the back of an old photo. The mother dies, but Jing-Mei travels to China, rejoins her sisters, and takes up her place in the book's closing image—a Polaroid in which all three have taken on the mother's "eyes, her same mouth, open in surprise to see, at last, her long-cherished wish."

Among these four versions of the Kweilin story, the key element is the structure of the second. This is as full an account as the mother herself is ever able to give, and it leaves virtually everything out. The story of the separation of daughters from their mother, the first big story told in *The Joy Luck Club,* becomes paradigmatic and is repeated, with variations, in the accounts of the three other families. Yet the story is *not told*—at least, not by the mother. She does not tell her daughter how the babies were lost.

Tan's novel argues that there stands a bar to the direct fulfillment of maternal love, especially the love for a daughter. Beyond that, even telling the story of unfulfillment is barred because the cultural precedents that would recognize this story *as a story* and that would sanction the voicing of it are absent. While the traffic in women on which the culture of both East and West are founded comes under scrutiny here, and while Eaton, Wong, and Tan engage in a acute analysis of the sexual politics that continue to sanction it, these authors all return to the power and responsibility of writing stories, especially stories shared among women. These are books in which responsibility begins at home, in the recognition, as Wong Ah So put it in her Fresno letter, that "now I may be somebody's daughter, but some day I may be somebody's mother."

The key question is one that Suyuan Woo asks of her daughter Jing-Mei and that might be asked of all China Women—perhaps of all the women—who came to California because of the gold and stayed to live out a life: "Why do you think you are missing something you never had?" For female readers of Amy Tan's novel, the "something never had" is *daughterhood*. *The Joy Luck Club* exposes the cultural arrangements and historical forces that make it difficult for mothers to "mother" their daughters. The stories of the other three mothers-as-children in the novel's first section deal with the loss of self in concubinage, in unhappy marriage, and in neglect. Daughterhood is a fiction projected backward in order to make up for what was never had; from the start, in Tan's novel, the mother-daughter bond is irremediably broken. Daughters nevertheless mourn the absence of this bond; the purpose of story is to expose the ironies and pleasures of this mourning process, a process whereby the lucky mother-daughter pairs—those that survive—can create by an act of speaking and listening the bond they were never previously allowed to fully form.

In her first telling of the Kweilin story, Suyuan Woo says that "to despair was to wish back for something already lost." This sentence understands that the word "always" belongs before the word "already." Home is the something always already lost, and the longing for it we call nostalgia. Nostalgia has little place, these writers argue, in the emotional lives of women, although it is certainly an available emotion. The very logic behind the word "nostalgia" may demand the qualifying adjective "male." It is sons, these stories tell us, that are from birth given the status and value that can later be lost and therefore luxuriously mourned. Male self-pity proves much more stubborn and debilitating than its female counterpart because it is based on the revocation, by time or whatever else disconnects the son from Gatsby's "pap of life," of an actual and original gift. This is why, in our culture, men are so often passive and women so often angry; it is why Bret Harte remains the ever-popular chronicler of the Gold Rush. His stories retail a past that can be warmly remembered: they replace, for the uncritical reader, the pain of memory with the revisions of nostalgia. The story of the Chinese in California serves, in contrast, not only as the story of the daughter's arrival as a cultural force but, in its challenge to the most fully realized male fantasy about California's good gone past, as the story of history's return.

CHAPTER FOUR

THE SAN FRANCISCO EARTHQUAKE AND FIRE

The Culture of Spectacle

Thr San Francisco earthquake knocked William James out of bed. Lying awake at about half past five in the morning in his little apartment on the campus of Stanford University, he felt his bed begin to waggle. Before departing on his western tour, the philosopher-psychologist had been wished well by Bakewell, a friend from California:

"I hope they'll treat you to a little bit of an earthquake while you're there. It's a pity you shouldn't have that local experience." Well, when I lay in bed at about half-past five that morning, wide-awake, and the room began to sway, my first thought was, "Here's Bakewell's earthquake, after all"; and when it went crescendo and reached fortissimo in less than half a minute, and the room was shaken like a rat by a terrier, with the most vicious expression you can possibly imagine, it was to my mind absolutely an *entity* that had been waiting all this time holding back its activity, but at last saying, "Now, *go* it!" and it was impossible not to conceive it as animated by a will, so vicious was the temper displayed—everything *down,* in the room, that could go down, bureaus, etc., etc., and the shaking so rapid and vehement. All the while no fear, only admiration for the way a wooden house could prove its elasticity, and glee over the vividness of the manner in which such an abstract idea as "earthquake" could verify itself into sensible reality.

Writing four days after the earthquake, the working psychologist quickly translated the experience into an experiment where abstractions were verified. James even insisted on visiting the epicenter of the disaster and so boarded the only train that reached San Francisco on April 18. In an essay published two months later, "On Some Mental Effects of the Earthquake" (in *Memories and Studies,* 1911), he translated the California events into a parable of morale.

In the essay James made two important modifications to his initial account: "Sitting up involuntarily, and taking a kneeling position, I was thrown down on my face as it went *fortior* shaking the room as a terrier shakes a rat." In the letter there was no mention of being thrown on his face or of doing anything involuntarily. Perhaps James decided to play up his vulnerability so as to highlight the moment when he would assume control. In the letter James heard the earthquake saying, "Now, *go* it!" In the essay he himself says this, in response to the delight and welcome he feels in the middle of all the shaking: " '*Go* it,' I almost cried aloud, 'and go it *stronger!*' " In assuming the voice of the earthquake, James aligns himself with the disaster and its telluric power.

Both the letter and the essay personify the earthquake; it is animated by a will. Of course James knew that the event was one without an actual intention and that from the point of view of science "earthquake is simply the collective *name* of all the cracks and shakings and disturbances that happen." But since, as a psychologist, his concern was with subjective phenomena—with our way of taking things—James felt liberated to explore the immediate data of consciousness. His openness to the irrational and primitive nature of his own responses produced some of the best writing about the earthquake, imposing conflict and suspense on an otherwise random, physical event in order to give it the "overpowering dramatic convincingness," as he put it, of a story.

There is no significant "literature" of the San Francisco earthquake and fire, and for this, perhaps, we should be grateful. Of my five fires, it is the only catastrophe instigated by nature. Writing is not much given to elaborating events that are brief, sudden, and inexplicable. Movies have had better luck with the subject, since it does afford plenty to watch. In novels like *Storm* (1941) and *Fire* (1948), George Stewart attempted to make personified meteorological events into active protagonists. He located the action in California because California is the place where such events are located. It is a naturalist's paradise: to live with the prospect of earthquake and forest fire and drought and "the Santa Ana is to accept," Joan Didion argues, "consciously or unconsciously, a deeply mechanistic view of human behavior." In order to live with this view, as James showed, we must also repress it.

James and the Californians he wrote about survived the earthquake and fire by subsuming the experiencing into the spectatorial self. At a moment when nature most dramatically asserted herself, James draws attention to the cultural mediation of the event. The process begins with the first tremor. In the letter James feels "no fear, only admiration." In the essay his first consciousness is of "gleeful recognition." Recognition and admiration are not components of overcoming terror. Delight and welcome, rather, are James's portion. He maintains in the essay that "sensation and emotion were so strong that little thought, and no reflection or volition, were possible in the short time consumed by the phenomenon." Yet his own detailed and shapely verbal account of the "short time" belies this claim. The gap between James's emotions and his awareness of them is so distinct that it impressively conveys the ever-present power and composure of the human *watcher*.

Once he arrives in San Francisco, James witnesses a city rapidly recomposing itself. He chooses to say nothing of the material ruins. Two things strike him instead. The first is "the rapidity of the improvisation of order out of chaos." Everyone who can work is at work. The second is the "universal equanimity" he sees. People's faces are "inexpressive of emotion," and he hears not a pathetic or sentimental word. "The terms 'awful,' 'dreadful,' fell often enough from peoples' lips, but always with a sort of abstract meaning, and with a face that seemed to admire the vastness of the catastrophe as much as it bewailed its cuttingness." Admiration, then, is present on every hand, and the conversion of the catastrophe into something to be admired suggests that Californians have learned to cope with loss by casting themselves into the distanced, dimensionless space of a photograph.

I begin with James's two accounts of the earthquake in order to establish that even during the most overwhelming catastrophes, people will make representations of the event. Robert Altman makes this point at the end of his 1992 *Short Cuts,* where the audience of the movie watches an audience in the movie watching on TV an earthquake through which they are living. James's two versions underscore that even a single watcher can generate a plural response. And such responses take on a life as enduring as the physical consequences of the event—consequences from which San Francisco, in any case, quickly recovered. With the earthquake and fire, San Francisco began an immediate translation of the text into the myth. The distinction is Gary Snyder's: the text is the given particulars of an event, the facts on the ground; the myth is their transformation into the dramatic convincingness of a story. The particular story that San Francisco told itself about the earthquake and fire was of a city coolly eyeing its own destruction, a city acting "casual," as Kathryn Hulme describes a man blowing drifting char from his hands, "casual when you knew he wasn't feeling so." The conversion of catastrophe into spectacle depended, in turn, on the emerging technologies of still photography.

"OH, IS THAT A STILL from a Cecil De Mille picture?" This question was actually asked about the most famous photographic image produced of the San Francisco earthquake and fire—Arnold Genthe's shot down Sacramento Street taken on the morning of April 18, 1906. Photography played a unique and sometimes peremptory role in recording the event, and the surviving books about the disaster display, for the most part, a preference for image over word. The Roebling Construction Company's commissioned volume, *The San Francisco Earthquake and Fire* (1906), does not immediately recommend itself as an adequate account of those four April days; the book sits dusty and unconsulted on a few university library shelves. Yet even this market-driven document maintains a kind of mute eloquence through the sheer power of its photographs, images that convert an otherwise tedious report into a visual representation of the vanity of human wishes. Here are steel uprights melted into themselves like ribbon candy. A large entablature supported by two columns stands, like a vestige of the Roman Forum, before the ruins of City Hall. In some photographs, the only vertical shapes are the outlines of still-standing chimneys.

Roebling sent engineer A.L.A. Himmelwright to San Francisco as soon as it was "possible to visit the burned district." That area covered 4.11 square miles, virtually all of San Francisco's old downtown. Water mains had been severed by the earthquake, and fire burned virtually unchecked throughout the city until the U.S. Army began dynamiting. After three days the fire was stopped as it threatened to jump the Van Ness corridor. By that time 435 people had lost their lives, and 514 city blocks had been burned.

Roebling had pioneered fire-proof construction methods, especially the use of reinforced concrete. After examining more than sixty buildings, Himmelwright concluded that the most resilient building design was a steel skeleton with reinforced-concrete curtain wall construction. As proof of this he produced a photograph of the Hotel St. Francis, a building remarkably uninjured. The St. Francis had been built with Roebling segmented-concrete floors and concrete column protection.

This photograph was first published in A.L.A. Himmelwright's The San Francisco Earthquake and Fire *(1906). A structural engineer, Himmelwright was sent to the city immediately after the fire to assess the efficacy of reinforced concrete construction. Courtesy of the University of Virginia.*

But most of the book's photographs, taken by R. J. Waters and Company, tell a different story. They depict a shock and heat so intense that the notion of prevention looms only as a supreme fiction. If the Crocker Building stood relatively intact, it was because it was "subjected to normal fire only." In his conclusion, "The Lessons of the Earthquake," Himmelwright brings his argument into line with the visual evidence. As a structural engineer, he draws conclusions about overly high chimneys, mortar quality, and roofing tiles. But his primary conclusion radically expands the notion of prevention: It entails the depopulation of the two major cities in the state. Striking at the very heart of California as a site for human architecture, Himmelwright suggests that builders should henceforth "Avoid Locations in Close Proximity to Geological Fault Lines." His suggestion has not been followed. By 1990 more than 20 million people lived within twenty miles of the hundreds of California earthquake faults.

Photographer Arnold Genthe might have been sympathetic to Himmelwright's conclusions. He was certainly in a position to admire the resiliency of Hotel St. Francis. After wandering about on the morning of the quake, he found himself hungry and made his way to the hotel.

There he discovered a crowded lobby and dining room. His last meal, the night before, had been a supper after Enrico Caruso's performance in *Carmen*. Now, near the entrance to the hotel, he saw the opera singer himself in a fur coat and pajamas muttering to himself, " 'Ell of a place! 'Ell of a place!" Despite the lack of gas and electricity, the hotel coffee was hot. After a breakfast of bread and butter and fruit, Genthe asked his waiter for a check. "No charge today, sir," he replied. "Everyone is welcome as long as things hold out." The equanimity with which Californians today coexist with the imminence of natural catastrophe can be explained, in part, by the pathos of such moments, in which the loss of property is offset by the temporary gain of a felt sense of community.

Genthe had arrived in San Francisco in 1885. Trained as a draftsman, he wandered into Old Chinatown and attempted to make some sketches of it. But his subjects refused to sit still, disappearing into cellars and doorways. So he "decided to try to take some photographs." Knowing that the Chinese saw any camera as the "black devil box," he bought one small enough to conceal, with a Zeiss lens.

Because of the darkness of Chinatown's narrow streets, the reserve of its inhabitants, and the slow speed of his plates and films, Genthe learned to efface himself so as to capture his subjects without being seen. The result, *Pictures of Old Chinatown* (1908), is the most enduring visual record of the eight blocks of the Chinese district that went up in the 1906 fire.

The fire that destroyed Chinatown also opened up California to a new wave of Chinese immigration, since the fire also destroyed the municipal records that controlled the flow of newcomers from China. According to the laws in force in 1906, any Chinese who could claim U.S. citizenship by birth or derivation was allowed to enter the country. After the fire, a thriving trade in "paper sons" grew up, since an invented genealogy now had as much standing, given the loss of the paper record, as a real one. Before the earthquake, immigrants claiming the right to admission had been subjected to a cross-examination at the port of entry until an identity could be verified. Now, for immigrating Chinese, these interviews now took on the quality of an elaborate and deadly serious game in which the inventiveness of the immigrant was matched against the suspicion of the interviewer. "Every paper a China Man wanted for citizenship and legality burned in that fire," Maxine Hong Kingston writes. "An authentic citizen, then, had no more papers than an alien. Any paper a China

Arnold Genthe's "Street of the Gamblers." The German-born Genthe discovered San Francisco's Chinatown in the early years of the century and photographed its inhabitants with a concealed camera. His Pictures of Old Chinatown was published in 1908, a little over a year after the eight-square-block neighborhood had been destroyed by fire. Courtesy of the Library of Congress.

Man could not produce had been 'burned up in the Fire of 1906.' Every China Man was reborn out of that fire a citizen."

Thus began the Angel Island period. Before the earthquake, Chinese arriving at San Francisco had been detained at a two-story shed in the San Francisco harbor. With the increase in immigrants after the fire, Chinese leaders called for a more accommodating structure. A barracks was built on Angel Island, and until 1940 all Chinese immigrants were detained and processed in this facility.

While the Angel Island story may appear a digression from the drama of the earthquake, it proves, instead, to be the heart of the matter. For already existing San Francisco communities, earthquake and fire, as ordeals to be endured, were an opportunity to cope in style. The movie *San Francisco* has given this resiliency its most enduring, sentimental, and apolitical treatment. Yet beyond the immediate and terrible losses suffered, the fire had lasting consequences for the lives of Californians. The

"U.S. Quarantine Station (Port of San Francisco). Several views showing shops, foreground, laundry, bathing barracks, and disinfecting plant." After 1910, when the Angel Island facility was opened, Chinese immigrants were detained at the facility and subjected to rigorous questioning about their claims to citizenship status. Some were held on the island for months and even years. This and the following four photographs were taken by the National Health Service and are published here with their original captions. Courtesy of the National Archives.

"Aliens arriving."

"Packing baggage after disinfection."

"View aboard vessel showing partial result of fumigation from destruction of rodents."

"View aboard vessel."

spectacle of San Francisco watching itself burn was elaborated, in part, to obscure these consequences and to suggest that in its aftermath the city was required simply to rebuild.

For Chinese immigrants, the fire resulted in far more—it radically improved their odds at achieving entry. Those odds were complicated, however, by the screening measures enforced at the new immigration station. "There are two islands in San Francisco Bay which contain ruined buildings with doors four inches thick," Shawn Wong writes in the 1979 novel *Homebase*. "The islands are Alcatraz and Angel Island. Alcatraz is a National Park and Angel Island is a California State Park. Both were places of great sadness and great pain." On Angel Island the Chinese were separated from the immigrating Japanese and other Asians. The sexes were also segregated; up to three hundred Chinese men and fifty Chinese women were held on the island at any one time. Visitors were forbidden, in order to prevent coaching of the newly arrived. But every immigrant required coaching, since even those with valid claims were asked detailed questions about the number of steps to Father's house in Canton or the location of Uncle's rice bin. Judy Yung reports that "one Chinese woman who was illiterate resorted to memorizing the coaching information on her family background by putting it into a song." Immigrants arriving at Ellis Island in New York were asked, typically, twenty-nine questions; at Angel Island those seeking entry could be asked from two hundred to one thousand. The answers they gave had to be corroborated by witnesses. The Chinese kitchen staff on the island surreptitiously helped families keep their stories straight by ferrying messages to and from the city. By the 1920s the average period of detention lasted two to three weeks, although in some cases it could stretch into months or even years.

In 1970 park ranger Alexander Weiss noticed some Chinese characters inscribed on the walls of the long-abandoned island barracks. It turned out that the walls were covered with poems. Weiss arranged to have the walls photographed. Mak Takahashi's photographs recovered the text of some 135 poems that had been written on the barracks walls by detainees. But the first act of recovery had begun in 1931 and 1932, when detainees Smiley Jann and Tet Yee copied most of the poems then on the walls. These manuscripts, along with Takahashi's photographs and rubbings and additional copies made over the years, have been gathered by Him Mark Lai, Genny Lim, and Judy Yung into *Island: Poetry and History of Chinese Immigrants on Angel Island, 1910–1940* (1980).

This photograph shows one of the poems carved in the wall of an Angel Island barracks by a male Chinese immigrant. Courtesy of Chris Huie.

To a Western eye, the original poems comprise, on the page, beautiful squares and rectangles of calligraphy. All of the poems are written in the classical style. Most are brief, from four to eight lines long, with five to seven characters per line. Only poems by male detainees have survived. The first translation reads as follows:

> *The sea-scape resembles lichen twisting and turning for a thousand li.*
> *There is no shore to land and it is difficult to walk.*
> *With a gentle breeze I arrived at the city thinking all would be so.*
> *At ease, how was one to know he was to live in a wooden building?*

The Chinese character for "wooden building" recurs frequently in these poems; the men who wrote them clearly thought of their time on the island as an imprisonment. Fantasies of revenge and return to China are also linked throughout. The shortest of the sixty-nine poems refigures the difficult journey to California as a conquest in which the Chinese occupy the United States (the land of the Flowery Flag) and make historic preservation of the barracks their ultimate payback:

If the land of the Flowery Flag is occupied by us in turn,
The wooden building will be left for the angel's revenge.

GENTHE'S PHOTOGRAPHS OF old Chinatown testify to a survival in discontinuity, a remnant saved from the fire. The techniques he developed in making them also enabled his future career. Struck by the beauty of California women, and aware of the money to be made from San Francisco's vain *nouveau* oligarchy, the handsome German émigré decided to apply his new method to society portraiture. He thus made the transition from documenting the elusive or invisible "other" to representing the already-prominent rich. "Perhaps, I thought, if they were photographed in the unobtrusive manner which worked so well with my shy and unsuspecting Chinese subjects, if they were not allowed to become self-conscious by artificial posing, if they could be kept from knowing the exact moment the exposure was being made—then something more of their spirit might be brought out by the camera." Genthe opened a studio in 1898. His first client was the wife of W. H. Crocker, and as he succeeded in pleasing her, the industry of modern celebrity photography in California was born.

Genthe's memoir of his years in San Francisco, *As I Remember* (1936), contains 112 of his photographs, including images of Mary Pickford, Isadora Duncan, and Sarah Bernhardt. The book also contains a chapter called "Earthquake and Fire." The prose of this chapter measures the adequacy of verbal accounts of catastrophe in the age of photographic reproduction.

Genthe begins by describing the "terrifying sound" of Chinese porcelains crashing to the floor—an event that marks his social status but also establishes his tone of dandified chagrin. The earthquake becomes, for him, an inconvenience that requires a sporting response. The question of dress being paramount in his mind, Genthe starts to disrobe but decides "that the most suitable 'earthquake attire' would be my khaki riding things—I was to live in them for weeks."

The psychologist and the photographer: Could the city have been more fortunate than to have these professional witnesses on hand that day? Like James, Genthe converts the event into an allegory of morale, and like James, he maintains his own morale by distancing himself from the experience, turning it into a spectacle to be watched. "The streets presented a weird appearance," Genthe writes, mothers and children in their nightgowns, men in pajamas and dinner coats, women scantily dressed with evening wraps hastily thrown over them. Many ludicrous sights met the eye: an old lady carrying a large bird cage with four kittens inside, while the original occcupant, the parrot, perched on her hand; a man tenderly holding a pot of calla lilies, muttering to himself; a scrub woman, in one hand a new broom and in the other a large black hat with ostrich plumes; a man in an old-fashioned nightshirt and swallow tails, being startled when a friendly policeman spoke to him, "Say, Mister, I guess you better put on some pants."

What counts here is what meets the eye. Understanding this, Genthe has his breakfast, then returns to his studio to get a camera. But there he discovers that falling plaster has damaged everything. He then walks to Montgomery Street and borrows a #A Kodak Special from George Kahn and hits the streets. "For several weeks I did not concern myself with any thought of the future. I blithely continued to take photographs."

Genthe's society portraits had used soft focus and deep shadows to flatter his subjects. He applied this method to the earthquake and fire as well, as in "Steps that Lead to Nowhere," a moonlit shot of chimneys and other verticals against the twinkling lights of distant hills. But in one fortuitous image he abandons the picturesque and captures something more. In *As I Remember* the photograph bears the caption "San Francisco: April 18th, 1906." Genthe gives it this description:

> Of the pictures I had made during the fire, there are several, I believe, that will be of lasting interest. There is particularly the one scene that I recorded the morning of the first day of the fire (on Sacramento Street, looking toward the Bay) which shows, in a pictorially effective composition, the results of the earthquake, the beginning of the fire and the attitude of the people. On the right is a house, the front of which had collapsed into the street. The occupants are sitting on chairs calmly watching the approach of the fire. Groups of people are standing in the street, motionless, gazing at the clouds of smoke. When the fire crept close, they would just move up a block. It is hard to believe that such a scene actually occurred in the way the photograph represents it. Several people upon seeing it have exclaimed, "Oh, is that a still from a Cecil De Mille picture?" To which the answer has been, "No, the director of this scene was the Lord himself."

This extraordinary question could not have been asked in 1906; De-Mille began making movies only in 1913. In 1906 the more apt reference

"San Francisco: April 18th, 1906," Arnold Genthe gave his photograph this caption in his memoir, *As I Remember,* published in 1936. *Courtesy of the Library of Congress.*

would have been to San Francisco–born producer and playwright David Belasco. Belasco's turn-of-the century theater productions were noted for their melodramatic plots and ambitiously realistic sets. His 1905 *The Girl of the Golden West* became famous for the special effects in a storm scene; in a play staged in the year of the earthquake, Belasco insisted that real oranges be hung on the set's artificial trees.

Belasco gave DeMille his start in the theater. The filmmaker transferred Belasco's obsession with mimesis to the screen and received, for his 1923 production of *The Ten Commandments,* his teacher's highest accolade: "At last! A spectacle that out-Belascoes Belasco!"

Genthe's position in this evolution is pivotal. His famous photograph of the earthquake marks the transition from the realism of three-dimensional theatrical space to the surrealism of two-dimensional film projection. In this progression the world viewed—and especially its arresting catastrophes, since DeMille loved shipwrecks and surging mobs—is steadily internalized into a manageable and manipulable image. The sense of something staged, as if Genthe had taken a picture of people acting in a movie; the repetition of words like "watching" and "gazing" in Genthe's prose; the emphasis upon "the attitude of the people" rather than on the content of what they see—all this marks the full emergence, on California soil, of the culture of the spectacle.

"I'M A CALIFORNIA PHOTOGRAPHER": Ansel Adams introduced himself to Alfred Stieglitz with these words in 1933, on the occasion of their first meeting in New York. Adams had trained for a career in music, but in 1930 Paul Strand convinced him to commit to photography after seeing his negatives at a dinner party in Santa Fe. Adams soon became the center of Group f/64, a gathering of Northern California photographers who were opposed to the reigning pictorialism of the day and dedicated to "straight photography." The membership included Adams, Edward Weston, Imogen Cunningham, Willard Van Dyke, and Weston's son Brett. While he would later call Weston the "top man" in photography, it was Adams himself, through his monumental images of the Sierra Nevada and especially of Yosemite, who became the state's most visible exponent of camera work. As his service with the Sierra Club and his association with the national parks transformed him into a national figure, Adams met with presidents—he befriended Ford, photographed

Carter, and spent fifty minutes arguing with Reagan about the environment in 1983—and developed friendships with artists like Mary Austin, Georgia O'Keeffe, Walker Evans, and Dorothea Lange.

Adams had lived through the San Francisco earthquake at the age of four. In the first chapter of his autobiography, Adams reprints Genthe's famous "April 18th" photograph, although he identifies the shot as taken down Clay rather than Sacramento Street. Later in the volume, Adams writes of curating the first exhibit for the department of photography at the Museum of Modern Art in 1940. Wanting to include Genthe but finding no adequate prints, Adams nervously approached the famous man, who agreed with enthusiasm to Adams's printing of both "The Street of the Gamblers," a Chinatown photograph, and the now-renamed "View Down Clay Street, San Francisco." Instead of using Genthe's greenish textured paper and warm-toned developer, Adams decided upon glossy paper toned in selenium. The result was so good that Genthe exclaimed, " 'Why didn't I print them that way in the first place?' "

So Adams revisited and retouched the famous image of the earthquake and fire. In *An Autobiography* he represents the earthquake as his most profound early memory, and Genthe's is the only photograph of it that he chooses to include. As Adams tells his story, here and in *Letters and Images,* the earthquake provided for him both a point of departure and an object of reaction, a managed trauma that helped him to consolidate a countervailing artistic vision.

In 1906 the Adams family lived in a spacious house in the dunes beyond the Golden Gate. From his room Ansel could hear the waves crashing on Baker Beach. The evening of April 17 was quiet; Ansel slept in his child's bed next to Nelly, his nanny, while Kong, the Chinese cook, slept in the basement.

> At five-fifteen the next morning, we were awakened by a tremendous noise. Our beds were moving violently about. Nelly held frantically onto mine, as together we crashed back and forth against the walls. Our west window gave way in a shower of glass, and the handsome brick chimney passed by the north window, slicing through the greenhouse my father had just completed. The roaring, swaying, moving, and grinding continued for what seemed a long time; it actually took less than a minute. Then, there was a eerie silence with only the surf sounds coming through the shattered window and an occasional crash of plaster and tinkle of glass from downstairs.

The family regrouped outdoors, after preventing the dazed Kong from starting a fire in the kitchen stove. Adams quickly learned to wait for aftershocks, to hear them building: "It was fun for me, but not for anyone else." The call came for breakfast, and as he ran to answer it, a severe aftershock threw him to the ground. "I tumbled against a low brick garden wall, my nose making violent contact with quite a bloody effect." A doctor advised that the nose be left alone until Adams matured, and it was never fixed. Hence the famous Adams nose: "My beauty was marred forever—the septum was thoroughly broken."

Despite the disfigurement, Adams refrains from claiming the earthquake as his own. A day later, after a trip to Chinatown, Kong returned looking grim: "He had found no one and fire was everywhere. He never discovered what happened to his family." In retrospect, Adams imagines Kong's losses: "I have heard an estimate of four hundred lives lost; it was also said that the real total was closer to four thousand, as it is probable that the Chinese had never been counted." He also understands "the intense anxiety my father must have felt, thousands of miles away." Arriving in the city six days later and unable to rent a horse and buggy, Charles Adams walked and ran the five miles to his family's home.

Adams ends the chapter called "Beginnings" with the following paragraph:

> My closest experience with profound human suffering was that earthquake and fire. But we were not burned out, ruined, or bereft of family and friends. I never went to war, too young for the First and too old for the Second. The great events of the world have been tragic pageants, not personal involvements. My world has been a world too few people are lucky enough to live in—one of peace and beauty. I believe in stones and water, air and soil, people and their future and their fate.

The will toward affirmation in these words makes it possible to conclude that Adams, like Emerson, lacked a vision of evil.

Such a conclusion is supported by looking at his work. Adam's photographs, like his writing about his life, betray an inability or an unwillingness to register pain. "America is a land of joy," he wrote in 1938, after studying Walker Evans's photographs of the Depression. "The promise of the world—the dawn wind and the smell of orchards, the inherent sweetness of simple people, the great *possibilities* of a reasonable life—

these things are important and Art (except in a few instances) consistently bypasses them." Adams would bypass neither the sweetness nor the light. "Perhaps we must go through a real fire of some kind to re-establish a sense of reality," he wrote in 1948, but Adams himself seems to have avoided such a fate. His life was singularly loss-free and productive, and he is to be believed when, in his early forties, he called himself "happier than almost anyone I know." His relentlessly affirmative and even anthemic images suggest that for Adams the big shock came early, left its mark on his face, and then insulated him against any comparable "suffering."

John Muir arrived in California in 1868 and drove a herd of sheep into Yosemite Valley in the following year. Believing that glaciers had shaped his beloved valley, he roamed the high country in search of the living glacier which he discovered in 1871. Muir founded the Sierra Club in 1892. Courtesy of the John Muir Papers, Holt-Atherton Department of Special Collections, University of the Pacific Libraries. Copyright 1984 Muir-Hanna Trust.

The style and content of Adams's mature images certainly cannot be reduced to the after-effects of an early trauma. Still, his work does make a case about the place of catastrophe in our lives. By choosing Yosemite as his central subject and shooting it so consistently, Adams took sides in the debate between John Muir and Clarence King, one rooted in conflicting geological visions, about the beneficence of creation itself.

Muir, who founded the Sierra Club in 1892, was the writer who popularized and fought to protect, through the creation of Yosemite National Park, the Range of Light. King, who served as the first head of the U.S. Geological Survey, conducted, in the 1860s, the initial survey of the major peaks of the Central Sierra. His 1872 *Mountaineering in the Sierra Nevada* is as apocalyptic as Muir's 1894 *The Mountains of California* is benign. Both men loved the mountains, but they squared off over the question of how they had been made.

In the nineteenth century talking about geology was a way of talking about God. Muir believed in the slow work of glaciers, those powerful carving architects that create and then disappear. Glaciers operate as a "tender" hand from above rather than an unpredictable fault from below. Muir did live through a number of earthquakes while living in Yosemite Valley in the 1860s and 1870s, but he stubbornly maintained that glaciers had done the essential work of carving there. "Glaciers work apart from men," he wrote in his first newspaper article, published in 1871, "exerting their tremendous energies in silence and darkness, outspread, spirit-like, brooding above predestined rocks unknown to light." The language here intentionally echoes the Book of Genesis; Yosemite is a "readable glacier manuscript," and God its invisible and loving author.

King, by contrast, reasoned that Yosemite Valley had been precipitated by earthquakes. The high mountains of California, he came to believe, had been formed by sudden and discontinuous events rather than by a gradual and steady evolution. While King did admit that the "terrible ice-engines" called glaciers had done some work in the Sierra Nevada, he sided with his boss, Josiah Whitney, head of the California Geological Survey, in identifying earthquakes as the primary architects of the valley. The geology of the West "was distinctly catastrophic in the wildest dynamic sense," and Yosemite survived as its most vivid emblem.

Clarence King climbed the major peaks of the Central Sierra for the California Geological Survey during the mid-1860s. A Catastrophist rather than a Uniformitarian, King believed that the geology of the West, and of the Sierra in particular, has been formed by violent and discontinuous "moments of catastrophe." He favored earthquakes over glaciers as the primary architects of Yosemite Valley. Courtesy of the Bancroft Library.

Muir wanted to believe that creation was a tender rather than a terrible affair; but nineteenth-century geology and biology had upset the notion of a creator presiding with love. The way of the glaciers allowed him to fuse traditional creationism with the insights of modern science. Adams shared Muir's passion for tenderness, a quality in made things that lay even beyond technique. After meeting Stieglitz in New York, he wrote: "I will always remember what you said about the quality of *tenderness* (it's a rotten word for a deep cosmic quality) in things of art. Tenderness—a sort of elastic appropriation of the essence of things into the essence of yourself, without asking too many intellectual questions, and the giving of yourself to the resultant combination of essences. The soup stirs the cook—perhaps that's what happens in Art." The particular challenge Adams set himself was to choose as his subject a world of rock and to give it, through his "neat, clean, clear-cut technique," the quality of tenderness.

In the summer of 1916, after reading J. M. Hutchings's *In the Heart of the Sierras,* Adams insisted that his family visit Yosemite. On the morning of their arrival, his parents gave him his first camera, a Kodak Box Brownie. The first shot he took was of Half Dome, upside-down; Adams fell while shooting and accidentally hit the shutter. "There was light everywhere," he later wrote, and the valley and the high country beyond it were to become his spot. Photography began for Adams as a visual record of his mountain trips. "From that time on," he told Nancy Newhall in 1944, "things became crystallized in a far more healthy way." Adams lived in the valley during the 1930s and 1940s, and after discovering it as a boy, he visited Yosemite in every year of his life. He met his wife Virginia there in 1920 and married her at Best's Studio, run by her father, in 1928. While on a Sierra Club outing in 1933, Adams missed the delivery of his first child, who was born in the valley.

Like Muir, Adams often hiked the high country for days alone. Like Muir, he sometimes camped in snow. Neither man favored fancy equipment; Adams's preferred footwear in the mountains was rubber-soled basketball shoes. Both men sought in the mountains the clarity of "crystal days." The metaphor of crystal is Adams's, but it originated in Muir. In *The Yosemite* (1912), Muir wrote:

No pain here, no dull empty hours, no fear of the past, no fear of the future. These blessed mountains are so compactly filled with God's beauty, no petty personal hope or experience has room to be. Drinking this champagne water is pure pleasure, so is breathing the living air, and every movement of limbs is pleasure, while the body seems to feel beauty when exposed to it as it feels the campfire or sunshine, entering not by the eyes alone, but equally through all one's flesh like radiant heat, making a passionate ecstatic pleasure-glow not explainable. One's body then seems homogeneous throughout, sound as a crystal.

Crystal is the sublime essence of rock, matter pressured into transparency, a solid trembling on the brink of spirit. For Muir, crystal embodied the promise of a life beyond tension and of a body in seamless harmony with its world. For Adams, crystal became the figure for his "transcendental" art. He sought "crystallization of perception," the "crystal incisiveness" of those brittle-blue distances above and beyond the horizon of the sea off his childhood home. Crystal finally became a figure for the integrity of the man himself: "I remain the same old rock, taking pictures of the same old rocks. . . . I seem to have changed least of all the photographers I know."

What would a crystal photography look like? It would be a photography purged of people. Adams did take wonderful portraits, and to the complaint that his images typically contain no human figures, he responded: "There are always *two* people; the photographer and the viewer." Yet we can no more imagine salient human figures in Adams's landscapes than we can imagine Edward Weston's without them. In *California and the West* (1940), Weston juxtaposed the curves of his wife's body with the curves of California earth, thereby establishing a continuity between human and natural forms. Adams's work argues for a discontinuity; his recurring subject is a peak or monolith, a shape that stands alone and dwarfs and instructs the viewer. "What is lonely is a spirit," A. C. Bradley wrote in his lecture on Wordsworth, and Adams's photographs attempt to evoke and celebrate that loneliness.

A crystal photography would prefer line over form. Weston's vegetables, dunes, and bodies are endowed with a palpable weight; Adams's shapes glow with an unearthly light. They contain not a hint of sex. His mountains, trees, and water exist to affirm a bounding outline, where line becomes the token of a master engraver. In 1920 he wrote his father from the valley: "Even in portraying the character and spirit of a little cascade one must rely solely upon *line* and tone. Form, in a material sense is not only unnecessary, but sometimes useless and undesirable." "Elevation" is the goal, and to a height greater than the Sierra's maximum 14, 495 feet. Adams achieves it by way of a kind of hyperexposure; he opens the camera to light and then filters it out. The blacks and whites that do burn through seem to vie for space in the finished print. In looking at an Adams photograph, the salient effect is of sharp and even surreal contrast. The contrast sets up a shimmer that destabilizes the solidity of the subject. As late as 1967, he could write: "I wonder if I am printing too strong and tone-full!!! My prints all seem to have about 2x the silver of most others I see."

A crystal photography chooses as its subject, then, a recalcitrant hardness, like granite, and works to sublimate that hardness into the affective *"equivalent,"* to use Stieglitz's word, of the power of mind. "The subject is absolutely secondary" to its effect. The photographic image that best reveals this theory put into practice was taken by Adams on April 17, 1927, exactly nineteen years to the day (minus one) after the chimneys fell in on his childhood home.

"One bright Yosemite day in 1927 I made a photograph," Adams wrote in the autobiography, "that was to change my understanding of the medium." It was to become "my first true visualization." With Virginia and three friends Adams had hiked to the Diving Board, a slab of granite on the west shoulder of Half Dome. Arriving at the spot at noon, he found the face of the monolith in shade. He exposed all but two plates while waiting for the light. At 2:30 he placed a K2 filter over his Zeiss Tessar lens and composed the shot. "The shadow effect on Half Dome seemed right, and I made the exposure." "As I replaced the slide," Adams continued,

Ansel Adams, "Half Dome with K2 yellow filter, 1927." This is the first of the two photographs Adams took on the afternoon of April 17, 1927. Copyright © 1995 by the Trustees of the Ansel Adams Publishing Rights Trust. All Rights Reserved.

I began to think about how the print was to appear, and if it would transmit any of the feeling of the monumental shape before me in terms of its expressive-emotional quality. I began to see in my mind's eye the finished print I desired: the brooding cliff with a dark sky and the sharp rendition of distant, snowy Tenaya Peak. I realized that only a deep red filter would give me anything approaching the effect I felt emotionally.

I had only *one* plate left. I attached my other filter, a Wratten #29(F), increased the exposure by the sixteen-times factor required, and released the shutter.

The second and last shot resulted in the "desired image: not the way the subject appeared in reality but how it *felt* to me." *"How it felt to me"*: this is Joan Didion's phrase, used in *Slouching Towards Bethlehem,* for why she keeps a notebook. Like Adams, Didion knows that feelings are hard to have, honor, and express, and like Adams, she defines her California-centered art as a deeply affective one.

The image that Adams produced in his second shot had little to do with accurately recording the world. "The sky had actually been a light, slightly hazy blue and the sunlit areas of Half Dome were moderately dark grey in value. The red filter dramatically darkened the sky and the shadows on the great cliff." The resulting image offers a viewer day-for-night, a high-resolution glimpse of the rock face that seems to coincide with a near-eclipse of the sun. This is not a light ever seen on land or sea. It is a light that brings into focus the power of photography to create a world answerable to the shape and scope of human desire.

Like Muir, Adams conducted a lifelong campaign on behalf of his beloved Sierra, using both photographs and political action to make his case. Both men created through their activities a popular demand for access to the very wilderness they sought to protect. In 1940 Adams's images, shown to President Roosevelt, helped secure passage of the bill that created Kings Canyon National Park. "Public presentation is a game," Adams wrote Weston in 1934, "and none of us can neglect that attitude towards it." Adams played the game so well that he became, by the 1970s, the most famous photographer in America, a man who had converted the lineaments of the mountains into the portable spectacle of calendar art. In 1981 a mural-sized print of *Moonrise, Hernandez, New Mexico, 1941* sold for $71,500, the highest price paid for a photograph up to that time. Adams estimated that a million copies of his books had been sold before the 1979 publication of *Yosemite and the Range of Light.* By

Ansel Adams, "Monolith, the face of Half Dome," Yosemite National Park. The second photograph taken of Half Dome on April 17, 1927. In his autobiography, Adams called it "a personally historic moment in my photographic career." Copyright © 1995 by the Trustees of the Ansel Adams Publishing Rights Trust. All Rights Reserved.

1985, that volume had sold a hundred thousand copies in paper and another hundred thousand in hardback. As the Adams industry grew, his household came to include two cooks, a photographic assistant, a computer operator, a bookkeeper, and a manager-biographer.

In 1949 Paul Strand wrote Adams a letter about "the whole problem of establishing a proper value for a photograph." Strand complained that Adams had set too low a price for a run of a portfolio, a price that undermined the basic concept of the value of a photographic print. In a cheerful reply Adams wrote, "To me the essence of the photographic process is its reproducibility." By way of his reproductions, more tourists have visited Yosemite than could ever have crowded into the valley in fact. Through his consistent practice and vast productivity, Adams converted California into a hard-edged, idealized, and above all an *available* version of itself, an image that usurps the need for physical travel.

When Beaumont Newhall was removed from the directorship of the department of photography at the Museum of Modern Art, Adams wrote a letter of protest against "a *regime* which is inevitably favorable to the spectacular and 'popular.' " Yet these were precisely the aspects of twentieth-century photography with which he became firmly associated. Few would argue the sheer appeal of Adams's images; they are, by any standard, beautiful things. A question that remains is whether his photographs adequately reflect, in Didion's words, "the price of things."

The catastrophes that shaped Adams's beloved Yosemite—and, for that matter, his own life—remain invisible presences in his panoramas of composure. The irony of his Yosemite Valley images is that they minutely record the aftereffects of the very natural processes they set out to suppress. Modern geologists agree that earthquakes had a prominent role in creating the present spectacle of the valley. Arrested by this catastrophic production, Muir and Adams choose to focus on a theory of making that left out shock and pain. But catastrophe *produces* spectacle; this is the hard lesson imparted by California history and geology. For evidence of this fact, Adams had only to refer to Genthe's career, which was made by the opportunity provided by an earthquake. It was after San Francisco had been split open that Genthe had gone out into the streets and produced "pictures," as he wrote, "of lasting interest." The metaphor of crystal, so dear to Adams and to Muir, compensated for the fact of a primal fracture, a break that also had the power to make a landscape of surpassing force. Adams's is a vision haunted by the very forces it would exclude, and it is possible to read his photographs as the equivalent of an immense anxiety, one generated by the carefully managed awareness that he lived in a land of faults as well as beauty.

SEVEN YEARS AFTER the earthquake, the water that was to enable the development of the modern city of Los Angeles arrived in Southern California from the Owens Valley. In a pattern that continues today, California agreed to drain its north in order to irrigate its south. The water made subdivision possible, a story told in Roman Polanski's *Chinatown* (1974). Meanwhile oil was discovered in 1921 at Signal Hill, north of Long Beach. The oil lubricated a building boom, a story told in Jack Nicholson's *Two Jakes* (1990). "There's one thing about Los Angeles that makes it different from most places," the oil man played by Richard Farnsworth says, "and that's two things. You got a desert with oil under it. Second, you got a lot of water around it." Unfortunately the water is salt and the oil is largely gone. What thrives is the culture of spectacle, one in which an entire region can shut down its major north-south freeway in order to cheer the televised escape, in a white Ford Bronco, of a celebrity fugitive.

In 1910 D. W. Griffith moved Biograph's winter operation to Los Angeles. In less than three months he shot twenty-one films, most of them using Southern California settings. Cecil B. DeMille located his operation in Hollywood in 1914, after the successful shooting of *The Squaw Man*. The most familiar image of the earthquake and fire was generated some twenty years later in the Clark Gable/Jeanette MacDonald film *San Francisco* (1936). Richard Rodriguez, writing from the Castro district in the 1990s, remarks in *Days of Obligation* on the abiding and usurping power of the film's images: "Few American cities have had the experience, as we have had, of watching the civic body burn even as we stood, out of body, on a hillside, in a movie theatre. Jeanette MacDonald's loony scatting of 'San Francisco' has become our go-to-hell anthem. San Francisco has taken some heightened pleasure from the circus of final things."

San Francisco contains no image equal to Genthe's. But it owes much, indirectly, to the precocity of northern California camerawork. San Francisco can rightly claim, along with New York, to be the agora of modern American still photography, having fostered the careers of artists like Carleton Watkins, Eadweard Muybridge, Weston, Adams, Cunningham, and Genthe. It can claim more, since the world's first "moving" pictures were in fact created by Muybridge, to resolve a bet made by Leland Stanford over the motion of the feet of a horse. Stanford believed that at some point in the trot all four feet of a horse are in the air at the same time. In order to prove this, he hired Muybridge, a Bay Area photographer known for his gigantic images of the Pacific Coast landscape, to make his case. The results were recorded in J.D.B. Stillman's *The Horse in Motion* (1882).

In order to prove the case, Muybridge had a building erected on the west side of Stanford's racetrack in Palo Alto. He then placed twenty-four cameras in the building, in a row, at the level of a trotting horse. Opposite the building were strung trip wires at an interval of every twenty-one inches. As the driver guided his horse and sulky along a grooved track, a wheel of the carriage would trip each wire in turn. The wires fired the shutters, as Muybridge explained in an appendix, until the whole series was taken. Run together at high speed on one of Muybridge's crude projectors, the series of still photographs merged into a motion picture.

In 1887 Muybridge published his eleven-volume *Animal Locomotion*, but he failed to capitalize on the experiments he made in animating these images on what he called his "zoopraxiscope," a circular metal device that,

Eadweard Muybridge's photograph of the apparatus, built on Leland Stanford's Palo Alto farm, to capture the movement of a trotting horse. Using shutter speeds up to one-six-thousandth of a second, Muybridge projected the resulting photographs through a device that gave the illusion of continuous movement and so produced the world's first "moving pictures." Courtesy of the University of Virginia.

*"Edgerton—Trotting, Stride, 18FT, 3 IN." This series of photographs by Muybridge shows
the carriage wheel and horse as they move across numbered trip wires. From* The Horse in
Motion, *with text by J.D.B. Stillman and an appendix by Muybridge. Courtesy of the
University of Virginia.*

when rotated, projected a series of still images onto a screen in order to
create the illusion of motion. San Francisco after Muybridge remained
the center of still photography, leaving Los Angeles to commercialize the
image in motion with an industry that gave spectacle an unprecedented
luminosity and scale.

The San Francisco earthquake and fire mark the eclipse, in California,
of a world of dimension and depth, a world replaceable by the image of it.
As the century turned, both still and moving photography were beginning to create an alternative universe. Any understanding of how life was
lived either in San Francisco or, especially, in its rival city to the south
would yield increasingly to the amplified and the two-dimensional; Los
Angeles was to become the most "filmed" city on earth. As a result, it was
images of Los Angeles that increasingly showed audiences around the
world how life was lived in cities. Those who would express and analyze
the history of this emerging metropolis learned to articulate themselves
against the gathering pressure of a vast visual mediation. Between hearing and seeing—between the claims of voice and the power of
spectacle—those who lived in Southern California would henceforth be
required to make their unsolitary way.

CHAPTER FIVE

THE POLITICS
OF WATER

The Shift South

THE SAN FRANCISCO EARTHQUAKE and fire is an event whose meaning is largely self-enclosed. It presents something of a dead-end for historical analysis, a happening unproduced by human agency and therefore one in which responsibility gives way to response. What figures in the accounts of it is the feel or shape or look of the thing. The fire did break the city's continuity with its Gold Rush origins and "cleared the way," as Kevin Starr has it, for the building of the modern city of San Francisco. But during the rebirth of the city out of the flames, there also occurred a displacement of energy east and especially south. The Moore Shipbuilding Company moved from San Francisco to Oakland in 1906 and inaugurated the first boom in the modern East Bay economy. Los Angeles experienced even more significant growth after the fire. This southward shift was not a case of moving directly into some suddenly opened economic or cultural breach. Rather, all the forces that had been gathering to shift California's wealth and power southward came together in the next two decades. At the center of this story was not fire but water.

The water that brought life and expansion to Southern California also brought deep political hurt. Yet unlike the visitations of fire, the workings of water's power were often invisible. They took effect slowly, over decades, as a kind of occluded spectacle, one whose dimensions are still

being debated. The heroic building of the Los Angeles Aqueduct provided, of course, spectacle enough, even while diverting the public from
the project's real human and economic costs. The enterprise of piping
water across deserts and mountains for more than 250 miles delivered so
many compelling images and moments of high drama that it may seem
counterintuitive to claim that the truths of the event were largely hidden
from the eye. The irony is that for all the pages of text that have attempted
to bring this experience to light, one of the most sophisticated treatments
of it took place in a medium devoted to the visible, in a film called
Chinatown.

The story of the aqueduct still plays itself out—as recently as December 1993 *The Washington Post* ran an article entitled "Redirection of
California Water Proposed," quoting a resistant Governor Pete Wilson.
But the epic can be seen as beginning in 1904, the year Los Angeles city
officials first visited the Owens Valley in search of water, and as ending
some twenty-five years later, with the collapse of the Saint Francis Dam.
As far as catastrophes go, the Saint Francis Dam disaster killed as many
people as had the San Francisco earthquake and fire. For those who died

*The central core of the Saint Francis Dam on the morning of March 13, 1928. Designed
and built by the chief engineer of the Los Angeles Department of Water and Power,
William Mulholland, the dam collapsed near midnight and sent a wall of water some fifty
miles to the sea. The dam had been built in 1926 as a reservoir to hold the waters of the Los
Angeles Aqueduct. Courtesy of the Los Angeles Department of Water and Power.*

in the flood, it was perhaps more sudden and more terrifying, since a wall of water came sweeping down in the night. In *Water and Power* (1982), William Kahrl labels the event the "greatest unnatural disaster in California history." The dam broke three minutes before midnight. Twelve billion gallons of water poured through Castaic Junction and over the towns of Piru, Fillmore, Bardsdale, and Santa Paula. A twenty-five-foot wave carrying huge pieces of concrete flattened schools and ripped away bridges. The water traveled over fifty miles before reaching the sea between Oxnard and Ventura. The human remains that would be discovered over the next fifty years brought the death toll to nearly five hundred.

The dam gave way in the spring of 1928, when my father was three and two years after his family had emigrated from Oklahoma to South Los Angeles. He spoke often of the quake of '33, when the roofs of the Compton schools collapsed and when he saw the palm trees cross and uncross in his Lynwood front yard. He talked more about earthquakes than about floods: what was a Southern Californian to do with the idea of *too much* water? The dam disaster did not lodge itself in his sense of place any more than it did in the popular consciousness of his region. The politics of water in California remain a manmade affair, and any catastrophe in which they figure cannot easily be transposed into a melodrama of the plucky human withstanding a nature "animated," in James's phrase, "by a will."

The melodramas that do arise from competing human interests we call "political," and while California endures its share of these, it shows little interest in memorializing them, especially those so directly related, as was the Saint Francis Dam disaster, to the costs of development. Located forty-five miles north of Los Angeles in the Santa Clara Valley, near what is now Magic Mountain, the Saint Francis Dam had been completed in 1926. The largest arch support dam in the world, it measured nearly two hundred feet high and some two hundred feet long. The dam had been designed and built by the superintendent of the Los Angeles Department of Water and Power, William Mulholland. Its purpose was to create a reservoir for the waters flowing southward from the Owens Valley and across the Mojave Desert through the Los Angeles Aqueduct. As a result of the water provided by the aqueduct—a structure completed in 1913 and also designed and built by Mulholland—Los Angeles County had become, by 1920, the major agricultural county in the nation and home to the largest city in California.

Yet these waters were by no means secure. They had been procured in the early years of the century through a carefully orchestrated city campaign. The aqueduct delivered considerably more water than the plan originally promised; not until the drought of the early 1920s and the rapidly increasing demands for irrigation in the San Fernando Valley, annexed by Los Angeles in 1915, did water in the Owens Valley begin to run short. The first dynamite attack on the aqueduct occurred in May 1924; that November, Owens Valley residents, led by bankers Sam and Wilfred Watterson, seized control of the Alabama Gates and temporarily halted the flow of water to Los Angeles. Hundreds gathered at the scene and began a four-day camp-out, complete with bonfires and a pig roast. Movie star Tom Mix, filming on location in nearby Bishop, rode over with a mariachi band and joined the party. The Wattersons were eventually jailed for embezzlement; the Owens Valley, once a rich farming and ranching region, dwindled into a high desert in which people made a living pumping gas. Feelings there ran so high against the city that when they drove up Route 395 on fishing trips to the High Sierra, in the 1930s, my father and his brothers taped over the identifying words "Los Angeles" on their license plate.

While Mulholland preferred to store water in underground aquifers rather than in surface reservoirs, the city leaders, in the wake of recurring sabotage against the aqueduct, insisted that he build a surface reservoir as a visible monument to the capacity for supply. Despite his awareness of geologic weaknesses at the Saint Francis Dam site, Mulholland proceeded. At the trial that followed the collapse, a University of Southern California geologist testified that the dam's underlying conglomerate formation had become saturated and had given way. "The failure was due to defective foundation material," he concluded. The stricken Mulholland responded that there had been "no more reason to believe there might be a catastrophe than a babe in arms."

THROUGH THE FIGURE of Hollis Mulwray, Roman Polanski's *Chinatown* deals with the consequences of Mulholland's career. It begins with the end of the story and proposes to have Mulwray build a second dam. He refuses. He will not make "the same mistake twice." He is murdered, by his ex-partner and city-builder Noah Cross, for his refusal. Detective Jake Gittes, tricked by Cross into smearing Mulwray, does not escape the compulsion to repeat. As Gittes tries to "find out" what happened to Mulwray, he falls for Mulwray's wife, Evelyn. He tells Evelyn about a woman he loved, in Chinatown. "I was trying to keep someone from being hurt," he says. "I ended up making sure that she was hurt." In attempting to keep Evelyn from being hurt, and in trying to "know" her, Jake ensures that she will be killed, as she is with a bullet through the eye in the movie's last scene. He makes the same mistake twice.

Chinatown focuses on the fate of Mulholland, "the one universally acknowledged Founder of Los Angeles," as Kevin Starr calls him. The written histories of water and the Southland center on three men: Mulholland, Fred Eaton, and J. R. Lippincott. Each was a man obsessed by the dream of bringing "the water," as Noah Cross puts it, "to L.A." Eaton, a former mayor of Los Angeles, introduced Lippincott and Mulholland to the Owens Valley in the early years of the century. His purchase of options on the key Long Valley site later thwarted the city's plans for building reservoirs upstream and so led to the construction of the Saint Francis Dam. Lippincott worked for the U.S. Reclamation Service during the period when Los Angeles set about acquiring the Owens Valley

The Big Three in 1906: J. R. Lippincott, Reclamation Service engineer for California; Fred Eaton, ex-mayor of Los Angeles; and William Mulholland, chief engineer of the city's Department of Water and Power. Courtesy of the Los Angeles Department of Water and Power.

lands. He supplied information to both Eaton and Mulholland and paved the way for the city acquisitions by encouraging suspension of federal claims to the waters of the valley.

One of the valley residents whose ire Lippincott managed to arouse was a man named Stafford Wallace Austin, register of the U.S. General Land Office in Independence. In 1905, upon learning that the city had quietly purchased all the potential land within the federal government's proposed reservoir site and riparian rights along the Owens River, Austin wrote President Roosevelt, charging fraud and conflict of interest. Two years earlier Austin's wife published the classic treatment of life in this "long brown land," *The Land of Little Rain*. In her autobiography, *Earth Horizon* (1932), Mary Austin provides a lucid if not disinterested survey of how things stood in the valley two years before work began on the aqueduct:

> Strange things had happened in Inyo. In July, 1903, investigation was begun for the reclamation of arid lands there under the National Reclamation Bureau. All reports and estimates of costs demonstrated that the Owens Valley project promised greater results than any other for the cost. Individual owners made transfers of rights and privileges. And all this time the supervising officer of the Owens Valley project and Mulholland, chief engineer, had been working to secure a new water supply for Los Angeles. Suddenly it burst upon the people of Inyo that they were trying to secure the waters of Inyo. Everything had been done. The Reclamation Service had been won over. The field papers had changed hands. Transfers had been made. . . . There were lies and misrepresentations. There was nothing any of us could do about it, except my husband, who made a protest to the Reclamation Bureau.

Austin here draws Mulholland, Eaton, and Lippincott ("the supervising officer") into a web of "lies and misrepresentations." Subsequent histories have been more concerned to sort out blame, assigning core responsibility for the water project and what followed to one individual, or constructing a hierarchy of error. In doing so, these histories seek to manage, to varying degrees, an anxiety about the indeterminacy of the city's origins. The Owens Valley story is the origin-tale for modern Los Angeles—Kahrl begins *Water and Power* by asserting that "the history of California in the twentieth century is the history of a state inventing itself with water"—and the refusal of that history to yield up a master narrative or even verifiable evidence about human acts and intentions raises questions about how much we can come to know about the past.

CHINATOWN BEGINS with a detective telling a spouse concerned about adultery, "You're better off not knowing," and it ends by repeating this advice: "Forget it, Jake, it's Chinatown." What do we *know* about Eaton, Lippincott, Mulholland, and the water? The question can be answered by consulting the many popular and academic histories about the bringing of water to Los Angeles. The best of these works use archival records to create a detailed chronology of the events. Yet this kind of "straight history," as Michael Herr calls it in *Dispatches* (1977), does not entirely satisfy. In "straight history," as Herr describes conventional attempts to comprehend the Vietnam War, "something wasn't answered, it wasn't even asked. We were backgrounded, deep, but when the background started sliding forward not a single life was saved by the information. The thing had transmitted too much energy, it heated up too hot, hiding low under the fact-figure crossfire there was a secret history, and not a lot of people felt like running in there to bring it out." But in the film Robert Towne and Roman Polanski made in and about Southern California, a secret history is brought out, and something does get answered.

We know that Mulholland arrived in Los Angeles in 1877 and worked as a *zanjero,* or ditch tender, for the city. He wrote about the discovery of Los Angeles in an autobiographical fragment: "The Los Angeles River was the greatest attraction. It was a beautiful, limpid little stream with willows on its banks. . . . It was so attractive to me that it at once became something about which my whole scheme of life was woven. I loved it so much." We know that Fred Eaton worked for nine years as the Los Angeles City Water Company's superintending engineer, served as mayor, campaigned for the municipalization of the water system, and saw the city gain control of its domestic water supply in 1902. We know that Mulholland, who succeeded Eaton as head of the privately owned water company, fought the city's purchase of the company but then agreed to assume directorship of the public system. (The only map of that system existed in Mulholland's head.) We know that Lippincott took Eaton to the Owens Valley in 1904, and that Eaton took Mulholland on a visit there some months later. Lippincott, chief of operations in California for the Reclamation Service, had visited the valley a year earlier and had recommended that more than 500,000 acres be withdrawn for possible development of a local public water project. We know that Lippincott and his superiors from the Reclamation Service met with Eaton, Mulholland, and the city attorney in November 1904 and asserted that Reclamation would step aside only if the proposed aqueduct was "public owned from one end to another." We know that city officials and even the publishers of Los Angeles's newspapers were sworn to secrecy about the city's plans so as to prevent a speculative run on Owens Valley land values. We know that in March 1905 Lippincott, while still working for the Reclamation Service, signed a private contract with the Los Angeles Water Commission to prepare a survey of "the possible sources the city could tap for additional water." And we know that in the same month Lippincott gave Eaton a letter directing him to prepare a personal report on rights-of-way in the valley. Eaton used the letter to buy up options on the Long Valley reservoir site, options over which he also retained some private control and which he would eventually offer to the city at a price it refused to pay.

Why did L.A. want the water? Even this brief summary of the jockeying that occurred before the aqueduct construction began suggests a profound mixture of motives. "Los Angeles is a desert community," former mayor Sam Bagby argues in the second scene in *Chinatown*: "Without water the dust will rise up and cover us as though we never existed." The film takes place during a period of drought—a drought engineered, it turns out, by the water department. In reality, Los Angeles voters supported a bond issue for Mulholland's aqueduct, in part, out of a chronic fear of water shortages—a fear manipulated by the water department. Mulholland campaigned for the bond issue by concocting drought conditions that did not, in fact, exist; 1905 was an especially wet year in Los Angeles. He imagined a system that would serve a population of 390,000 residents, a figure he estimated the city might reach in 1925. By 1925 the population of Los Angeles was three times that number.

Water was and is brought to Los Angeles less to meet a necessary demand than to provide an infinite supply. William Kahrl establishes that from that time to this, the city has been able to secure far more water than its citizens have proven able to consume. In the early 1980s only seven percent of the water provided by the Colorado River was used by the city; the remainder went to the surrounding municipalities that had helped

fund the Hoover Dam project by
joining with Los Angeles in 1928
to form the Metropolitan Water
District.

Despite the vagaries of demand, the building of the aqueduct was to prove so heroic an
enterprise that its success tended
to eclipse second thoughts. Work
on the project began in the fall of
1907. The planned route was to
carry 260 million gallons of water
a day over a distance of nearly 250
miles. Arising near the back entrance to Yosemite National Park,
the aqueduct was to divert the
water of the Owens River into
some sixty miles of open canals
and concrete ditches. Gathered
into the fifteen-square-mile Hai-
wee Reservoir, these waters
would then flow or be pumped

*Pipe for the Los Angeles Aqueduct as it passes
over one of the mountain ranges on its 250-
mile route from the Owens Valley to
reservoirs above the San Fernando Valley.
Courtesy of the Los Angeles Department of
Water and Power.*

through steel siphons and closed tunnels 125 miles across the Mojave to
the Fairmont Reservoir, at the base of the Coast Range. The Elizabeth
Tunnel was to carry the waters five miles through the six-thousand-foot-
high Sierra Madre, after which they were to tumble through twenty-
three miles of turbines and conduits to reservoirs above the San Fernando
Valley.

By the time Mulholland stood at the Owensmouth Cascades in 1913
and declared to the gathered populace, "There it is—Take it!" he had
built the longest aqueduct in the Western Hemisphere. To support the
five years of construction, the Bureau of the Los Angeles Aqueduct had
laid 120 miles of railroad tracks, graded five hundred miles of highways
and trails, and erected its own cement-manufacturing plant to produce a
special mixture made with Owens Valley tufa stone. Excavated in 1,239
days, the 26,800-foot Elizabeth Tunnel set a record for hard-rock tunneling. A potential labor shortage was averted when, in 1907, a financial
panic led to the closing of mining operations throughout the West; four

The Owensmouth Cascades on the morning of November 5, 1913. "There it is—Take it!"
William Mulholland said as he formally opened the aqueduct that allowed water to pass
through its terminus at the Owensmouth Cascades. The cascades are located near the present
site of Magic Mountain. Courtesy of the Los Angeles Department of Water and Power.

thousand experienced tunnelers and diggers descended upon Mulholland's desert labor camps. A strike over food service in 1910 coincided
with a cash shortage in construction funds. Mulholland weathered the
crisis by dismissing eighty percent of his workforce and then hiring re-
placements once the city was able to float a new set of bonds.

Mulholland's labor troubles coincided with the trial of the union-
organizing McNamara brothers, arrested in October 1910 on charges of
dynamiting the offices of the *Los Angeles Times*. Largely through the
efforts of *Times* publisher Harrison Gary Otis, Los Angeles had remained
an open-shop town. It was a city as resistant to working-class solidarity as
San Francisco was hospitable to it. The trial of the McNamara brothers
thus became an allegory of the battle between capital and labor in
Southern California, with a mayoral election hanging in the balance.

Throughout the country the progressive spirit had elected more than five hundred socialists to various public offices in 1910 and 1911. In the Los Angeles mayoral campaign of 1911, Socialist candidate Job Harriman portrayed Mulholland's aqueduct as built for the benefit of the San Fernando Mission Land Company—a cartel, formed one week after Lippincott's secret 1905 meeting with city officials, that had managed to buy up, before the arrival of the water needed to develop it, most of the available land in the as-yet-unincorporated valley. The land includes the present-day towns of Van Nuys, Canoga Park, Reseda, Sherman Oaks, and Woodland Hills. Harriman portrayed the water project as carried out for the benefit of an owner class; the cartel included Otis, his son-in-law Harry Chandler, a former Los Angeles water commissioner, the vice president of the Title Insurance Company, and H. J. Whitney, the land developer who built Hollywood. "Perhaps more than any other city," Roger Lotchin writes in *Fortress California*, "Los Angeles was the product of a development conspiracy by its leadership." "They've been blowing these farmers out of here and buying their land for peanuts"—this is Jake Gittes's assessment of the syndicate's effectiveness after he is knocked out by the crippled farmer in a San Fernando orange grove.

Having tied himself to the labor cause, the success of Harriman's mayoral candidacy depended upon the acquittal of the McNamara brothers. Clarence Darrow agreed to handle the McNamaras' defense. He also concluded that his clients were guilty of bombing the *Times* offices. Using Lincoln Steffens as a go-between, Darrow brokered a deal in which the McNamaras agreed to plead guilty in exchange for reduced sentences. The result was a lost election for Harriman, the discrediting of the labor movement in Los Angeles, and the assurance to Mulholland that the aqueduct would be completed in relative peace.

The story of water and Los Angeles divides itself into countless sub-plots. Historians have sometimes managed the proliferating narrative by reducing it to a melodrama. A signal contribution to this process was made in 1931 by Andrae Nordskog in a pamphlet printed by the California State Printing Office. His *Communication* advanced a conspiracy history and accused "the Mulholland political crowd" of "gross mis-management." Two years later Morrow Mayo relied on Nordskog's primary research in his chapter "The Rape of the Owens Valley," published in his book *Los Angeles*. "*The Federal Government of the United States held Owens Valley,*" he concluded, "*while Los Angeles raped it.*" Here Morrow paraphrased the earliest contribution to the controversy,

W. A. Chalfant's *Story of Inyo* (1922, 1933). Publisher of the *Inyo Register,* Chalfant had maintained that "the government held Owens Valley while Los Angeles skinned it." Books like Remi Nadeau's *Water Seekers* (1950) and Vincent Ostrom's *Water and Politics* (1953) took a more positive view of the actions of the city, championing its developer-engineers and even describing them as "great creators." Abraham Hoffman's *Vision or Villainy* (1981) went so far as to attempt a rehabilitation of Lippincott, arguing that he was a "far more complex person than the caricatures have shown," the "unwitting victim of later historiographical distortions."

While it does not take sides, Kahrl's *Water and Power* does deign to judge. "Probably no character in this narrative has appeared so villainous as J. B. Lippincott," he writes in his conclusion. "He alone consistently broke faith with his public trust and then lied to cover his actions." Kahrl tempers this claim by allowing that Lippincott was correct about Los Angeles's water needs and "sincere in his belief that he was serving some higher public duty by encouraging the Reclamation Service to abandon the Owens Valley in favor of Los Angeles." His closing dismissal of Eaton as "comically ineffectual" pales next to his prior claim that Eaton "never conceived of the project as anything other than a private scheme that would work to his personal profit." The San Fernando land syndicate he describes as "somewhat less than corrupting." Mulholland's story devolves, for Kahrl, into a "tragedy." As Kahrl's subtitle suggests, he views the story as a "conflict." The drama he restages with thoroughness and balance serves as a model of the historian's truth.

In *Chinatown,* Polanski and Towne conduct an inquest into the power of cinematic truth. Director and screenwriter invoke many of the incidents and figures from the Owens Valley story. But they are finally concerned less with what we know than how we know. Film confers a certain kind of knowledge; watching it, we take in the world with our eyes. This amplified visual evidence has an immense authority—it capitalizes on the cliché that seeing is believing. What is seen on the screen fills the being before the mind can think; the assent we give to a movie is more sensual and visceral than critical or analytical. *Chinatown* chooses to expose rather than to exploit this process. While it holds up cinema as a legitimate vehicle for historical memory and critique, it also cautions the viewer that "truth," as Jake Gittes calls what he wants from Evelyn Mulwray, is always more than meets the eye.

Chinatown was by no means the first movie to appropriate the Owens

Valley story; in the 1935 *New Frontier* John Wayne and the Mesquiteers rode to the aid of ranchers in the New Hope Valley, beset by a water project for Metropole City. But *Chinatown* is the first movie to link the historical and narrative materials of the story with the formal limits and properties of film. Water serves as the vehicle for this process because its history and movements are transparent yet subterranean, ubiquitous while also hidden from view. Los Angeles works as the site for the inquiry not only because of Polanski's personal experience of the city—the 1969 Manson-Tate murders, in which his pregnant wife was brutally slain—but because of the plot-ridden character of the local politics. The intersections between film and history are many, despite Towne's claim that "I didn't base a single character in *Chinatown* on any person I read about in the Owens Valley episode." Script and camera focus on a heroic Mulholland-figure; they collapse into Noah Cross the shadier aspects of Eaton, Lippincott, and even Mulholland (he, like Cross, fought a custody battle with his daughter over a granddaughter); they play up the role of the land syndicate; they play down the city's labor problems; they start with the failed dam rather than the successful aqueduct; and they shift the entire action into the waning years of the Depression, ten years after the dam gave way and over thirty years after the "rape" of the Owens Valley first began.

TRICKED BY AN IMPOSTER into smearing Mulwray, Jake Gittes sets out to secure his revenge. While he does develop some feeling for Evelyn Mulwray as the movie proceeds, his prime motive in solving the presumed mystery is to get back at the people "who set me up." "I want the big boys who are making the payoffs," he says. *Chinatown* unfolds as a movie about pride, especially the pride of knowing.

As a private eye, its protagonist makes a living by selling information. The first shot in the movie is of a photograph, "grainy but unmistakably a man and a woman making love." We hear a voice moaning offscreen. What sounds like sex noises turns out to be the groans of an anguished husband, Curly. His lamentations provide the sound track as photographs are leafed through on the screen, and the viewer is taken in by the synchronization. The movie immediately establishes and exploits, as it will throughout, a gap between the heard and the seen. Within the confines of Curly's story, Jake succeeds in selling him adequate information about his wife's adultery. Curly confronts his wife, blackens her eye, and sinks back into his routine. But in the world inhabited by Noah Cross, truth does not so easily yield to surveillance. Jake's investment in what things "look like" upholds him in the fatal belief that adequate knowledge can be gained from the world viewed.

"No script ever drove me nuttier," Towne was to say; he felt overwhelmed by the abundance of data on the politics of water in Los Angeles. "I tried one way and another casually to reveal mountains of information about dams, orange groves, incest, elevator operators." He was also influenced by another writer about a gone Los Angeles: "reading Chandler filled me with such a sense of loss that it was probably the main reason why I did the script." Polanski viewed the material as more personal, more existential. "I was in L.A.," he said, "where every street corner reminded me of tragedy." He insisted that Towne add a love scene between Jake and Evelyn, as well as an unhappy ending. "Evelyn had to die," he maintained. Towne, for his part, had imagined Evelyn in jail after shooting Noah Cross, with daughter Katherine escaping to Mexico. For Towne, the tragedy arose from the corruption of place. He smelled sage and eucalyptus and felt prompted to write about the despoliation of California land. The two visions happily converged; the incest between father and daughter became a compelling metaphor for our betrayal by those to whom we have given our private or public trust.

Directing their skepticism back at their own medium, Polanski and Towne also ask whether we can trust the truth delivered by an art so overwhelmingly visual. For Jake, who routinely misinterprets what he sees, experience proves an uninstructive spectacle. Polanski surrounds him with aids and obstacles to sight: the binoculars and camera with which he spies on Mulwray; the photographs of Curly's wife and of Noah Cross and Mulwray; the various kinds of clear and broken "glass" or "grass," as the Japanese gardener calls it in another misheard aural cue; Mulwray's spectacles and Cross's bifocals; the eye of a fish and the "flaw" in Evelyn's iris. Eyes get shot out; lenses and taillights broken. So Jake continues to see but has no perspective on what is seen. As both Cross and Evelyn say to him, "You may think you know what you're dealing with, but believe me, you don't."

Jake begins as superior to the action and to his client. He doles out sympathy and information to Curly and agrees that Curly is right only in order to get rid of him. The viewer, coming in at the end of the investigation, is placed in the role of voyeur. We share with Jake a sense of distanced knowing, even delectation. In the following scenes, we watch Jake watch Mulwray: at City Hall, in the bed of the Los Angeles River, and at the outfall at Point Fermin Park. The next day, back at the office, we are treated to a second set of photographs that show Mulwray outside a restaurant with an older man. Jake tosses them down in disgust, accusing his assistant Walsh of having wasted his time. These photographs refuse to yield information. Walsh mentions that the two men argued. "What about?" Jake asks. Walsh answers: "I only heard one word—apple core."

Jake cannot hear the clue in "apple core" ("albacore," the name of Cross's yacht club), and the viewer has as yet no idea what the words might mean. But the gap between the seen and the heard has been introduced a second time, and it suggests that what Jake needs to do is not to look but to listen. Throughout the film he proves remarkably deaf to the tones and inflections of speech. He cannot hear the falseness in Ida Sessions's impersonation of Mrs. Mulwray. Nor can he detect the obvious and sincere distress in Evelyn's voice as she gamely attempts to divert him from discovering the identity of her daughter.

Jake's futile attempt to catch up with the past is measured out by the movie's persistent ticking sounds, as in the scene just after he and Evelyn make love. Provocative little noises, like the sexy squeak of a car being polished or a name being scraped off an office door, frequently distract him. The telephone interrupts lovemaking and sleep. Jake's refusal to heed the messages carried by sound culminates in a silent movie of his own staging the scene where he watches Evelyn and her daughter arguing through a bungalow window, and where, for the lack of a sound track, he draws all the wrong conclusions.

Late in the film, and long after we have begun to question Jake's skill as a detective, Polanski introduces another scene that enacts the persistent lag in Jake's response to sound versus sight. Jake has been called to Ida Sessions's apartment and walks through it, finding a wilted head of lettuce, spilled groceries, and then Ida dead on the floor. A hand-held camera shakily follows him. Jake turns toward a dark closet. At this moment Jerry Goldsmith's score produces a loud screech, one that we hear but that Jake does not. A light suddenly comes on in the closet, revealing the hidden police officers Loach and Escobar. While the scene is meant to scare us, it also contains a built-in warning device that blunts the shock. The sound track gives us the aural before the visual cue; it is as if the thunder arrives before the lightning. By inverting the normal timing of cues, the scene not only points to an alternative method of gathering evidence but to the viewer's increasing distance from and even suspicion of the adequacy of the hero.

Until Faye Dunaway turns up as the real Mrs. Mulwray, the viewer accompanies Jake in gathering the data. Her appearance marks the beginning of our divergence from him. We first see her as she stands behind Gittes while he tells Walsh and Duffy the joke about the "China-man." As he finishes the joke, Jake laughs, turns, sees Mrs. Mulwray, and chokes. After this sequence, our relation to him shifts: We are no longer willing to look at the world through his eyes, and when we see him in the frame, he is increasingly shot from behind. Jake's back becomes part of the scenery; the camera situates him in the field he means to survey and master, while we look over his shoulder. Jake may continue to view himself as uninvolved, but we *see* him as part of the action, a man who continually gets ahead of himself and who gets in the way.

Yet although we learn not to trust Jake or his point of view, we are not granted any other angle of access. There are no scenes without him, and he increasingly becomes the moving force in bringing about the conclusion—the very one he means to prevent. His final summons to Noah Cross is not only gratuitous, based solely on Jake's desire to *know*, but will place Cross at the scene of his daughter's attempted escape. By subjecting Jake to this series of humiliations and uncertainties, Polanski withholds from his film an authoritative and knowing point of view. The director's mistrust—even renunciation—of authority culminates in the cutting of Jake's nose: Polanski casts himself as the "Man with Knife." By making the behavior of the character he plays so capricious and unattractive, he positions himself within the ugly confusions of his film rather than beyond them.

Anyone who drinks a glass from the tap in Los Angeles accepts Mulholland's gift. Water connects; even the Mexican boy on the horse who consults with Mulwray knows that, and he knows that to follow the appearings and disappearings of water is to acquire the deepest and most complex knowledge of his city. Yet it is not a knowledge that enables or empowers. The knowledge delivered by the movement of water implicates and entangles; it reveals experience as interrelation. Such knowledge does not afford a privileged perspective, and Jake's attempt to enjoy such a position is what kills.

Given its view of life as mutual entanglement, the movie rejects the metaphor of rape that governs so much of the discourse about Los Angeles and the Owens Valley. When Jake asks Evelyn, "Did he rape you?" she pauses, then quietly shakes her head back and forth. As an adult, Evelyn fights her father out of a desire to protect her daughter/ sister, not out of a sense of prior victimage. She accepts her own implication in the events of her past. The original script even allowed for a kind of sympathy for Cross, in lines that were eventually cut from the movie:

> EVELYN (*continuing*): he had a breakdown . . . the dam broke . . . my mother died . . . he became a little boy . . . I was fifteen . . . he'd ask me what to eat for breakfast, what clothes to wear! . . . it happened . . . then I ran away.

Towne's language here represents incest between father and daughter as a response to a need. It also attempts to imagine the misery of Mulholland's life after the collapse of the dam and to meet it with a strange kind of solace. The filmed version replaces these lines with Jake's question about rape. Evelyn does not nod yes to his question. The assumption of responsibility by a character who could so easily have been cast as a victim complicates any response to the film that looks to separate out innocence and guilt. Given the horrors of his personal losses—born in 1933 and raised in Poland, he saw his parents taken to a concentration camp in 1940—Polanski persists in viewing the world as a place in which people—and by this he means everyone—are "capable of anything."

Polanski's, then, is finally not a political vision. While the actual history of governments may be complicated, politics depends on people making a distinction between better and worse, on acting and deciding. Towne had wanted a movie in which the good guys got away. But by including everyone in his landscape of despair, Polanski created an image of Los Angeles as a site of continuing holocaust. He used the unique history of water in California to make a general case about the ubiquity of collaboration and evil. "He has to swim in the same water we all do," Jake says about Escobar. Not even the viewer of *Chinatown* escapes the implications of this claim.

While much is lost in this cinematic adaptation of California history— especially the informed anger that could make for political change— something is also gained. In *Chinatown* Polanski creates a powerful vision of life in which relations stop nowhere and in so doing makes a direct challenge to the historicizing imagination. When we attempt to understand the film as a historical artifact, as pointing toward or influenced by some earlier historical occurrence, *Chinatown* in fact invokes an infinity of contexts. The most obvious is the Mulholland story—surely this is a movie about bringing the water to L.A. But why, then, is it set in the 1930s? Perhaps it is a movie about the promises and failures of public works in and since the New Deal. The film is, as Polanski writes, "about the thirties seen through the camera eye of the seventies." Jake's failed attempt to save the woman he loves—a mistake he makes twice—cannot be ignored: the futility and impotence and even the guilt Polanski may have felt after the murder of his pregnant wife provide the context here. But if any work of art necessarily expresses the received truths of its moment of production, then the context that comes to mind is the corruption and betrayal of Watergate. Nixon resigned less than a month after the film was released. The film's message, however, is not that we must pursue corruption to its lair. Although the catastrophe here is the coverup, Jake only inflicts more damage by trying to uncover the "truth." But why, then, is it called *Chinatown*? Yes, "Chinatown" becomes a metaphor for the unmanageable, a kind of universal and negative signifier. And if there ever was a situation in which the United States thought it knew what it was dealing with but didn't, it was Vietnam. The final image of the Asian faces crowding onto the screen, as well as the salient yet marginal figures of the Chinese butler and the Japanese gardener— these may provoke some to consider the film's context as not only the long history of the oppressed "Oriental" in California but the Asian war from which America had withdrawn in 1973 and which was to end with the fall of Saigon in 1975.

By so deftly invoking these and other contexts, Polanski opens up a free space. Not for action or emotion: these remain for the characters in the film, at least, a dead end. The space *Chinatown* opens onto is the space of interpretation itself, a space Polanski creates and protects for the viewer. *Chinatown* refuses to allow the onlooker to remain comfortable in the belief that a city or a life or even a movie can be fully understood by invoking its generating historical context. Yet the film also understands and accepts that such narratives and attempts at inter-connection are necessary fictions by way of which we control our anxiety about the ambiguity of experience. This mordant negative capability reminds us that works of art that dramatize the past without apportioning blame, or even establishing firm lines of cause and effect, do as much as the histories to keep stories like the one shared by Los Angeles and the Owens Valley unforgotten and alive.

CHAPTER SIX

WORLD WAR II

Los Angeles and the Production of Anger

I N 1992 DIRECTOR ROBERT ALTMAN revived his career by making a movie about the devolution of hope in the post–cold war economy. *Short Cuts* did not immediately present itself as an anatomy of a martial culture in decline; its setting was, after all, Southern California, a fat and sunny place reputedly at peace. The movie's concerns appear to be more technical than political: while the lives it shows share a common condition—the struggle to make a living in Los Angeles—their resemblances depend upon a highly manipulative and self-conscious camera eye, not on an openly argued cultural analysis.

Altman's deeply sly film diverts attention from the incisiveness of its vision with the virtuosity of its style. *Short Cuts* foregrounds the power of film to edit continuity into lives that lack it. The shapelessness of these individual stories is amplified by the number of them—a cast so large as to suggest a random collection. The camera manages this overload with a recurring pattern of portentous cuts—from, say, a live and naked female body floating in a swimming pool to a dead and naked female body floating in a river. Not every act in the film is overdetermined by such visual rhyming; it is precisely the intermittence of the pattern that reinforces in the viewer a taste for and conviction of the connection between shots.

While these "short cuts" produce the movie's central effect—a sense of willed or formal connectedness—Altman relies on two further scenic choices to achieve his ends. Both have to do with Southern California as a mise-en-scène. The Raymond Carver stories on which the movie is based are located in a vaguely invoked Pacific Northwest; Altman relocates them to the Los Angeles of the late 1980s, overlaps plots that never converge in Carver, and makes the place the main protagonist. Scenes begin with a camera sliding across or moving slowly into a Los Angeles exterior. Finally, at the movie's end, Altman gathers his characters together through the event of the earthquake. The moving of the plates is the one thing that everybody in the film indubitably shares. Waiting for and living through the "big one" binds Californians into a casual sense of common ordeal, even if their primary means of connecting is by watching it—as Fred Ward and Anne Archer and Matthew Modine and Julianne Moore do—on TV.

Altman's movie appears to be all transitions, and its characters are linked momentarily by them. Editing is a property of film, not of the world it registers. The only experience consciously and universally shared in Altman's Los Angeles is the earthquake, and it *means* nothing. Any meaning or pattern or even shape in Altman's cinematic world is conferred by the camera, a continually tracking, zooming, and cutting eye. In a landscape of such transience and amnesia, the burden of creating a world shifts to the watcher. As Julianne Moore says, about her paintings: "They're about seeing. And the responsibility that goes with it."

A viewer of the film may watch the final sequence in horror: it looks as if a man killing a woman with a rock actually produces the earthquake. Chris Penn lifts the rock and brings it down on the woman—and the world and the frame of the film begin to shake. The characters in the movie take it all with a suspicious calm. "It's not the big one," someone says, almost in disappointment. Altman's Southern Californians are spoken for by a voice called Stormy Weathers, a helicopter pilot who tells the TV watcher, given the statistic of only one death, "just how lucky he or she is to be living in L.A."

As a movie, *Short Cuts* might seem condemned by the amplified and continuity-ridden conventions of film to divert attention from the strains of its historical moment. But spectacles are not defined simply by their size or luminosity, just as modes of representation do not provoke, simply because of their formal conventions or means of material production, any single or guaranteed effect. Spectacle can be defined as the *use* of form that sets out to distance its audience from the represented event while mystifying that audience about the event's contexts and possible causes.

Film can certainly be used to do this, but it remains as available as any other art form to the spirit of critique.

Short Cuts is an example of an antispectacular film—one, like *China-town,* that illuminates rather than obscures the relations of life. As early as 1886, Josiah Royce complained that Californians have "too often come to love mere fulness of life and to lack reverence for the relations of life." By the time Altman made his movie, even the "fulness" had departed. Everything about the film directs our attention to the way it, and the society it images, is put together. The effect is finally to provoke analysis rather than rapture or rationalization.

Precisely by using the power of cinematic form to establish relations between the seemingly unrelated, Altman's movie analyzes the compelling structural similarities between the lives it represents. The movie's characters do share a world, one with highly limiting features. Here people are isolated in unaccommodating spaces: trailers, tract houses, monstrosities in the hills. Proximity has replaced community; no longer are these Angelenos free to move or expand. Work is entirely separated from play; the competent doctor in the hospital is the incompetent husband at home. Drugs and alcohol lubricate personal unhappiness, while sex has been replaced by talk about it. Men head for the hills in order to avoid women. Race, relegated to the periphery, can intrude into the most ordinary evening out. Life is lived in a perpetual state of alert— on a virtual wartime footing—but the anxiety derives from the fact that a war (and the money to be made from it) is ending. The government, embodied by its helicopters, remains addicted to readiness—"The time has come to go to war again" are the film's first spoken words—and routinely sprays its own civilians. These people live, that is, in the unique yet representative nexus that is contemporary Southern California.

Short Cuts captures the moment when the postwar economic boom began its decline into downward mobility. That boom had transformed California's economy into the seventh largest in the world. Even though that economy was located in a region devoted to the pleasures of peace, it was based on war. Once the defense cuts of the late 1980s began their devastating work, the social contract experienced the dramatic collapse that has allowed Los Angeles to replace New York, in the public mind, as the nation's most criminal and ungovernable metropolis. The 1996 summer movie was not about escape from New York, but from L.A.

This chapter, however, traces the price of expansion rather than the process of decline. It ends, as it begins, with a contemporary jeremiad—in this case Joan Didion's "Trouble in Lakewood," which echoes Altman in its portrayal of a defense-based economy as a costly, temporary, and finally illusory short cut. Meanwhile, the story of the postwar expansion is told by two other writers, one a longtime resident, the other a wartime immigrant. Raymond Chandler arrrived in Los Angeles before the First World War and experienced the Second as the final destruction of a sleepy, good-hearted place; Chester Himes, migrating from Ohio to California in 1942, spent most of his time in Los Angeles in a frustrating search for work. The Zoot Suit Riots fill out the story, not only because they predict the cost to civic culture of a permanent military presence, but because they inaugurate, however painfully, the long-deferred return to public life of the city's Mexican-American population.

The movie industry that sprang up before World War One did not alone make Southern California rich. Tourism, agriculture, real estate, oil, and—especially—the federal government also played a role in the dramatic expansion of the region. From the beginning of its settlement, the trans-Mississippi West had enjoyed a level of governmental subsidy and land ownership so extensive that Patricia Limerick justifiably calls it a "federal captivity." Army forts had been the initial settled presence in the West—outposts with names like Laramie, Bridger, Hall, Leavenworth. It was federal money that had opened and maintained the routes west, and its presence only expanded as the world rushed in. The region's aridity required a Reclamation Service, with its dams and canals; a Department of Agriculture, with its willingness to farm the wilderness; its deserts and harbors and unclaimed spaces a navy and army and an air force, with their military reservations and bombing ranges. In 1980 forty-five percent of the land in the West was still federally owned.

In California the problem of large-scale land ownership, public and private, was especially pronounced. By the 1960s Los Angeles could claim to have the largest number of free-standing private homes of any city in the United States, but the region also contained large landholdings like the vast Irvine Ranch, one-fifth the size of present-day Orange County. Such patterns could be traced back to the original ranchos, five of which once divided up the Los Angeles basin. But they had much more to do with development practices and federal incentives that allowed firms like the Southern Pacific Railroad to acquire huge tracts of land, and with the topography and climate of California's inland valleys, where aridity and unbroken expanses favored irrigation and planting patterns based on vast economies of scale. In 1947 Freeman Champney could thus write of California that "in its extremes of wealth and destitution, in the absence or impotence of any middle group representing the public interest, and in the domination of the organs of civil life by irresponsible private greed, it has been one of the few areas of American life that has closely approximated the Marxian predictions about capitalist society." At the same time that California attracted immigrants with a dream of home ownership, a good job, and a place in the sun, it indentured many of them into an economy precariously based on growth and bigness. No concentration of power played a larger part in this dynamic than did the industry of defense.

In 1993 Joan Didion observed that "the distress in which California now finds itself has as its proximate cause the withdrawal of the federal money that kept the defense industry afloat and the subsequent decision by the surviving prime defense contractors to concentrate operations out of state." The 300,000 aerospace jobs held in Los Angeles County in 1987 had dwindled, by April 1993, to 174,000. The direct product of World War II, California's defense industry certainly changed the East Bay, but it had its most profound effect on the city of Los Angeles.

In 1900 Los Angeles was home to 102,000 people. That figure tripled in the next decade, almost doubled in the next, and rose to 1.2 million by 1930. In those thirty years San Francisco merely doubled in size; by 1930 its population was only half that of its rival to the south. Sustained by Mulholland's water, the annexation of the San Fernando Valley—Kevin Starr calls it the city's Louisiana Purchase—the discovery of oil, and a 1920 boom in real estate, Los Angeles had grown by 1930 into a major industrial, agricultural, and maritime center.

On the eve of World War II, California ranked eighth among the nation's manufacturing states. In the next five years, the value of its manufactures quadrupled. Ten percent of all federal monies spent during the war were spent in California, an influx of capital that established the nation's largest urban military-industrial complex. The Bay Area expanded into the nation's leading shipbuilding region, while Los Angeles—through the efforts of Douglas, Lockheed, Northrop, and North American—became its aircraft-manufacturing center.

California's wartime economic boom triggered a massive national migration. In the 1940s the state added 3.5 million people, with 72.2

percent of the growth due to in-migration. The problems of reception that had been anticipated by Steinbeck in *The Grapes of Wrath* compounded during the war. In 1943 the cities of San Francisco and the East Bay faced an influx of half a million war workers and a breakdown of municipal services. The boomtown of Richmond resorted to the rental of "hot beds," beds in which workers took turns sleeping, using them around the clock. In 1942 and 1943 the rate of venereal disease in San Francisco rose by more than 75 percent. The 85 percent of aircraft employees who commuted to work by car in Los Angeles led to massive traffic jams and the first "daylight dimout"—a smog alert—in 1943.

Earlier migrants were drawn into the vortex as well. My maternal grandmother, who had come to California from Texas after World War I, worked in her fifties as a riveter on airplanes known as Liberators. My father James, brought to Lynwood from Oklahoma at the age of two in 1926, drafted assembly procedures for C-47s at Douglas before joining the Army Air Corps. After coming back from the war, his brother Bill bought out his brother Lynn's interest in a machine shop, surfed the cold war demand for precision-tooled aircraft parts, and by the early 1970s was golfing at the Bel-Air Country Club and owned part of a bank.

Nathanael West was the John the Baptist of the boom. *The Day of the Locust* (1939) faces backward, toward the Depression and the midwestern migrations of the 1930s. At the novel's end disappointed migrant Homer Simpson tries to get out of California as unsuccessfully as the Joads, invented in the same year, try to get in. Both Steinbeck and West wrote out of a social sorrow that longed for a great day; that day would come neither as a flood nor as a fire but as a catastrophe even more transforming. The anger and poverty of purse and spirit that erupts into West's "The Burning of Los Angeles" was sublimated into a war effort that substituted for the problems of scarcity the anxieties of abundance.

Virtually everybody made money. The war and the expansion that followed created a culture of mobility and middle-class affluence unmatched in the history of the world. Yet few books or movies affirm this good life. Carolyn See has written brilliantly about Southern California's industries of hope, but her characters must pay for their happiness by surviving the catastrophes: auto accidents in *Making History,* and in *Golden Days,* the terminal catastrophe of nuclear war. Perhaps the ironic and hard-boiled conventions of the Hollywood novel already laid down by James M. Cain, West, and Fitzgerald preempted innocent celebrations of affluence. The continuities between pre- and postwar Southern California fiction are, in any case, remarkably clear. By contrast, the discontinuity in the region's material conditions—the supersession of lack by excess—is merely recorded without being celebrated. In writers like Raymond Chandler and Chester Himes, West's and Steinbeck's militant anger modulates into the depiction of a culture of illusion and rage. It was their firsthand experience of work in the oil and shipbuilding industries that compelled these two novelists to create two of the most powerful and mordant representations of the birth of Southern California's military-industrial complex.

CHANDLER ARRIVED in Los Angeles in 1912 after an adolescence spent on the green playing fields of an English preparatory school. A poem he wrote twenty years later expressed his abiding nostalgia:

> *There are no countries as beautiful*
> *As the England I picture in the night hours*
> *Of this bright and dismal land*
> *Of my exile and dismay.*

The phrase "bright and dismal" not only captures Chandler's permanent ambivalence about California but alludes as well, perhaps, to his having been fired, in 1932, from his job as vice president of the Dabney Oil Syndicate. The oil boom in Los Angeles actually began in the 1890s, with production of the city wells peaking before World War I. The Bolsa Chica well opened at Huntington Beach in 1920; a year later came the big strike at Signal Hill. With the capacity to pump out a quarter-million barrels a day, Signal Hill inaugurated the oil decade. Shipping through the Panama Canal doubled in 1923, and in the next year oil temporarily surpassed agriculture as the leading industry in the state. Chandler rode the Signal Hill strike into prosperity, and then, in the depths of the Depression, after prolonged bouts of drinking and absenteeism, he rode it out.

"Depression" is perhaps too small a word for the lived conditions of the next seven years, years that culminated in the publication of *The Big Sleep,* Chandler's first novel, in 1939. The unemployed Chandler and Cissy, his aging wife—he was forty-four in 1932 and she was sixty-one—

began to move from rented room to rented room. Silver Lake, Big Bear, Cathedral City, Pacific Palisades, Riverside: what makes Chandler's career so moving is that he actually drifted through the depths he wrote about. He started reading pulp fiction in the year he lost his job and began producing mystery stories based on its formulas. In a good year, 1938, he made only $1,275. "I never slept in the park," he was later to say, "but I came damn close to it."

In 1943 Billy Wilder asked Chandler to collaborate on the script of *Double Indemnity,* and in 1946, after fourteen years of life constantly on the move, the Chandlers bought their first home and settled in La Jolla. Four of Chandler's seven novels were published before or during the

Raymond Chandler with his cat Taki at his home in La Jolla in 1948. Born in Chicago in 1888 and raised in England, Chandler arrived in Los Angeles in 1912. After losing his job with the Dabney Oil Syndicate in 1932, he began to write fiction. In 1939 he published his first novel, The Big Sleep. *Courtesy Department of Special Collections, University of California at Los Angeles.*

war. As his fortunes rebounded along with the region's, his vision grew darker. His stubbornly elegiac sense of things culminated in the 1949 *The Little Sister:*

> A long time ago. There were trees along Wilshire Boulevard. Beverly Hills was a country town. Westwood was bare hills and lots offering at eleven hundred dollars and no takers. Hollywood was a bunch of frame houses on the interurban line. Los Angeles was just a big sunny place with ugly homes and no style, but goodhearted and peaceful. It had the climate they just yap about now. People used to sleep out on porches. Little groups who thought they were intellectual used to call it the Athens of America. It wasn't that, but it wasn't a neon-lighted slum either.

It was not only England but prewar Los Angeles that Chandler had lost; his obsession with the fragility of place converted his first five novels into a tragedy of development. He saw clearly the rampant sprawl that was to come, the connection between the brutality with which money is made and the insularity with which it is spent. His is a sociology as prescient as Mike Davis's in *City of Quartz,* a book that virtually predicted the 1992 riots in South-Central Los Angeles. In *The Big Sleep* the Sternwoods live in view of the spot that made them rich, and, in the sump, the murdered man lies buried. The site of the family's success is also the grave of its crimes. Chandler convicts himself of collusion as well: the novel focuses on the profits the Sternwoods have made in oil.

Like an old-fashioned psychoanalyst, Chandler saw his task as the dismantling of illusion. His eloquence about the literal false fronts in which Angelenos willingly encase themselves is equal to West's. As the city mushrooms into Moorish apartment houses and Tudor villas, the owners, Chandler argues, perfect the art of hiding from themselves. The resulting deep distrust provoked by social surfaces leaves Chandler unimpressed by anything as literal as an economic recovery.

As Marlowe leaves the Sternwood mansion for the last time, he notices that "the bright gardens had a haunted look." The mystery has been solved, but the sense of implication has only spread. If Marlowe openly manipulates simile and synecdoche, it is because he experiences the phenomenal world as haunted by repressed histories and fugitive truths. The Sternwoods refuse, on the other hand, to see that in Los Angeles "everything is like something else," a statement that prefigures Noah Cross's warning to Jake Gittes, "You may think you know what you're dealing with, but believe me, you don't." It is Marlowe, that stern rhetorician, who must search out the hidden connections between act and consequence and whose response to the place—paranoia—is as adaptive as it is disabling. In *The Little Sister* this state of mind is given full play. That novel represents the region's endless fabrication of plots and identities as a crisis of production. California now offers "the most of everything and the best of nothing." Chandler's protest is that of a traditional modernist invested in the conventions of integrity, recognition, and depth who finds himself on the streets of a city not so much mean as unreal, a postmodern mall of proliferating images where the imperative is simply to shop.

UNTIL THE IN-MIGRATIONS of the 1930s, Los Angeles remained a predominantly white city. In 1926, out of a population of more than 1.2 million, the census counted 45,000 Hispanics, 33,000 blacks, and 30,000 Asians. In 1941 there were four black production workers employed in California's aircraft industry. Between the spring of 1942 and 1945, 340,000 blacks migrated to California. Lockheed eventually hired some 7,000 black workers, but according to Gerald Nash, "most of the aircraft plants were resolutely opposed to hiring blacks." The resistance to hiring blacks and Mexican-Americans proved a boon to white women; by 1943, forty percent of the labor force in California aircraft was female. The ship-building industry proved much more welcoming, and it was there, first in the Kaiser Shipyard No. 1 in Richmond, and later as a shipwright's helper in San Pedro, that Chester Himes found a job.

Himes was born in Jefferson City, Missouri, in 1909. In 1934 *Esquire* published a piece he had written while serving a prison term on a charge of armed robbery. "At the detective bureau" after his arrest, Himes's feet had been bound, "his wrists were handcuffed behind his back, and he was hung upside down on an open door and pistol-whipped until he confessed." Paroled in 1936, Himes married Jen Jackson in the next year and researched a history of Cleveland for the Ohio Writers' Project before moving to Los Angeles in 1942.

Himes had come to Los Angeles with a list of contacts from Langston Hughes and the intention of doing some screenwriting. He soon saw that there was no place for him in Hollywood. In all his years in Los Angeles, he worked twenty-three jobs, only two of them involving skilled work. In *The Quality of Hurt,* Himes later wrote that "Los Angeles hurt me racially as much as any city I have ever known—much more than any city I remember from the South." This experience generated his first novel, *If He Hollers Let Him Go* (1945), the story of Bob Jones, Madge, and the Atlas Shipyard.

What Bob Jones does is drive and dream. The first chapter begins with the words "I dreamed" and ends with the sentence "All of a sudden I began rushing to get to work on time." Driving releases his anger, and dreaming refigures it. The two activities converge on the issue of control. *If He Hollers* unfolds as an ordeal of pace, a five-day headlong rush toward the imprisonment of its hero in the army.

In this deeply internal book, Himes confines the reader within the wariness of a mind. Through the character of Bob Jones, he delivers the self as a mood. "I felt better"; this, for Bob, is the token of life. Yet his endless mood shifts are merely a weather that blows through him. As

Chester Himes in the 1940s. The Missouri-born writer arrived in Los Angeles in 1942, part of the wartime migration that brought 340,000 African Americans to California. After a series of odd jobs, Himes found work as a shipwright's helper at the Los Angeles Shipyard at San Pedro. In 1945 he published a novel about the shipyard, If He Hollers Let Him Go. Yale Collections of Western Americana and American Literature, Beinecke Rare Book and Manuscript Library, Yale University.

the story unfolds, character and reader experience the daunting Emersonian recognition that "our moods do not believe in each other." Emerson made this claim in an essay called "Circles," and the circle of the moody, impulsive self is what Bob runs in. In the climax of the book, Bob notices a closed door. Madge, the blonde, is behind it. "I noticed a closed door, put my hand on the knob, and pushed inside to see what it might hold." What appears to be a choice here is actually a compulsion. While Himes's hero does pursue an inescapable "racial" destiny, in his status as a human being he is run ragged by his attempt to escape the dead end of a mood-ridden consciousness.

The external world through which Bob Jones moves denies continuity as ruthlessly as does his inner one. Virtually every pleasurable experience in the novel is interrupted. The alarm lifts Jones out of his dream-ridden sleep; the red light catches him at Manchester; a racial insult breaks up his winning crap game; a typed note ruins his dinner with Alice. Himes notates this pattern in sentences that are either joltingly brief or breathtakingly unpunctuated. Despite Bob's continual rushing about, however, the novel devotes itself largely to his argument with himself about race. "The pressure" that builds in him is released by a ball-peen hammer his co-workers take to his head, after Madge cries "rape": "I didn't feel the blow; just the explosion starting at a point underneath my skull and filling my head with a great flaming roar." Jones's opening dream about the Irishman comes true, except that it is his head that gets busted.

"To me it was racial," Bob says, about his experience of driving to work. Race frames the novel's every move. It is neither an obsession nor a projection of his mind, although it certainly does compel him. Jones begins by saying that "race was a handicap, sure, I'd reasoned. But hell, I didn't have to marry it." The social fact of race nevertheless announces itself on the same page when he sees "them send the Japanese away. . . . Little Riki Oyana singing 'God Bless America' and going to the Santa Anita racetrack with his parents next day." Bob wants to marry Alice, not race, yet in the scene where he proposes to her, he also admits that "in any incident that might come up a white person can use his colour on me and turn it into a catastrophe and I won't have any protection." Himes completes the racial frame on the novel's last page, where Jones, forcefully inducted into the army, finds himself in the company of "two Mexican youths": "They were both brown-skinned, about my colour, slender and slightly stooped, with Indian features and thick curly hair." They fall in beside him and start up the hill to the induction center, the cop bringing up the rear.

Bob Jones loses his job but not his socially conferred vocation, the one-man defense industry in which he has always been employed, full-time. Himes imagines a world conditioned by anxiety over personal safety, where the greatest threat to that safety comes from within. Jones attempts to displace his self-destructive anger into dreams. But the war has so raised the social stakes—the president of Atlas Shipyard tells him after his trial for rape that "you were the first Negro to be employed in a position of responsibility by our corporation and you were in a position to represent your race"—that he is unable to contain his emotions within a merely psychological frame. The endlessly advertised promise of Los Angeles has made its rejections too painful. Chandler hated the disfigurations of growth, the replacement of memory with *more;* Himes endured the deeper frustration of seeing that the more was not for him. From his side of the racial divide, the ordeal of mobilization proved simply redundant. This is why the Mexican youths who walk off with Bob Jones are moved to say, "Looks like this man has had a war."

THESE MEXICAN YOUTHS have had a war as well. One of the major stateside civil disturbances during World War II occurred in Los Angeles: the 1943

Zoot Suit Riots, during which U.S. military personnel invaded the barrio. As Pachuco says to Henry Reyna in Luis Valdez's *Zoot Suit* (1978), "Your war is on the homefront." While the outlandish zoot suits worn by the pachucos were later held up as provocative, the riots had their source as much in the friction between two groups of cultural outsiders: the young men who had been brought to Southern California for their basic training or to await shipment overseas, and the young male Mexican-American residents of the city who had not been and were not likely to be incorporated into any sanctioned cultural institution.

The riots began on June 3, 1943, but their roots lay in the Sleepy Lagoon case of 1942 and in the patterns of immigration that had begun during the Mexican Revolution. By 1910, the number of persons of Mexican descent in California had declined to 51,000. In that year the revolution began, and cotton was first planted in the Imperial Valley. The uncertainties of life at home, along with rising opportunities for agricultural labor to the north, combined to launch the first wave of Mexican immigration to California: 224,000 between 1910 and 1920; 436,000 between 1920 and 1930; 293,000 from 1950 to 1960. During the 1930s and 1940s the numbers decreased, since these years saw the "repatriation" of Mexican laborers: from 1931 to 1933 one trainload of workers per month was shipped from Los Angeles to Mexico. The 1940s also saw the beginning of the bracero program. Braceros (from the word *brazo,* "arm") were hired hands, temporaries, and so were not counted as immigrants. The program was instituted to deal with a shortage of agricultural labor during World War II. From 1942 to 1947, 250,000 braceros were imported into California. In the postwar period from 1948 to 1964, the year the program ended, 4.5 million braceros crossed the border to pick lettuce, cotton, orchard fruits, and table grapes.

Mexican farmworkers typically "followed the fruit." Cantaloupes needed to be harvested in the Imperial Valley in May. The laborers then moved north to the San Joaquin to thin peaches and apricots and later to pick them. As the season warmed, they entered the orchards of the Santa Clara and the vineyards of the Napa Valleys. August brought the grape harvest, centered in Fresno. The workers began to scatter in September, some to the walnut and citrus harvests in Southern California, others back to the Imperial Valley to pick cotton and lettuce.

Their toil was onerous. At congressional hearings held in 1926, an

"Mexicans who have been accepted for farm labor in the United States follow their contracts down a long row of tables," 1944. This and the following photographs were taken by the Department of Agriculture and are published with their original captions. Courtesy of the National Archives.

Idaho representative averred that "white men," required to pick sugar beets, "might stand it two hours a day." A citrus grower who shipped his fruit through Covina singled out a Francisco López as his "top picker"; during the boom period of 1928–29, López "was called to labor 225 days. He missed only two possible working days in those eleven months. For that period he earned $830.41." Indispensable to the California agricultural industry—which became during the early twentieth century the most profitable industry of its kind in the world—these workers lived in substandard housing, and their children had little or no schooling. Access to public services and facilities like restaurants, theaters, barbershops, and swimming pools was routinely denied them. In *Scene from the Movie Giant* (1993), Tino Villanueva captures the sensation of living in but not of a culture that makes movies about him. His entire book is constructed of poems out of his boyhood memory of being frozen in front of the screen by the scene, in *Giant* (1956), where Rock Hudson must defend the right

"Mexicans who have signed contracts for work in the United States await the final roll call."

"Mexicans leaving to work on farms and ranches in the United States wave good-bye to their families."

of his Mexican daughter-in-law to receive diner service against the refusal of the gigantic Sarge.

Attempts to unionize agricultural workers through strikes at Wheatland (1913), El Centro (1928), Corcoran (1933), and Orange County (1936) met with the staunch opposition of the *Los Angeles Times* and the Associated Farmers. Only in the 1960s, under the leadership of Cesar Chavez and the United Farm Workers, did agricultural labor in California organize itself into an enduring political force. To invoke the long history of labor struggle in California, the Boycott Day Proclamation issued on May 10, 1969, revived the central metaphor applied to another group of migrants who had come to California to pick fruit: "In the souls of the people the grapes of wrath are filling, and growing heavy," Steinbeck had written in chapter 25, "growing heavy for the vintage." Appropriating and inverting the metaphor of ripening fruit, the Boycott Day Proclamation argued that history was now ripe for harvest:

> Grapes must remain an unenjoyed luxury for all as long as the barest human needs and basic human rights are still luxuries for farm workers. The grapes grow sweet and heavy on the vines, but they will have to wait while we reach out first for our freedom. The time is right for our liberation.

When the Second World War began, the Mexican-American male in California found himself in an awkward position. In 1940 defense workers were granted draft deferments, but agricultural workers were not. Mexican males were drafted in considerable numbers; one-fifth of the casualties from Los Angeles were to have Mexican names. The first number called in the national Selective Service lottery was that of Pedro Aguilar of Los Angeles. Even when subjected to literacy tests that many were bound to fail, Mexican men were drafted anyway. A Los Angeles police lieutenant testified in 1942 that despite a labor shortage in "defense plants" Mexicans were barred from jobs there and even from joining most unions. While seventeen Mexican-Americans were earning the Congressional Medal of Honor, the Los Angeles Police Department maintained files according to the race of the perpetrator—a practice it did not abandon until 1950.

The pachuco developed out of these contradictions and represented a rejection of both official American and traditional Mexican culture. He was a kind of male Malinche figure, one who insisted on otherness rather than on accommodation. The zoot suit became his primary symbol. In *Zoot Suit Murders* (1978), Thomas Sanchez describes the look: "The Zoot suits they wore clashed in color and cut, broad-shouldered baggy coats of yellow and chartreuse draping below their knees, flared green and purple pants cuffed skin tight around ankles above oversized waxed shoes." In the wake of the Depression and wartime rationing, such clothing paraded the right of individual excess. In an age of compulsory wearing of uniforms, the zoot suit accomplished an antithetical stylization of the self.

And at a time when the LAPD was publicly arguing the "biological" basis for Mexican behavior, the zoot suit could become a metaphor for race itself, but race as an artificial category subject to the control of the user—race that could be put on or taken off.

The Sleepy Lagoon case of 1942 served as the first act of the zoot suit affair. Sleepy Lagoon was a swimming hole in Baldwin Park frequented by Mexican-American youths. Two incidents that occurred there in August of 1942 involved purported clashes between groups that the press called "boy gangs." In one clash, according to the *Los Angeles Times,* eleven "hoodlums" attacked "five youths" at the Sleepy Lagoon site, chasing one into the water and beating him with tire chains. On the same day in nearby Montebello, "three girl hoodlums joined nine youths in breaking up a birthday party" and started a "free for all" in which José Diaz "was beaten to death." More than three hundred teenage Mexican-Americans were arrested in the ensuing police dragnet. Twenty-three were indicted, with twelve eventually convicted of murder and five of assault. Eighteen months later an appellate court reversed the convictions and criticized the conduct of the trial judge and the prosecution. Even the

On August 2, 1942, a Mexican-American boy, José Diaz, was found dead at a reservoir in East Los Angeles. More than three hundred Mexican-Americans were rounded up in what came to be called the Sleepy Lagoon murder. Shown here are twelve of those indicted. They are, from left to right: Gus Zammora, José Ruiz, Henry Ynostroza, Victor Robert Thompson, Henry Leyvas, Ysmael Parra, Angle Padillo, John Y. Matuz, Joe Carpio, Victor Segobia, Eugene Carpio, and Robert Telles. The resulting guilty verdicts were later reversed by an appellate court. Courtesy of the Regional History Center, University of Southern California Library.

original reporting of the incident came under review, since it turned out that Diaz had not been "beaten to death" in Montebello but, after heavy drinking at Sleepy Lagoon, had fallen asleep in the road and was probably run over, accidentally, by a car.

A year later, when the Zoot Suit Riots occurred, they were merged with Sleepy Lagoon as a continuing example of the unmanageability of Mexican-American youth. In *North From Mexico* (1968), Carey Mc-Williams lays out the chronology of events. On Thursday, June 3, the Alpine Club met in a police substation in Los Angeles. The group was composed of "youngsters of Mexican descent" interested in averting gang warfare. On the way home from the meeting, the group was set upon by assailants "not of Mexican descent." On the same evening, eleven sailors were attacked by a gang of Mexican boys on North Main Street. After hearing of the second attack, the police, much later in the evening, failed to find anyone to arrest.

On June 4 two hundred sailors in rented taxicabs entered the barrio and beat four young men wearing zoot suits. The Shore Patrol later arrested seventeen sailors. On the following night the sailors were joined by soldiers and marines in a similar venture. As they moved through downtown Los Angeles, the servicemen attacked zoot suiters and sometimes stripped them of their clothes. By the next night, as McWilliams writes, "the police had worked out a simple formula." Thomas Pynchon gives it a fair summary in the second part of *Gravity's Rainbow* (1973), after Blodgett Waxwing hands Slothrop a zoot suit:

> The zoot suit is in a box tied with a purple ribbon. Keychain's there too. They both belonged to a kid who used to live in East Los Angeles, named Ricky Gutiérrez. During the Zoot Suit Riots in 1943, young Gutiérrez was set upon by a carload of Anglo vigilantes from Whittier, beaten up while the L.A. police watched and called out advice, then arrested for disturbing the peace.

Through the consistent application of this formula, the police, by the morning of June 7, had placed some forty-four Mexican boys, all severely beaten, under arrest.

The serious rioting came on the evenings of June 7 and 8. The *Times* for June 7 carried a headline that read "Zoot Suiters Learn Lesson in Fights with Servicemen." The bias of its coverage paled, however, in comparison with that of the *Daily News* and the Hearst press, both of which had long conducted a campaign to influence public opinion against the city's Mexican-American population. "Zooters Planning to Attack More Servicemen," the *Daily News* headlined. The Hearst *Herald & Express* claimed that "Zooters Threaten L.A. Police." On Monday evening, June 7, thousands of Angelenos, inflamed by such coverage, marched through the downtown area attacking zoot suiters and ripping off their hated garments. Half-page photographs in newspapers would later show the bodies of stripped boys. By midnight on the seventh, downtown Los Angeles had been declared out of bounds for military personnel. Rioting occurred for two more days in the suburbs; the city council adopted a resolution making the wearing of a zoot suit a misdemeanor.

The Zoot Suit Riots were one of Los Angeles's media-created events: a synergy clearly had developed between the escalating rhetoric in the press and the responses of the men in the military. A *Time* magazine article of June 21, 1943, entitled "Zoot-Suit War" referred to one taxicab brigade as a "*Panzer*-division" and made it plain that the local press had chosen to represent the event as a patriotic battle. It is easy to see that the fight was between two groups of young men who had chosen or been forced to choose widely divergent forms of engagement with the larger war. To the rioting servicemen, the pachucos appeared to be at leisure *not* to fight. They were in fact at leisure to do far more: to enjoy the complex world of Mexican-American life, one that had long tantalized the onlooking culture with a host of exotic and forbidden meanings. They appeared uniquely free to engage, in the words used as the title of a 1993 book edited by Norma Alarcón, *The Sexuality of Latinas*.

The press coverage of the 1942 and 1943 events situated the Mexican-American in a world of wayward women and ungoverned desire. Dress was a mere index of this image. Even the grand jury investigating the Sleepy Lagoon case was treated to a disquisition on Aztec "disregard for human life" and on the protocol of a Mexican in a fight, whose "desire is to kill, or at least let blood." Constrained by the Good Neighbor Policy with Mexico, the *Times* avoided use of the word "Mexican" when it began covering Sleepy Lagoon. Its initial article of August 3, 1942, entitled "One Killed and 10 Hurt in Boy 'Wars,' " made no mention of race at all. On the next day the word "Mexican" did slip into the coverage, as did the subhead "Girls To Be Held." "The boys and even the girl friends wear a distinctive dress," the article states. The emphasis on "girls" is consistent throughout. "Girl gangs also exist in certain districts of Los Angeles city and county," the *Times* reported in a separate article in the same issue.

"Three Teen-Age Girls Held in Boy-Gang Slaying Inquiry," reads the caption for an August 5 *Times* article. Accompanying it is a photograph of three Chicanas looking away from the camera and talking to each other. The article presents the girls as unable to focus on their legal situation. "A little bit puzzled, three teen-age girls . . . ," it begins. In the photograph the intense focus of the three girls on each other rather than on the viewing eye reinforces the claim that "they didn't seem to comprehend they were involved in an investigation of such a serious crime."

These *Times* articles seamlessly segued into the further coverage that began in June 1943. In an article published on June 2, a day *before* the riots began, the *Times* brought out its fourth in a series of articles on the rise of juvenile delinquency in Los Angeles. "Fresh in the memory of Los Angeles is last year's surge of gang violence that made 'zoot suit' a badge of delinquency," the story begins. The article is divided by subheadings that read: "Language Makes Difference," "Girls Unique Problem," "Sex Cases Increase." "Girls are becoming delinquent mostly in sex matters and as runaways," the article tells us. Such cases are hard to solve because of the "eagerness on the part of family and friends to shield a young girl's honor." In the same issue, the *Times* ran a piece entitled "Four Suspects Seized in Attack on Women." Those arrested were suspected of participating in a "zoot suit orgy in Elysian Park."

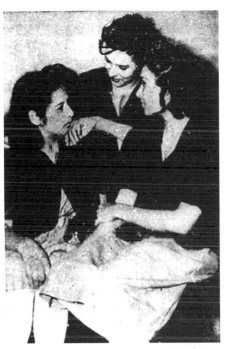

IN CUSTODY—Dora Barrios, 18, left; Frances Silva, 19, center, and Lorena Encinas, 19, are under arrest in connection with boy gang killing of Jose Diaz.   *Times photo*

Three Teen-Age Girls Held in Boy-Gang Slaying Inquiry

This photograph and caption, from the August 5, 1942, edition of the Los Angeles Times, *are typical of the newspaper coverage given to the Sleepy Lagoon case. Copyright 1942, Los Angeles Times.*

Meanwhile, the *Herald & Express* carried articles on the "weird sexual activity" engaged in by girl gang members, calling pachuquitas "little tornadoes of sexual stimuli, swishing and flouncing down the streets." "The Mexican *pachuquitas* were very appealing to American servicemen," Patricia Rae Adler wrote, "and jealously guarded by the Mexican-American boys. They scandalized the adults of the Anglo and Mexican communities alike, with their short, tight shirts, sheer blouses, and built-up hairdos." The June 7 article, in which the *Times* celebrates the lesson being taught the zoot suiters, begins with the phrase, "Those gamin dandies, the zoot suiters." The article concludes with the bizarre admission that "Lifeguards Can't Tell 'Zoot Suit' Bathers" at the beach. The ending not only undresses the zoot suiters by imagining them in bathing suits but, in the feminizing language of its opening phrase, continues to treat them as a threat to the stability of gender roles and relations and to the integrity of the physical body.

The riots themselves had set out to strip the zoot suiters of their clothing and thereby undress a culture. Those in military dress unclothed those in zoot suits. The police, a mostly spectatorial element here, are dressed in a uniform representing civil authority and even the possibility of civic life. But they are merely marginal figures that mostly clean up the mess. During the riots white women also play an important part; numerous accounts mention the onlooking Anglo female who, once the soldiers and sailors have stripped the pachuco, dons his clothes and displays her new look before the assaulting men. The character Danny describes such a moment in the short story "In the Flow of Time":

> Those kids were getting it all right, with busted heads and bleeding faces, those kids were getting it. Pretty soon, a black coat was thrown up and got passed around with people catching it and tossing it. Then the pants came and another coat, a tan one. . . . A blonde girl near us jumped and caught the tan coat that went sailing by. She grabbed it, then she squirmed until she got it on. She danced around in a circle yelling, "I'm a Pachuca, I'm a Pachuca." She was laughing and kissing the sailor next to her like she was nuts.

Chicanas appear to be missing from this scene, but they are of course invoked in the blonde's chanted words. They play, in fact, a crucial role in these transactions. Like the black woman in a slave narrative, the Chicana remains here an abiding if sometimes invisible medium of exchange. In

Incidents in the Life of a Slave Girl (1861), Harriet Jacobs narrates a stunning moment in which the white wife of her owner comes to her bed at night and whispers into her ear "as though it was her husband." Jacobs has been fighting off the husband's sexual advances, but the wife is not convinced. The encounter exposes a system in which brutalization results for everyone: for the master, by the insatiability of his will to power; for the master's wife, by her desperate identification with the aggressor; for the "dark" woman, by the violence of the continuous assault; and for the "dark" man, by his marginalization in or exclusion from the dynamic.

Chicanos were never slaves in the United States, although they have been called by some "The Slaves We Rent." Jacobs's story nevertheless has a parallel for Chicanas in that it reveals that power relations, in a culture like California's, depends on the sexualization of the nonwhite female. This pattern dates back to the earliest encounters between United States and Mexican culture. George Kendall, a veteran of the Texas–Santa Fé expedition of the 1830s, observed in the women of New Mexico "a roundedness, a fulness, which the divinity of tight lacing never allows her votaries." The "Anglo-Saxon traveler," he continued, "feels not a little astonished at the Eve-like and scanty garments of the females he meets." Compared to the women with whom Kendall was familiar, these women looked *loose*.

In this dynamic the light woman is set against the dark woman by the fact or fantasy of the latter's sexual availability or desirability. The dark woman's "man" is left powerless either to avenge the actual rape that results or to counter the prejudice that narrows, for his people, the range of permitted public and private behavior. The dominant male seeks to possess the Chicana or, as the next best thing, to humiliate her male counterpart in a dramatic physical way.

The opening of the 1992 movie *American Me* makes explicit the connection between the Zoot Suit Riots and the envy or possession of the Chicana. It begins with a rape—which invokes, of course, the primal myth of Mexican-American California, the Joaquín Murieta story. In John Ridge's version of that myth, one of the events that turned Murieta toward banditry was the rape of his wife. In the movie sailors gang-rape the beautiful Esperanza, while her husband, dressed in a zoot suit, is carried into the street, stripped, and beaten.

Both movie and myth argue that Mexican-American culture is infused with a hedonism that must be punished by violence against its women.

Since their earliest encounters the onlooking American has eroticized Mexican-American culture. "The women have but little education, and a good deal of beauty, and their morality, of course, is none of the best. . . . The women have but little virtue, but then the jealousy of their husbands is extreme, and their revenge deadly and almost certain." So wrote Richard Henry Dana in *Two Years Before the Mast*. This ongoing and massive cultural projection could be called the Californio Complex since it dates far back—at least to the 1830s, when a Californio wedding stirred up disturbing feelings in Dana. Here the women were less a show than the men, who danced "with grace and spirit." A Californio named Don Juan Bandini drew Dana's special attention:

> He was dressed in white pantaloons, neatly made, a short jacket of dark silk, gaily figured, white stockings and thin morocco slippers upon his very small feet. His slight and graceful figure was well calculated for dancing, and he moved about with the grace and daintiness of a young fawn. An occasional touch of the toe to the ground, seemed all that was necessary to give him a long interval of motion in the air. At the same time he was not fantastic or flourishing, but appeared to be rather repressing a strong tendency to motion.

The juxtaposition of repression and free bodily motion, the Spanish-speaking male dressed in an attention-getting way, the presence of women both "loose" and "bare"—all this suggests a long and complex history of associations that culminated in the Zoot Suit Riots. In the presence of Mexican-American culture, Dana and his heirs came up against a vision deeply threatening to the Yankee work ethic and found themselves disturbingly drawn to its unsettling celebration of the pleasure principle.

The Zoot Suit Riots can be read as an eruption of machismo, as a fight between two groups of men over turf, manhood, and women. They can also be read as an attempt to go beyond machismo—at least on the part of the pachucos, whose exaggerated costume, like Juan Bandini's, asserted the physical self-regard normally associated with women. Either way, the affair appears to have been one between men. Any "mockery of the patriarchy," in Renato Rosaldo's phrase, is probably unintended. Such mockery would be accomplished rather by women themselves, especially, as Rosaldo argues, in the short-story cycles authored by women in the 1980s. "The Mexicans . . . don't like their women strong," writes Sandra

Cisneros in the best known of these cycles, *The House on Mango Street*. Ever since the stigmatizing events of the 1940s, it has been the work of Chicana writers to claim that strength.

A significant body of writing by Chicana lesbians like Cherríe Moraga and Gloria Anzaldúa rejects the abiding machismo of their culture in favor of alternatives to heterosexual bonds. They do this, in part, to avoid the "rigid sex role expectations" that typically develop during "a difficult migration process." As Yvette Flores-Ortiz argues, such "cultural freezing" hearkens back to the fantasy of an ideal Latino family in which "stereotypic cultural patterns of machismo prevail."

A writer like Sylvia Lopez-Medina attempts to revise the culture of machismo toward her own ends. In her novel *Cantora* (1993), the narrator defies her family and *"eight-hundred years of carefully arranged marriages,"* marries for love, and then leaves her husband for another man. The woman of color has a complex fate: in dealing with the dominant culture, her prevailing issues, like those of the Chicano, are those of race, while in living within her culture of origin, her prevailing issues are those of gender. Emma Perez argues in a seminal essay that for Chicanas the questions are "who do we choose to love and to have sex with, and how do we make those choices." Two works of the 1990s, a memoir and a novel, use antithetical strategies to work toward an answer to the questions. Mary Helen Ponce's memoir of growing up in the San Fernando Valley in the 1930s and 1940s suspends the issue of sex altogether. Alma Luz Villanueva's *Naked Ladies* (1994) makes its more difficult way through a vertigo of sexual partners and experiences. Together the two books test what can be gained and lost by insisting on either innocence or experience.

Ponce's *Hoyt Street* (1993) narrates the story of growing up in Pacoima, from her earliest memories to the day of her first period, when she became a "señorita." With her innocence fully intact even at the end of her narrative, she is a figure of pure potential, undetermined by any traumatic encounter that might have shaped, for better or for worse, her pursuit of happiness. For the heroine in *Naked Ladies* (1994), by contrast, sex resolves into a routinely orgasmic encounter that quickly diffuses into an autoerotic sublime: "she reached the very edge of nothing, darkness, and flew higher, higher, higher into this pure gold light, screaming without restraint." In its unapologetic explicitness, Villanueva's language challenges the reticent proprieties of a culture of machismo. While Ponce and Villanueva may share little in the way of decorum, both allow their characters a large measure of control. Writing like theirs stakes out territory in which women, Chicana or not, are no longer required, in order to maintain their selfhood and their status and their self-respect, to become madonnas of denial.

FOR BOB JONES, questions of pleasure are a luxury; what he wants to do is work. This desire defines life in the city where he seeks work—a city, as Jan Morris argues, "essentially of the forties and the fifties, and especially perhaps of the World War II years, when the American conviction acquired the force of a crusade, and sent its jeeps, its technicians and its Betty Grables almost as sacred pledges across the world." Morris concludes that "somewhere near the heart of the L.A. ethos there lies, unexpectedly, a layer of solid, old-fashioned, plain hard work. This is a city of hard workers."

It was on the Plains of Id, as Reyner Banham calls vast, flat, industrial South Los Angeles, the area threaded by the Long Beach and Harbor freeways, that the country's postwar boom was centered. This is where my father and his five siblings survived the Depression by cultivating worms and raising dogs. By the mid-1960s my uncle had made enough money from his machine-tool business to build a plant in North Long Beach and to hire my father to decorate the new house he had purchased near the company town of Lakewood.

Joan Didion's 1993 *New Yorker* article "Trouble in Lakewood" converted the fortunes of this planned community into a parable of postwar Southern California. Lakewood lies north of Long Beach and southeast of Compton, its borders detectable only by a sign on the road. From its inception, however, Lakewood was set apart. In 1941 the federal government helped Donald Douglas finish his plant at the Long Beach airport. In order to supply contented workers for Douglas and other nearby defense industries, developers bought 3,400 nearby acres, called it Lakewood, and built the world's largest subdivision there. The plan included lots for 17,500 houses, the region's largest shopping mall, parks and playgrounds, and 133 miles of street. On the day in 1950 when the homes first went on the market, 30,000 buyers turned up.

"These Second World War and Korean War veterans and their wives who started out in Lakewood," Didion writes, "were, typically, about thirty years old. They were, typically, not from California but from the Midwest and the border South. They were, typically, blue-collar and lower-level white-collar. They had 1.7 children. They had steady jobs. Their experience had tended to reinforce the conviction that social and economic mobility worked exclusively upward." What attracted Didion to Lakewood, over forty years later, was the television coverage given to a band of aging adolescents known as the Spur Posse. In March 1993 nine former Lakewood High male students were arrested on various counts of rape by intimidation, unlawful sexual intercourse, forcible rape, and oral copulation. In the "posse" to which they informally belonged, points were assigned to boys for having sex with girls. As the story began its media career, the suspicion grew that members of the posse were responsible for a rash of other crimes: the theft of jewelry, credit cards, and guns; threats and intimidation involving automobiles and baseball bats; and in February 1993 the explosion of a pipe bomb.

In July 1993 *Rolling Stone* carried an article by Jennifer Allen that presented the story as a piece of dissonant, self-contained Americana. Didion's approach, by contrast, satisfies because the dialectical quality of her thought refuses amazement at the spectacle and insists instead on setting it within a context both political and economic. She has learned, perhaps from Chandler, that Southern California mysteries are over-determined.

Didion shuttles between the promise of California's past and the ugliness of its present, with the effect of condensing Los Angeles's war-based expansion into its decline. While this temporal foreshortening is a product of her narrative technique, it does argue that there was already some flaw in the expansion itself, that it was a boom that necessarily implied a bust. Yet the troubles in 1990s Lakewood do more than simply verify the cyclical nature of capitalism's business cycle. They are the product of a uniquely unstable approach to region-building, one in which even privileged white workers must depend on an untenable production regime.

In Didion's analysis little about the Spur Posse proves adventitious. It sprang up because Lakewood was dying. The premise on which the city had been founded was, from the beginning, adolescent and male-centered. The men were educated only through high school and were then sent to the defense plants. Women by and large stayed home to raise sons and daughters. The community channeled its energies into high school and team sports and their rituals; its central meeting site remained the playing field. "Males are encouraged to continue, after graduation and indeed into adulthood, to play ball (many kinds of ball, all kinds of ball) in the parks and on the school grounds where they grew up." Men in Lakewood did not so much grow up, then, as recycle their youth. They worked hard and made money and moved into the middle class, but any notion of self-making was founded on a certain illusion, since the money that financed the Lakewood way of life originated in Washington and could be cut off there.

"The sad, bad times began, most people will now allow, in 1989, when virtually every defense contractor in Southern California began laying off workers." In a typical Didion move, she withholds this sentence until the reader is three-quarters of the way into her article. She has by that time described the development of the city, told the story of the Spur Posse, explained the out-migration of the defense business. Her conclusion, when it comes, is therefore inescapable: The Spur Posse arose as the direct result of the sudden end of forty years of upward economic mobility nurtured in a claustrophobically structured civic space and subsidized by federal dollars. The young men of Lakewood are growing up into a future in which they cannot play ball. They respond by angrily turning upon and "scoring" against the women they can no longer impress and support.

If postwar California lacks a literature of celebratory abundance, it may be because at some level it grasps and dreads Didion's conclusion: that the state's prosperity is largely illusory, fragile, and time-limited. The ownership class that grew up in Lakewood—and, for that matter throughout much of California in the 1950s and 1960s—she deems, in a killing word, "artificial." "There are a lot of places like Lakewood in California. They were California's mill towns, breeder towns for the boom. When times were good and there was money to spread around, these were the towns that proved Marx wrong, that managed to increase the proletariat and simultaneously, by calling it middle class, to co-opt it."

But the situation to which Didion has applied her imagination of scarcity is filled with more possibility than she can perhaps allow. California will doubtless remain the nation's leading state for agricultural enterprise and high-tech industry, according to a 1994 front-page article in *The Washington Post*, and may already be bouncing back. In 1996 the *Post* found it possible to report that "the number of workers in entertainment and allied trades now surpasses aerospace," a number that had risen 50 percent since 1988 to 111,600 workers in Los Angeles County. For the children of the boom, however, such recoveries may come a little late. "In April," Didion writes, "the Bank of America estimated six to eight hundred thousand jobs lost since 1990, but made an even bleaker and more immediate projection: four to five hundred thousand more jobs lost, in the state's 'downsizing industries,' between 1993 and 1995. This is what people are talking about when they talk about the riot."

"The riot," here, or the urge to riot, is connected with the fact of unemployment, white unemployment. Didion's claim that such an urge exists seems a leap, since certainly it was the nonwhite citizens of Los Angeles who took to the streets in 1992, and they did so over a racial, not an economic issue. But Didion is interested in root causes, not in immediate provocations. For her, the anger expressed by black and brown rioters after the Simi Valley verdict exists on a continuum with that unleashed by a one-man white riot in a 1993 film set in Los Angeles. The Michael Douglas character in *Falling Down,* while cutting his swath across the city, explodes with racial rage, but the proximate cause of his distress can be located in the eulogy to his lost job on his license plate: D-FENS. The war of the races imaged by the movie is real enough, but that war also provides the spectacle that acts as a container for and diversion from the high costs, to everyone, of living in an economy based on the continual production of another and equally costly kind of war.

CHAPTER SEVEN

RELOCATION, THE JAPANESE, AND THE TWICE DIVORCED

I N 1964 YALE UNIVERSITY remodeled its central courtyard by hiring Skidmore, Owings, and Merrill to build the Beinecke Library, a state-of-the-art home for rare books and manuscripts. The building that resulted was a six-story box of Vermont marble squares hung in a granite grid; students called it the "egg carton" or the "toaster." The nearby Sunken Garden, built of the same materials, merged more gracefully with the neoclassical and gothic facades that bordered it. Unlike the library building, which challenged its neighbors, the garden seemed to be about the play of different styles nearby.

Rimmed by a waist-high balustrade, the garden sheers down some twenty feet. The rectangular pit contains three marble shapes rising from an incised marble ground: a pyramid, a cube resting on its point, and a doughnut-shaped disk. The standing forms are smooth and unadorned, mysterious, suggestive, conducive to meditation, and, during my years at Yale as an undergraduate in the late 1960s, I often walked over to the garden to stare at its unlocatable geography. The man who made the garden had sought, it turned out, an uncanny effect, writing in *A Sculptor's World* that "it is nowhere, yet somehow familiar." The quotation points toward a unique cultural burden, toward a sense of being caught in between, of not feeling, perhaps, at home at home.

182

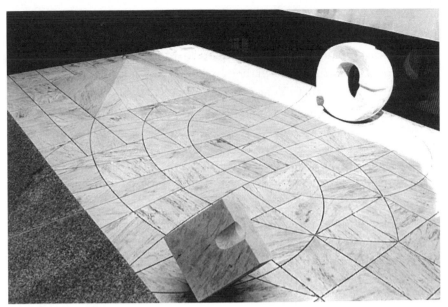

The Sunken Garden of Yale's Beinecke Rare Book and Manuscript Library, as seen from above. Built in 1964, the garden was designed by American-born sculptor Isamu Noguchi. Photograph by David Wyatt.

Isamu Noguchi was born in Los Angeles in 1904 to a Japanese father and an American mother. He lived in Japan from the age of two until his thirteenth year, when he returned to the United States for further schooling. Diverted from his studies by World War I, Noguchi began his apprenticeship as a sculptor with Gutzon Borglum, the designer of Mount Rushmore. Discouraged by Borglum, he took up medicine at Columbia. His mother supported his return to the world of art, and in 1927 he traveled to Paris on a Guggenheim to work with Brancusi. In the 1930s he began receiving commissions for seventy-two-foot murals in Mexico City and ten-ton stainless-steel sculptures in New York. He started designing sets for Martha Graham and would later work with George Balanchine and Merce Cunningham. In 1942 Noguchi voluntarily removed himself from his home in New York to spend six months with Japanese-Americans incarcerated at the concentration camp at Poston, Arizona.

Noguchi's is a story of crossings, suggestively fusing both with important movements in the world of modern art and with Japanese history in the United States, most dramatically during World War II. And it contains an intersection of East and West, as embodied in the marriage of

his father, Yone Noguchi, and Leonie Gilmour, a union that produced a
son of both Japan and California.

America / Japan / America: the pattern of Isamu's story is of birth,
departure, and return. His father lived out the complementary story:
Japan / America / Japan. Yone Noguchi arrived in San Francisco in 1893,
at the age of eighteen. He spent eleven years in the United States and in
Europe, returning to Japan in 1904. Despite his visits to the West,
Noguchi made his permanent home in Japan, marrying a second time,
raising his children, corresponding with Yeats and Pound, becoming a
respected teacher and man of letters. His story, like his son's, points up
that the Japanese in America, more than any other visiting or immigrating people, lived within a romance of return.

While going back to Japan remained for the immigrated Japanese a
livelier possibility than did a Chinese return to China, the vast majority
of *issei* who came to California came to stay. Yet a belief that Japanese
living in California could or wanted to go "home" and even that "all
resident Japanese were spies" was projected onto the Japanese with a
ferocity that led, finally, to their removal from the culture. Such percep-
tions arose from a number of ambiguous facts and notions. The Chinese
had long been an emigrating people, but not until the Meiji Restoration
of the 1860s was it legal for a Japanese citizen to emigrate. A number of
the Japanese who came to the United States brought with them the
means to return, or earned it once they arrived. While the Chinese lived
primarily in cities, the Japanese concentrated their efforts on farming
and so acquired California land. In the 1840s China began to fall apart
and entered a century of political instability and strife. The Japanese, on
the other hand, had a strong nation to which to return—a vigorous
emerging military and economic power on the Pacific Rim. Japanese
immigrants were denied, even longer than the Chinese, the right to
become citizens of the United States; for an *issei,* Japan necessarily
remained until 1952 the official "country." *California and the Oriental*
(1920), an official state publication with a preface by the governor,
contains headings like "Once a Japanese, Always a Japanese." The
report maintains that "every Japanese in the United States, whether
American-born or not, is a citizen of Japan and as such is subject to
military duty to Japan from the age of seventeen years until forty years
of age, unless expatriated."

Beliefs like these combined in the popular mind to create a fear of

Japan and to undermine belief in Japanese loyalty. "If Japan and the United States were to go to war tomorrow," the *Los Angeles Times* wrote, "or at any time beyond, almost every Jap in the land would hie himself away to Nippon to shoulder a gun against us." This sentence was written in 1908, not in 1941. Such prophecies became self-fulfilling; yet by taking action on anti-Japanese prejudices, the government set in motion a dynamic that would more deeply root the Japanese, and at a terrible cost, in American life. The relocation of the Japanese in 1942 made them exiles within the new culture of their choice, but it also broke the continuity with their Japanese origins. The government actions redefined return—or "re-entry," in Jeanne Wakatsuki Houston's word—not as a nostalgic going back to a mother country but as the assumption of full rights of citizenship in the adopted one.

In 1915 Isamu Noguchi's father published, in Philadelphia, *The Story of Yone Noguchi*. A frontispiece, despite the Japanese dress, gives us a Westernized profile of the author, complete with sideburns, aquiline nose, and square jaw. The memoir contains four chapters on the sojourn in America, two about Noguchi's years in London, and five on later life in Japan. Noguchi's writings and his lectures in London prompted Yeats to experiment with the Noh play and may even have spurred the composition of Ezra Pound's "In a Station of the Metro." His autobiography unfolds as one of the most original and vivid sojourn narratives written by a potential immigrant to California, a work eloquent in its portrayal of the strange mixture of hostility and hospitality displayed toward such visitors.

Noguchi structures his travels as a romance of literacy. He begins with a chapter titled "How I Learned English," which opens:

> My first sensation, when I got a Wilson's spelling-book in my tenth year, was something I cannot easily forget; I felt the same sensation when, eight years later, I first looked upon the threatening vastness of the ocean upon my embarking on an American liner, where I felt an uneasiness of mind akin to pain for the conquest of which I doubted my little power.

This brilliant beginning conflates culture and nature into the oceanic, a vastness awaiting the conquest of the writer's "little power." In what it

Yone Noguchi, young and old. The Japanese poet arrived in San Francisco in 1893 and returned to Japan in 1904. He described his sojourn with Joaquin Miller at the Hights in a memoir called The Story of Yone Noguchi. *His son Isamu was born in Los Angeles in 1904. Courtesy of Professor Yoshinobu Hakutani.*

says, the sentence poses the problem of the book; in what it does, it demonstrates the solution.

For the young Noguchi the unknown here creates an anxiety, an "uneasiness" that can be dispelled by travel and by articulation, by venturing to move and learning to spell. The predicament is primal; a man's story starts with it, it is his "first sensation." Life begins in the anxieties and delights of the acquisition of language. That first sensation is also evoked by the decision to embark, to go to America. All life begins in sensation, of course, but Noguchi renovates the term by aligning it not with the reflexes of the body but with the ambitions of the mind. His story begins, then, not with generation but with self-generation (one that resembles Gatsby's in its elision of the biological in favor of the constructed source). Sensations of babyhood and childhood are omitted in order to dramatize the encounter with English and with America that was to give birth to a new man. Noguchi's opening sentence concludes as much as it initiates; in its carefully structured introduction of the narrator to the reader, it announces the successful "conquest" of English and, by extension, of the country on the other side of the Pacific.

"A sudden turning" threw Noguchi into "the strange streets of San Francisco in the month of December of 1893"; the city presented a hell of noise and smoke. He gives no reasons for making the journey, except to say that he was "thrown, of course of my own free will." On arriving he first despairs over his "linguistic incompetency." He could not have been much helped by the instructor he had had back in Japan whose English had been limited to the names of wines and drinks he had served as a bartender in San Francisco. Noguchi clammed up and was often mistaken for a deaf mute: "Indeed if I had stayed as such, in the years of my Western life, with my thought in the golden silence whose other name is meditation, I might have stayed so much wiser." Instead of staying silent, however, Noguchi memorized Hamlet's soliloquy while working as a carrier boy. After stealing a book called *Dora Thorne,* he found that it did not engage his soul's curiosity and returned it to the bookstore. The bookseller befriended him, giving him a volume of Keats. Noguchi walked to Palo Alto and read Victor Hugo while picking strawberries. There, in the Menlo Park Hotel, he first heard the name Joaquin Miller.

Even more than Bret Harte, Cincinnatus Hiner Miller was California's first celebrity poet. Unlike Harte, he parlayed his way into fame on virtually no talent. Ambrose Bierce once remarked that Miller "requires no fewer than one hundred and fifteen lines to relate the landing of a ship in fair weather with nothing to prevent it." Today his strained Whitmanic bombast on the beauty of the Sierra or the wars against the Modocs is unreadable.

Miller emigrated from the Middle West to Oregon in 1852 and drifted south to California a few years later. He worked as a miner, teacher, and pony express rider before beginning to write his long, vaporous lines in the 1860s. During his apprenticeship he took an Indian wife and fought against the Modocs. His early writing defended Joaquín Murieta, and so he was given the nickname. While he did join the *Overland Monthly*'s stable of writers, it was only after decamping for England that he made his name. His flowing yellow locks, high-heeled boots jingling with spurs, and upturned sombrero gratified an English fantasy about some lost Wild West. The Pre-Raphaelites labeled him "the Byron of Oregon." In 1886 he returned to California and to the seclusion of the Hights, a tiny but well-sited rural retreat in the hills above Oakland. There he looked after his mother, grew roses, and insisted on the beauty of silence.

Noguchi walked to the Hights in 1894. After stints as a dishwasher and newspaperman, he was tired and looking for a place to sleep. Wearing a silken skullcap, Miller, who liked to loaf and invite his soul, stretched out his hand from bed and welcomed Noguchi to his "ridiculously small cottage." Miller was the first person in California to call the poet "Mr. Noguchi." Noguchi was to spend four years at the Hights, taking meals, working in the garden, barely speaking. He made no money there and was often required to walk to Oakland or San Francisco to borrow from friends. There he published his first book of poems, *Seen and Unseen; or, Monologues of a Homeless Snail* (1897). For all his celebration of Miller as "the most natural man," Noguchi also admits that the years spent with him were the hardest of his American life.

Books were not part of life at the Hights; Miller had given or hidden them all away. He "fully lived" poetry, Noguchi maintains, even though "he may not have been a great poet of words." Noguchi's fictionalized account of these years, *American Diary of a Japanese Girl*, treats Miller as a slightly daffy saint of hospitality. He was known by all as a generous and loyal friend; when Oscar Wilde came to America, for instance, the two men bonded over the discovery that they were both three-bottle-a-day drinkers. Later, when Wilde ended up in Reading Gaol, Miller organized a fund-raising campaign for him. In Noguchi's novel, Poet Heine and the American Girl eat frogs by candlelight. She then buries the frog bones, places a stone over them, and pencils onto the stone, "Tomb of the Unknown Singers." The Poet goes squirrel hunting with a pick and shovel, having no shot for his gun. His menu lists items like the Meat of Wisdom and the Potatoes of Simplicity. But the Poet interferes with the preparation of the meat and drops a can of red pepper into the broth. During a similar incident, as recorded in the autobiography, Miller remarks that all poets love "high seasoning."

After his years at the Hights, Noguchi drifted eastward, through Chicago, New York, and London. He sailed for Japan in August 1904, during the Russo-Japanese War. His patriotism jumped when he saw the

Rising Sun flag; "I felt in my heart to shout *Banzai.*" Later he looked forward with crane-neck-long longing to the arrival in Japan of his two-year-old son, the son born to his wife, Leonie, in the months after he had left America. The baby proved perfectly at home with Japanese food. He mastered the words *"sayonara"* and *"banzai."* Although Noguchi did not record it, he and Leonie never again lived together, since he had in the meantime taken a Japanese wife. Father and son lived apart and became estranged. In 1966, in response to a question about the women in his father's life, Isamu speculated, "Maybe he didn't marry either one of them." Yone Noguchi rarely saw his oldest son, and in his autobiography he does not detail Isamu's leaving for the United States, since the event lies beyond the horizon of his book. Yone's is a story of successful departure and return and of the blending of cultures and languages.

His son would mirror this motion, taking his sojourn not in America but in Japan. He would also complete the father's quest for "a language of silence." In Yone's memoir Miller is the first to impress this imperative on him, but in a late chapter, entitled "A Japanese Temple of Silence," Yone reminds us that silence, too, is "the real heart of Buddhism." As "the full urge of active actionlessness," silence represented for him a state of calm beyond the lifelong attempt to make oneself heard, often in an alien tongue. It is a state achieved and provoked by his son's quietly expressive sculpture, an art of fusion that gathers and holds in stillness the father's and son's travels and lives in both East and West.

THE NOGUCHI STORY yields a fairy tale of cultural hospitality and exchange. In the second generation this movement back and forth produced a fair amount of strain. Dore Ashton records that Isamu was shadowed "by the duality of his origins" and that he referred to himself in later life as a "waif," a "loner," and a "stranger." Yet in his travels the younger Noguchi was allowed to cross between cultures with a freedom unavailable to the typical Japanese who came to California. "More than any other immigrant group," Robert Heizer and Alan Almquist write, "the Japanese were regarded as temporary visitors." The federal government passed more legislation regarding the Japanese than any other immigrating people. Up until the turn of the century, Hawaii had been for the Japanese what California was for the Chinese—the point of entry and ordeal. The first Japanese arrived in California in 1869 and attempted an agricultural settlement near Sacramento. In 1886 Hiroshi Yoshiike began growing chrysanthemums in Oakland; in 1892 Sotaro Endo planted the first carnations and violets on Main Street in Los Angeles. By World War I, the Japanese would dominate the growing of flowers as well as many varieties of fruits and vegetables in California.

In 1900 a little more than 10,000 Japanese lived in California. By 1910, the number had climbed to 41,000; by 1920, to 74,000. These were also the years in which anti-Japanese agitation in California reached its peak.

The trouble began with the San Francisco School Board. In 1906 it ruled that the city's ninety-five Japanese students could no longer attend public school and would be sent to the segregated school for the Chinese. The Japanese government protested; President Roosevelt was drawn into the fray. In the resulting "Gentleman's Agreement" of 1907 the school board backed off in exchange for the Japanese government's agreement to halt further emigration of laborers by refusing to issue them passports.

The Gentleman's Agreement produced a flood of "picture brides," more than 20,000 between 1907 and 1920. The Japanese had always been, in the United States, a more marrying culture than the Chinese. In 1920, while the Chinese-American community was still 87 percent male, women made up a little over a third of the Japanese population. Since the Gentleman's Agreement was targeted at "laborers," Japanese women were still free to emigrate to join a husband in the years after 1907. The convention of the picture bride was invented to deal with this reality: A Japanese man in the United States exchanges a photograph with a woman living in Japan. "This 'interview' through photographs proving satisfactory to both parties, the nuptial knot is tied at a ceremonial dinner in which the groom, living in America, is naturally absent."

The arrangement did not favor the bride. A woman who entered such a union embarked, like Yone Noguchi, on a voyage of threatening vastness. She would arrive in California knowing little more about her husband than his looks, and *issei* men, typically ten to fifteen years older than the women they married, often sent doctored or obsolete photographs. The first meeting between these strangers could easily produce a shock that reverberated throughout the marriage.

The exportation of picture brides was prohibited in 1919 by the "Ladies Agreement." In the meantime California had passed the Alien Land Law (1913), which barred Asians from owning agricultural land and which

Japanese picture brides arriving in San Francisco. Following the "Gentleman's Agreement" of 1907, which restricted the flow of "laborers" between Japan and the United States, Japanese women began emigrating as "picture brides." The women in this photograph are about to meet their husbands for the first time; the couples had been married at a ceremony in Japan when the groom was absent and his photograph present. Courtesy of the Japanese American History Archives.

was expressly aimed at the Japanese. In the years leading up to the Immigration Act of 1924, which effectively halted Asian immigration to the United States, California experienced a panic about the effectiveness of Japanese agricultural labor. On the one hand, Governor Stephens vowed that "the people of California are determined to repress a developing Japanese community within our midst." The volume to which his letter served as a preface admitted, on the other hand, that "sudden removal" of the Japanese would be "Not Wise": "Any sudden removal of the Japanese from their present agricultural pursuits in California would affect our food supply very seriously." The food products they produced were "indispensable." According to the governor, between 80 and 90 percent of California vegetable and berry products were grown on Japanese farms.

The Japanese had created the state's rice industry "out of nothing"; in the 1970s rice accounted for 30 percent of all tonnage shipped from

Sacramento. A Japanese who controlled some 28,000 acres in the Sacramento delta, George Shima, became known as the "potato king" of California. Yet most Japanese-American farmers did not have such large holdings. In 1920 they owned only 458,000 acres out of the 29,365,000 under cultivation in the state. Their holdings fell by nearly half between 1920 and 1937; in that year the Japanese made up 1.7 percent of California's population and owned only 0.9 percent of the state's land.

If there is a crucial date for the Japanese in California, it is not 1907 or 1924 or even 1941 but February 19, 1942. On that day President Roosevelt signed an order authorizing the War Department "to prescribe military areas ... from which any or all persons may be excluded." Executive Order 9066 did not specifically name the Japanese, but it was aimed at them, and its rapid enforcement led to the removal of 120,000 *issei* and *nisei*—first- and second-generation immigrants—to ten concentration camps.

In 1943 the government required all interned Japanese to answer a set of "loyalty questions," which came to be known as Questions 27 and 28. The first asked, "Are you willing to serve in the armed forces of the United States on combat duty, where ever ordered?" The second asked whether the respondent would swear "unqualified allegiance" to the United States, renounce allegiance to the Japanese emperor, and defend the United States from "any and all attack." The questions were asked of all male *nisei* by the war department; answering them was voluntary. The war relocation department drew up a similar form that it required all adults in the camps to answer. *Issei* who answered yes to Question 28 would find themselves stateless, since the United States was asking them for allegiance but not offering them citizenship. Question 27 asked *nisei* to agree to serve in the army or nursing corps of a country that, although it conferred citizenship upon them by virtue of their birth within its borders, had deprived them of basic civil rights. Those who found it impossible to answer yes to the two questions came to be known as "no-no boys," although it is doubtful that any Japanese-American applied the term to himself. "Disloyal" Japanese were thereafter sent to the Tule Lake Segregation Center, near Lava Beds National Monument. The center had been created after disturbances caused by the questionnaires.

At Tule Lake 5,589 *nisei*—under pressure from underground pro-Japanese groups and in some cases from their parents, who believed they would be left in the safety of the camps if their children renounced—gave up their citizenship. Most of those who did so soon attempted to withdraw their renunciations. These cases remained in the courts for twenty-two years, but in the end 4,978 appeals for the restoration of citizenship were granted.

Questions 27 and 28 created the very crisis they were meant to avert. Possibly a few die-hard Japanese-Americans living in the West hoped for a Japanese victory in the war, but after the Japanese defeat at the battle of Midway in June 1942, any threat to the West Coast had vanished. Any Japanese-Americans who were, as it was imagined, signaling submarines or conducting short-wave radio broadcasts would have been working in vain. In *Nisei Daughter* Monica Sone remembers "Edgar Hoover's special report to the War Department stating that there had not been a single case of sabotage committed by Japanese living in Hawaii or on the Mainland during the Pearl Harbor attack or after." Despite this report, Governor Olson, in a broadcast on February 4, 1942, accused Japanese residents of California of engaging in fifth-column activities. California's attorney general, testifying before a committee headed by Congressman John Tolan, felt compelled to agree that "the very *absence* of subversive activity," as Donald Hata, Jr., and Nadine Hata write, "was proof of Japanese American cunning." Such suspicions were widespread: "I believe," Earl Warren said, "that we are being lulled into a false sense of security and the only reason we haven't had a disaster in California is because it has been timed for a different date."

Toshio Mori's *Yokohama, California* was the first book by a Japanese-American to deal with the camp experience. But for a lag in publication caused by the war, his volume would have missed the story of the camps. Mori, who was born in Oakland in 1910 and lived in San Leandro, had written stories in the 1930s about his life there. They were originally scheduled for publication as a book in 1941. The war delayed these plans; in 1942 he was shipped to the camp at Topaz, Utah, where he became camp historian. When *Yokohama, California* first saw print in 1949, Mori had added two stories, both of them written in the camps.

The temporal gap between the proposed and the actual publication of Mori's book mirrors the breach that the war had created in the Japanese-American experience. The challenge Mori faced, in the final version of *Yokohama, California,* was to reconcile two orders of time and to defend the possibility of a life in a "present." In *Farewell to Manzanar* Jeanne

Wakatsuki Houston gives an account of the predicament. In 1944, when she and her family returned to Los Angeles, she expected to see hatred in the faces of her non-Japanese neighbors:

> In our isolated world we had overprepared for shows of abuse. If anything, what greeted us now was indifference. Indeed, if the movements of this city were an indication, the very existence of Manzanar and all it had stood for might be in doubt. The land we drove away from three and a half years earlier had not altered a bit. Here we were, like fleeing refugees, trekking in from some ruined zone of war. And yet, on our six-hour drive south, we seemed to have passed through a time machine, as if, in March of 1942 one had lifted his foot to take a step, had set it down in October of 1945, and was expected just to keep on walking, with all the intervening time erased.

Manzanar and the nine other camps figure as *the* crucial event in the Japanese-American experience. The removal constituted an interval with a before and an after, but the interval itself can prove fugitive in the mind. "My memories of Manzanar, for many years," Houston writes, "lived far below the surface." She calls her book a farewell because she is physically going back to Manzanar, in 1972, to recover the memory of that time and therefore release it: "Now, having seen it, I no longer wanted to lose it or to have those years erased. Having found it, I could say what you can say only when you've truly come to know a place: Farewell."

Manzanar is the best-known of the camps the government hastily threw up, in 1942, in swamps and in the deserts of the West. The order for the evacuation of the Japanese was posted on April 30, 1942. Prominent male *issei* had been shipped out as early as December 7 of the previous year. Held in prisoner-of-war camps, some of the men were later reunited with their relocated families. Before being sent to the camps, Japanese families were held for days or even months in Assembly Centers like the Tanforan and Santa Anita racetracks.

The two most famous images of Manzanar focus on place rather than on people. Manzanar was located in what had become, after the building of the Los Angeles aqueduct, the high desert of the Owens Valley. To the west stood Mount Whitney and the 14,000-foot wall of the Sierra. Dorothea Lange's photograph shows a line of barracks and telephone poles receding toward the mountains. A lone distant figure walks down the road that bleeds across the lower margin of the photograph. Ansel Adams visited Manzanar in 1943 and 1944 and produced out of the experience a book of photographs and commentary called *Born Free and Equal*. "I have been accused of sentimental conjecture," he wrote in *An Autobiography*, "when I suggest that the beauty of the natural scene stimulated the people in the camps." The "grand view" of the Sierra from Manzanar excited Adams, and his photograph, "Mount Williamson, Sierra Nevada, from Manzanar," captures this mood. The foreground consists of a field of boulders, backlit by the sun. The setting sun streams over the peaks of the Sierra that fill the background. The photograph has its beauty, but it was perhaps also meant to look "Japanese" in its indirection and its austerity. To live with this view is not to live in the land of the rising sun. Adams gives the viewer a garden of stone. The boulders lie together, but each is also resolutely alone.

Dorothea Lange's photograph of the Japanese relocation camp at Manzanar, taken in 1942. Some 93,000 Japanese in California were removed to ten concentration camps in the West after the issuance of Executive Order 9066 on February 19, 1942. Manzanar was located in what had become by the 1940s the high desert of the Owens Valley. To the immediate west of the camp stood the highest peaks of the Sierra Nevada. Courtesy of the Dorothea Lange Collection, The Oakland Museum of California, The City of Oakland. Gift of Paul S. Taylor.

"Mount Williamson, Sierra Nevada, from Manzanar, California, 1945." Ansel Adams took *this photograph while working on his book about Manzanar.* Copyright © 1995 by the *Trustees of the Ansel Adams Publishing Rights Trust. All Rights Reserved.*

THE JAPANESE WHO WROTE about Manzanar and the other camps express considerable resistance to converting the experience into a pleasing or a portable image. Mori's book registers this tension. Most of the stories in his book were written before the war and take place in a world of vital presences. But the meaning of these "prewar" stories was changed utterly by the subsequent events, so much so that their tone of celebration takes on a powerful if not wholly intended irony. While they savor many pleasures in the moment, their recurring drift into "sadness" and a sense of being "walled in" comes to feel almost proleptic, an anticipatory melancholy over a looming fate.

If Mori's book had been published in 1941, it would open with the story "The Woman Who Makes Swell Doughnuts." In its sense of uncanny hospitality, magically available food, and unhesitating female nurturance, the story resembles nothing so much as Steinbeck's 1934 "Breakfast." "This thing fills me with pleasure," Steinbeck's story begins. In it, a man lives out a fantasy of coming upon warmth and a woman and food in the middle of the road. Like the male protagonist in Mori's story, he gets to eat his breakfast and leave it too. Little talking occurs; these men can "taste the silence" during their sojourn in these "depots," where they live in a world that gives without taking. And both characters know, as Mori's speaker says, that "outside of her little world there is dissonance, hugeness of another kind, and the travel to do."

It is this "outside" that haunts the characters in Mori's prewar stories and that prefigures the loss to come. "Outside" proves less an alien space than an uncontrollable future. This is why the book ends with another story about a woman cooking called "Tomorrow and Today," a story set in the years before the war. We are free to read it under the shadow of tomorrow and an awareness of history, or immersed in today's immediate pleasures. Yet in the closing words of the book a sense of foreclosure triumphs: "it is her day that is present and the day that is tomorrow which is her day and which will not be."

Mori also signals that time is his misfortune in the lovely way he says farewell to the woman who makes swell doughnuts. "She is still alive, not dead in our hours, still at the old address on Seventh Street, and stopping the narrative here about her, about her most unique doughnuts, and about her personality, is the best piece of thinking I have ever done. By having her alive, by the prospect of seeing her many more times, I have many things to think and look for in the future." But "most stories would end with her death," he concedes.

Mori's book unfolds as a war of tenses, a struggle between being-present and nostalgia. The war *produces* nostalgia and suffuses even the most powerfully remembered pleasure with a sense of unreality. The opening story, which is one of the two that were added to the collection after the war, begins with a voice that says, "Long ago, children, I lived in a country called Japan." This story was first published in 1943 in the camp magazine *Trek,* both in English and in Japanese translation. Whatever it meant in 1943 has been superseded by its function as an introduction to the published collection. The unstoppable events of history—Pearl Harbor, the battles in the South Pacific, the relocation, Hiroshima, the Japanese surrender, the release from the camps—give the phrase "long ago"

Toshio Mori in his study, mid-1940s. Born and raised in the gardening culture of the East Bay, Mori was removed to the camp at Topaz, Utah, in 1942. There he finished writing Yokohama, California, *a collection of stories centering on Japanese life in San Leandro before and after the war. Courtesy of Caxton Printers.*

the power to conjure an endless recession of possibility. "Japan," in such a sentence, becomes as distant as the moon.

"Tomorrow Is Coming, Children" attempts to counter this felt loss with brave cheer. The grandmother-narrator is recalling her departure from Japan for California, where her husband awaits; she presents the journey as a thing she is determined and willing to do. Mori has her tell her story in such a way that her departure becomes a figure for the difficult response to the past the postwar Japanese will be called upon to make. "Turn back?" she says, remembering her doubts as the steamer crossed the Pacific. "A steamer never turns back for an individual. Not for death or birth or storm. No more does life." As she begins her story, she sounds nostalgic, but at every opportunity where she might turn back or even express regret at leaving her country behind, she renounces or moves quickly through that emotion.

Her story, it turns out, is being told from the middle of the conflict. On the last page of his story, Mori deftly establishes her specific location: "If there were no war we would not be in a relocation center." She will not indulge in bitterness but seizes the war as an "opportunity" to choose again, to reenact the commitment to America she and virtually all of the *issei* had long since made. In order to bring her fellow immigrants to this recognition, she shifts into the third person: "War has given your grandmother an opportunity to find where her heart lay. To her surprise her choice had been made long ago, and no war will sway her a bit." Not "*my* surprise" but "*her* surprise"; with this simple substitution, Mori renders the choice generic, representative.

"Come back," her sister and brother in Japan have written the grand-mother. "But I did not return," she says. It is difficult to imagine a writer giving a character a more painful and courageous sentence. Even in the wake of the camps, and in the sure expectation of opprobrium from those who would have her renounce the country that imprisoned her, the grandmother chooses that country. Hers is a story about rechoosing, about the second will more wise that confirms the initial commitment, even in the face of abuse and betrayal. Mori's strategy of delay—with-holding from the reader the knowledge that the grandmother speaks from the camps—gives us the nostalgia first. It sounds like nostalgia for Japan. But the longing here expressed, the longing so decorously controlled, is not for the lost country of origin but for the lost country of adoption, an America she hopes to reenter and that she will not abandon even if it has abandoned her.

MORI'S ENACTMENT of an abiding Japanese loyalty leaves little room for the emotion of anger. A number of the memoirs written by women about the camps are similarly muffled. "Today I would not allow my civil rights to be denied without strong protest," Yoshiko Uchida writes at the end of *Desert Exile*. But her story has been one of stoic endurance, and so she also ends by quoting the *sansei* or third-generation children who ask her and other *nisei*, "Why did you let it happen?" *Farewell to Manzanar* takes as its subject the successful management of pain: it proposes that for many, the emotions surrounding the camps have been blocked. The anger that would have led to resistance surfaces most powerfully in accounts that include the experience of the camps in a sorrowful indictment of the Japanese-American experience in California.

In *Seventeen Syllables and Other Stories* (1988) and in *Songs My Mother Taught Me* (1994), two women give a shape and a story to *nisei* rage. Hisaye Yamamoto, the author of the first book, was born in Redondo Beach in 1921; Wakako Yamauchi, the author of the second, in the Imperial Valley in 1924. The two women spent the war together at the Poston, Arizona, relocation camp. Yamamoto had already published her work in the Japanese-American vernacular press. "It was *before camp* that

This photograph was taken at the relocation camp at Poston, Arizona, in April 1944. The young woman at the far left is Hisaye Yamamoto; third from the left is Wakako Yamauchi. The short story cycles they wrote after returning to California deal with the fate of women in an emigrating culture. Courtesy of Wakako Yamauchi.

I knew her stuff," Yamauchi wrote of Yamamoto. "She taught me not to be ashamed of being Japanese in my writing." In 1949 Yamamoto placed her breakthrough story, "Seventeen Syllables," with *The Partisan Review.* Yamauchi began publishing her stories in *Los Angeles Rafu Shimpo,* the bilingual English-Japanese daily, in the 1960s.

Writing from an *issei* perspective, Yamamoto and Yamauchi work through the experience of the camps by focusing on the terrible logic and consequences of the culture of picture brides. The failure of marriage to satisfy women—their experience of it as a prison of endless labor—subsumes even the experience of the camps, in these stories, as a more persistent form of exile and alienation.

The refrain enunciated in Yamamoto's "Seventeen Syllables" is directed by a mother to a daughter: "Promise me you will never marry!" The story traces the incompatibility between husband and wife, culminating when he destroys a painting she has won in a haiku-writing contest. His act prompts the mother to tell the daughter her story. "Do you know why I married your Father?" she asks Rosie. Rosie answers no, but she knows, as all these daughters know, the answer. "Don't tell me now, she wanted to say, tell me tomorrow, tell me next week, don't tell me today. But she knew she would be told now, that the telling would combine with the other violence of the hot afternoon to level her life, her world to the very ground." The story gets told. *I had no choice;* this is what it comes down to.

The mother's telling is an act of psychological violence. In most of the stories by Yamamoto and Yamauchi, daughters are allowed to bring this knowledge to consciousness in their own time, in a way that does not level their lives

Wakako Yamauchi in her senior year of high school, Oceanside, California, 1941. Courtesy of Wakako Yamauchi.

to the very ground. In Yamamoto's "Yoneko's Earthquake" (1951) and in Yamauchi's "Songs My Mother Taught Me" (1976), the two writers who met in the camps tell essentially the same story, one in which a mother, watched by a daughter, escapes and confirms the limits of her life.

The two stories can be reduced to the following structure: A daughter lives with Japanese parents and at least one brother. A younger man works with the family, then leaves. The mother becomes pregnant. An abortion is performed, or a son is born. A son dies. The daughter loses her religious faith.

These stories choose to measure the price of things rather than to lay blame. They argue that the deepest understanding of the culture is that of the onlooking daughter and that the contradictions of that culture must be paid for with the life of a son. Desire finds its satisfaction outside of marriage, and the solace of belief breaks up against the pain of experience.

These stories also quietly rage against an order in which, as Janice Mirikitani writes, "our possibilities must be compressed / to the size of pearls." They argue that an emigrating population routinely forces men and women, given the ratios and the distances involved, into arranged and often loveless unions. The couples that result are marginalized as agricultural workers in an economy that craves their produce but will pay little for it. The inflexibility of gender roles, especially when compounded by differences in age and distinctions of class, trap the *issei* and even the *nisei* in a cycle of misunderstanding and abuse.

After such knowledge, what forgiveness? The answer may lie in the management of voice in the two stories. While the two writers tell the same story, they do so with differing effects. Yamamoto writes "Yoneko's Earthquake" in the third person; in "Songs My Mother Taught Me," Sachiko narrates her own story. Yamauchi rewrites "Yoneko's Earthquake" not to repeat its action but in order to unpack its meaning.

Yoneko, the subject of a narrator's voice, remains a prisoner of appearances, confined to registering outward events. She must make judgments based on signs that she does not even know are signs. Sachiko, by contrast, interprets the world around her in her first-person voice; she not only registers events but comments on them. She possesses the ability to notice that "there was a subtle change in the family." She can even pull back from her narrative with a kind of retrospective wisdom when her mother admits that she did not want the baby: "I know now what she meant: that time was passing her by, that with the new baby she was irrevocably bound to this futile life, that dreams of returning to Japan were shattered, that through the eyes of a younger man she had glimpsed what might have been, could never and would never be." The interpreting and sympathetic power of Sachiko's voice will give her access to a life that she not only suffers but understands.

Marriage, in these stories about women attempting to gain power over and within their marriages, becomes a metaphor for what is gained and lost in the immigrating Japanese experience. The powerlessness these women experience within their marriage becomes a measure of their inability, one they share with their men, to control the meaning ascribed to their political commitments. For such writers, marriage proves available as a subject in a way it could not have been, until years after the war, for the Chinese. When it comes to the politics of love, the Chinese story had been one of enforced loneliness, of China Men. The Japanese story more often focused on enforced union. In the literatures of both cultures, the daughter has been assigned the role of passionate witness. As she suffers the constrictions of a traditional culture in transition, she also discovers her answering voice.

But the Japanese-American daughter does not invest her hope, as might an Amy Tan, in the possibility of return. In their uncanny ability to move between countries, marriages, even freedom and incarceration, the Noguchis define the limits of the problem. Home for them becomes the oceanic silence of art; a place, like Isamu's sculpture garden, located nowhere, yet somehow familiar. The eventual uncanniness of any home is diffused into a sublime but ungrounded sense of belonging. Writers like Yamamoto and Yamauchi and even Mori do not so fully sublimate their losses. No "Japan" hovers behind their stories as does "China" in *The Joy Luck Club*. Perhaps this is because for most Japanese Americans, Japan has remained a more accessible and therefore a less compelling object of nostalgia. Perhaps it is because, in order to become "Americans," the Japanese were called upon publicly to declare their loyalty and to remake their choice. The resulting mourning for Japan diffuses itself into Mori's "sadness" or into what Sachiko calls "my mother's malaise." These are characters twice divorced: from their native country by the demands of an adopted one, from the adopted country by its suspicion of their abiding love of Japan. Even the happiest marriage, in the most fully lived immigrant life, cannot entirely make up for that.

CHAPTER EIGHT

FROM WATTS TO SOUTH CENTRAL

Internalizing the Fire

I N HIS MID-FIFTIES, during the last year of Jimmy Carter's presidency, my father began selling artworks made from shells and Lucite at the Orange County Swap Meet. During the week he and his companion fashioned the sculptures in a rented workshop in Costa Mesa, and on Friday night they loaded their van. Saturdays and Sundays they got up at three, drove to the fairground, and raced hundreds of other vehicles to the best asphalt space, where they pitched a tent, laid out Astroturf, and displayed their wares. People around them sold everything from avocados to bootleg Adidas. Transactions took place in cash. The management of the swap meet was eventually impressed enough by my father's industry to assign him a permanent space on a busy corner, a consideration that allowed him to sleep one hour later on weekend mornings.

My father married in 1944 at the age of twenty. When he left the Army Air Corps the next year, he started a pottery in a big shed at the back of my grandmother's acre of land in Lynwood. (Lynwood, where I was born in 1948, referred to itself until the early 1960s as "the friendly Caucasian city.") My mother, who had worked as a nurse during the war, grew up in neighboring Compton. During the early years of the marriage, she helped pour slip and finish pots. My father eventually moved the pottery to South Gate and finally to the San Bernardino

Taken in Lynwood, California, in 1945, the photograph shows, from left to right: Elinor Wyatt (aunt), Bill Wyatt (uncle), Eva Wyatt (grandmother), James Wyatt (father), and Joy Wyatt (mother). In the background is the family home my grandparents bought in 1926, after emigrating from Oklahoma. Courtesy James Wyatt.

Mountains. He made good money for a while from his original slipcast designs and glazes, selling his figurines and dinnerware to Gump's and Bloomingdale's. Then Japanese imports flooded the market, the pottery burned down, and in the mid-1950s we moved to South Pasadena, where my father began designing appliance advertisements for Gatters and Satler.

Before the war he rode the Red Car into Los Angeles and studied drawing at the Art Center. He talked most of his life about being a painter, and over the years he completed a few paintings. But the need to support a family and the anxieties of ambition encouraged his turn into commercial art. To be an artist in California after the war was to live outside the largess of federal subsidy while remaining dependent on it for a steady source of clients. (San Bernardino, where the family eventually settled, was an Air Force town.) This fact was perhaps brought home to my father in the early 1970s, when he became the first and probably the last interior decorator invited to appoint the quarters of a tank carrier, the U.S.S. *San Bernardino*. The job was a challenge, since unlike in the hundreds of houses he had draped and carpeted, everything—even the ashtrays—had to be bolted down or somehow secured in place.

In the years before this commission from the Navy, my father designed Southern California's first theme park—Santa's Village—started and lost a vacuum-formed plastics company, dressed windows for Crosley's Florists, and became the most sought-after designer for the Inland Empire's annual Headdress Ball. In 1971 my mother was killed in a car accident. My father went bankrupt a second time and left San Bernardino for Orange County. After various forays into retail, he returned to small-scale manufacturing and still is, at seventy-two and as of this writing, making his living with his hands.

My father's older brother Bill stuck with one thing, his machine shop. Before I left for college in 1966, I spent the summer working at Wyatt Automatics in North Long Beach. My job was to burr hexes. This meant holding the six sides of some ten thousand metal parts a day against a whirling sandpaper wheel. The parts were generated out of the bar stock that was fed into automatics that chewed the metal into nuts and bolts. Twenty men working the second-operation lathes and screw machines added threads and other refinements to the rough-cut parts. The parts then came to me, after which they were shipped to Lockheed or Douglas to make something that could fly over Tulsa or Hanoi.

The summer I worked for Bill, I lived with my grandmother in Compton. Compton still felt to me like a quiet, mostly white suburb with narrow cement streets shaded by carob trees. It had weather so cool and temperate that my grandmother was able to maintain a weed-free dichondra lawn, one we crawled across on foggy mornings to pick up, by hand, the fallen carob leaves. It was a place where things happened, as Didion might say, "typically." Compton had not been laid out, like Lakewood, in one fell swoop. But the houses and lifeways fell into similar patterns, closely spaced islands of stucco inhabited by families marooned in a privacy without intimacy.

On summer evenings, after I got home from work, my grandmother and I had dinner in the patio under the twenty-foot rubber plant, then played two-handed bridge or watched shows like *Peyton Place* on TV. Next door lived a Mexican girl that I took a fancy to; it was the summer of "Guantanamera." Angela's neighbors to the right were black, the first black family on the street.

Watts adjoins Compton on the north. It was a town built on a sandy, treeless area that once served as the water basin for Los Angeles. In 1926 the city annexed Watts in an attempt to control black migration into the area. In 1930, about the time my grandmother moved to Compton, the town had one black resident. By 1978, the year of my grandmother's death and some twelve years after the summer I lived with her, she remained the only white parishioner in the Compton Methodist Church she had attended for over forty years.

The changes that have come to these towns and their absorption into the term "South Central" can affect someone who knew them in his youth in a peculiar way. It is not a question of nostalgia, an emotion continually generated by California's always-disappearing landscape. Nor is it a question of wishing these towns magically restored to their prior condition; they were, in my experience, the heart of *Blue Velvet* country, home to a suffocating and uneasy domesticity dedicated to Canasta and good naps. What I feel rather is a kind of numb wonder that we could have so badly managed the transition from South Central's somnolence to its violence, especially since the end of somnolence at first appeared to be an expansion of possibility for its black citizens.

My quiet summer in Compton was lived out a year after the riot in neighboring Watts, an uprising coincident with the federal decision to send ground troops to Vietnam. It was the summer in which Richard Elman wrote *Ill-At-Ease in Compton,* a summer in which he noted that "if the white man was fleeing Compton for the outlying areas, the Negro was fleeing Watts for Compton." Between 1950 and 1960 Compton's white population declined by 18.5 percent, while nonwhites were increasing in numbers by 165 percent. By 1966, the "minority group," as the papers called it, had become Compton's majority.

After my grandmother's funeral, my father and I walked Compton's sunny, still-treelined streets and remarked that despite the changing population, the place looked much the same. What we could not see was that black migration into Compton had already crested. On Mayo Street my grandmother had been the last white homeowner on her block. She had held on there—despite two muggings—weeding her lawn, playing bridge, watching TV. In the year of her death, Compton looked black. Yet two years later the census recorded that there were more Latino and mixed neighborhoods in South Central than there had been in 1970. By 1994, Compton's population was 51 percent Latino.

Patterns of business ownership in South Central had also shifted.

Jewish shopkeepers had largely been replaced by Koreans, while manu-facturing, the mainstay of the area in the 1950s and 1960s, had fled to the San Fernando Valley and to Orange and San Diego Counties. By the early 1990s, black joblessness in parts of South Central ran as high as 50 percent. The jobs available to Spanish-speaking immigrants to the area were for the most part menial and low-paying. Asians had become a pivot group between the blacks and the Latinos. The 1980 census revealed that the rate of self-employment among Koreans in Los Angeles ran higher than for any other ethnic group. While the African-American and Korean-American conflicts that erupted in the 1992 riots derived from the troubled relationship between merchant and customer, the Latino-Korean conflict arose as much from tension over residence and work-place. Latinos, that is, typically encountered Koreans as landlords or employers. The destruction of Koreatown in April 1992 argued that once again, in California, an Asian population had been targeted as responsible for the plight of the state's economically threatened.

In August 1994 *The Washington Post* carried an article with the title "New Amateur Video Agitates L.A. Area: Black-Latino Confrontation Stretches Tensions." "It's racial *déjà vu*," a professor from the University of California is quoted as saying. What was being repeated, surely, was the beating of an unarmed minority male by a policeman. Except that this time the tape shown on the evening news contained footage of a black policeman beating a Latino teenager and jumping on the youth's back as he applied the handcuffs. "Everybody's fighting over turf," a black resi-dent of Compton ventures. Referring to "the Mexicans," she complains that "they're always playing that loud music and painting their houses sunshine yellow with tangerine orange trim. People here have always kept their yards nice, you know, and they let the grass grow all long and park a hundred cars on the lawn." The incident carried the ominous message that in the post–Rodney King era, solidarity among California's traditionally oppressed racial groups could not be depended upon or even easily imagined.

In *The Emergence of Los Angeles* (1986), B. Marchand argues that "Blacks structure space as they move much more strongly than do Whites." The claim bears directly upon the development of the ghetto called Watts, a space defined in the national consciousness by the behavior of a group that arrived there rather late. Originally part of a large Mexican land grant, the area that became Watts was first subdivided in the 1880s. During this time Mexican laborers moved into the area to work on the Southern Pacific Railroad, forming the village of Tujuata. Incorporated in 1907, Watts developed as a grid of small residential lots without the significant industrial base enjoyed by neighboring Compton. Blacks who moved into the area settled in a district called Mudtown. Los Angeles annexed Watts in 1926; Eldridge Cleaver was born there nine years later. Until World War II Watts remained racially balanced between whites, blacks, and Mexican Americans.

With the migrations sparked by the war, Watts became a primarily black city. It offered low-cost housing and was free of the deed restrictions that limited black access to other areas of Los Angeles. As blacks moved in, the other populations moved out. Between 1940 and 1960 the black population of Watts increased eightfold. In 1965 blacks made up

A restricted housing site in Los Angeles, about 1950. After the war, black Angelenos were prohibited from moving out of the city center by deed restrictions and other exclusive real estate arrangements. Not until 1963 did the Rumford Act prohibit discrimination in California's real estate dealings; the law was revoked by a public referendum in 1964. Courtesy of the Southern California Library for Social Studies and Research.

87 percent of the city's 34,000 residents. With an area of two and a half square miles, Watts had the highest population density of any city in Los Angeles County. The median black family income for 1964 was $4,669.

The movement of black Americans into Watts and their eventual diffusion throughout South Central was the product of neither accident nor choice. Legal and economic conditions provoked the initial settlement. The nearby industry of the war years held the community in place. When the war ended, the sudden withdrawal of federal housing subsidies strapped local governments and left the people of Watts trapped in place or displaced from any housing they could afford. In 1951 a group called Citizens Against Socialist Housing (CASH) organized a successful campaign against a public housing referendum, thus denying out-movement from the urban core. When Bebe Moore Campbell makes the heroine of her 1994 novel a black loan officer, she does so in direct and ironic response to a postwar history in which the FHA favored loans to the suburbs rather than the inner city. Federally supported loans were denied buyers in Boyle Heights, for instance, because it was held to be a " 'melting pot' area literally honeycombed with diverse and subversive racial elements."

The citizens of Watts did not possess the means, the power, or the cultural impetus to move to Orange County or to a home in the hills. Where money did not preclude such departures, traditional patterns of black migration often did. Marchand asserts that "residential expansion of the Blacks is by contiguity, from one block to the next, and not, like the Whites, by jumps to remote districts. As a result, the spatial effects of the black diffusion are particularly important in restructuring the urban space." The arrival in Watts of a significant black population thus set in motion a pattern of steady expansion outward from a central point and provoked a correspondingly powerful effort of containment.

THE WATTS RIOTS BEGAN on the evening of Wednesday, August 11, 1965, and were brought under "control" by the following Sunday. The curfew established north of Rosecrans and west of Alameda was lifted on Tuesday. During those five days thirty-four people were killed. The police made almost 4,000 arrests; the fire department registered between 2,000 and 3,000 alarms. Violence broke out in places as peaceful as Pasadena and as far away as San Diego. The police and sheriff's departments deployed more than 1,600 officers; by midnight Saturday close to 14,000 National Guardsmen were patrolling the streets of Los Angeles. Property damage from the riot was estimated at $40 million.

In December 1965 the Governor's Commission on the Los Angeles Riots delivered its official report. "The search for causes," the report maintained, "has been our primary objective." Yet the McCone Commission, as it came to be called, concerned itself more with explaining why the riot should not have happened than with why it did. "Why Los Angeles?" the report plaintively asked, and the answer consisted largely of ironies: "while the Negro districts of Los Angeles are not urban gems, neither are they slums. Watts, for example, is a community consisting mostly of one and two-story houses, a third of which are owned by the occupants. In the riot area, most streets are wide and usually quite clean; there are trees, parks, and playgrounds. A Negro in Los Angeles has long been able to sit where he wants in a bus or a movie house, to shop where he wishes, to vote, and to use public facilities without discrimination. The opportunity to succeed is probably unequalled in any other major American city."

Early in the century, Los Angeles had indeed provided a kind of haven for the some 7,000 blacks who lived there. In 1910 36.1 percent of black Angelenos owned their own homes, compared with 2.4 percent in New York City. Despite the restrictive covenants that so limited black mobility in the years after World War II, in 1964 the Urban League had even rated Los Angeles first out of sixty-eight cities "in terms of the ten basic aspects of Negro life."

The McCone report did proceed to amass some reasons for black discontent, the most persuasive of which was the repeal of the Rumford Fair Housing Act by two-thirds of California voters in 1964—the beginning of a swing to the right in California politics that would lead to the election of Ronald Reagan as governor in 1966 and the property tax revolts of the 1970s. Yet such larger contexts are perceived throughout the report only dimly. An allusion to the repeal of the fair housing law is followed by the claim that "when the rioting came to Los Angeles, it was not a race riot in the usual sense. What happened was an explosion—a formless, quite senseless, all but hopeless violent protest— engaged in by a few but bringing great distress to all." Here the report appears to back off from making a connection between cause and result and throws up its hands before the interpretative crux. Words like "few" and "all" inaugurate, however, its most determined argument: that the riot was the work of a tiny minority (two percent) of the city's otherwise 650,000 unprotesting black citizens.

The McCone report repeatedly breezes past hard facts while taking refuge behind unarticulated arguments like the "riff-raff theory." In the section entitled "Law Enforcement," for instance, it admits that the city police had been subjected by "many Negroes" to "bitter criticism." A page later we are told that "our society is held together by respect for law." The report appears content that such rhetorical gaps loom between the concrete evidence it amasses and the maxims it imparts. Recognizing that the Negro lived in extreme conditions, its anxious authors nonetheless felt particularly uneasy about "extreme statements." While the Negro was admittedly disadvantaged and excluded, he was nonetheless asked not to protest but to shoulder "a full share of the responsibility for his own well being." Reverend James Edward Jones, a member of the commission, issued a written protest against this Catch-22: "I do not believe it is the function of this Commission to put a lid on protest registered by those sweltering in ghettos of the urban areas of our country. . . . As long as an individual 'stands outside looking in' he is not part of that society; that society cannot say that he does not have a right to protest, nor can it say that he must shoulder a responsibility which he has never been given an opportunity to assume."

As Robert Fogelson argues in his edition of the report, those who accept its conclusions depart from the "conviction that no matter how grave the grievances, there are no legitimate grounds for violent protest." That violence was unacceptable obviated the need to search for a sufficient cause. The report thus retreated into the language of romantic capitalism and individual self-making, although the conditions under review fell much more readily into the worldview supplied by Frank Norris's naturalism. In *The Octopus* it is Shelgrim, the arch-capitalist and head of the Southern Pacific Railroad, who has the vision, however self-exonerating, to argue that history is a story "dealing with forces . . . not with men." Fogelson makes a strong case for applying a similar vocabulary in his account, which reads the riots as "manifestations" of intransigent racial and social problems rather than fixable economic and individual ones. Bayard Rustin also pinpoints the "moralistic" and rhetorical "bias" of a report that places an undue "emphasis on the decisions of men rather than the pressure of social forces."

In 1970 the Institute of Government and Public Affairs sponsored the

The National Guard sets up a machine gun in the streets of Watts, August 1965. The Guard was deployed after police and civic leaders, both black and white, proved unable to stop the rioting, which was to leave thirty-four people dead. Courtesy of the Bancroft Library.

publication of *The Los Angeles Riots: A Socio-Psychological Study*. Edited by Nathan Cohen, the study based its findings on interviews with 586 residents of the South-Central Curfew Zone. The study concluded that up to 15 percent of the Negro adult population, or about 22,000 people, were active at some point during the rioting. When asked what their grievances were, members of the sample group listed poor neighborhood conditions (33 percent), mistreatment by whites (14 percent), and economic conditions (13 percent). Twenty-one percent expressed no specific complaints. All this made sense, but the authors still thought there was a "disjuncture" between the "semitropical lushness of Los Angeles" and the "grim statistics." Again, as with the McCone Commission, surfaces belied depths. After speculating on a list of major causes, the authors concluded that "the one thread which ran through most explanations was a high level of discontent among the Negro population of the city."

What follows this conclusion is a massively detailed chapter called "The Structure of Discontent." For all the charts and statistics, however, something about the riots refuses to yield up more than circular or obvious conclusions. The chapter ends as it began, by asserting that "a high level of discontent seems to pervade the entire curfew community." Cohen and his team disdain the argument that the riots expressed the discontent only of the poor or the underclass: "Mistreatment or exploitation by whites . . . seems to be a source of riot support for all levels of the ghetto." Yet as blacks improve their class status and their contact with whites, they observe, frustration does not diminish. "We have also seen that discontent increases as social contact increases." Rising incomes and expectations lead to rising anger; economic improvement only makes things worse. In this cruel and compelling logic, to rise is also to fall.

After his visit to Watts in 1965, Martin Luther King, Jr., also interpreted the riots as a crisis of proximity. "Los Angeles could have expected riots because it is the luxurious symbol of luxurious living for whites. Watts is closer to it and yet further from it than any other Negro community in the country. The looting in Watts was a form of social protest very common through the ages as a dramatic and destructive gesture of the poor toward symbols of their needs." Such language suggests that the riots were less about forcing material change than about making symbolic gestures. At such a game, the black population of Los Angeles could not win, for the targets of the riots, symbolic or not, constituted the infrastructure of the black community and were destroyed. The net result of war making by way of symbols is to widen the actual gap between luxury and poverty.

The obvious and intolerable conclusion that must be drawn from the riots—that the system doesn't work—is superseded, after reading Cohen's study—by the mind-numbing and counterintuitive corollary that *fixing* the system doesn't work either. All the good ideas put forward in these reports will serve only to elevate more people into the region of discontent. Violence becomes, as a result, an appealing and even an inevitable result. Chester Himes had come away from Los Angeles angry in body and soul and believing that "in order for a revolution to be effective, one of the things that it has to be, is violent, it has to be massively violent."

But can violence alter the structure of discontent in a culture of desire?

Writing from Los Angeles in 1944, Max Horkheimer and Theodor Adorno argued that "the culture industry perpetually cheats its customers of what it perpetually promises." After a visit to the riot zone in 1965, Thomas Pynchon concluded in an article for *The New York Times* that "Los Angeles, more than any other city, belongs to the mass media." In such a place, illusion rivals economic disparity as an enemy to peace. The cultural machine that produces images of difference, and the discontent they breed, works faster and more efficiently than the political or economic system can work to eliminate actual material difference. As Martin Luther King in fact divined, all the citizens of Los Angeles are up against a system devoted to manufacturing needs that cannot be met, needs often predicated on the manipulation of symbols rather than on actual material lack. As if sensing this, the Cohen study, in "Implications for the Future," retreats behind an "If / then" construction whose circularity implies a kind of eternal return: "If the riots are viewed as a revolt against the System, as a crying out against the piling up of numerous grievances, and these conditions continue to fester, some pattern of violent response will emerge."

IN THE NEXT QUARTER CENTURY, as these conditions continued to fester, Watts expanded into "South Central." Black and Latino Angelenos living in this area experienced joblessness, gang warfare, urban blight. Yet these material conditions alone did not spark the next riot: in a place so dedicated to symbols, it was a symbol that did that work. The catastrophic violence that flared up in 1992 had its stimulus in a videotape and the reading of its contents by a jury in a Simi Valley court.

On April 29, 1992, four Los Angeles police officers were acquitted in state court on charges of beating motorist Rodney King. King's March 3, 1991, arrest had been videotaped by George Holliday. After the verdict was carried live on television, violence broke out in South-Central Los Angeles. Truck driver Reginald Denny was assaulted at the intersection of Florence and Normandie; this incident was also captured on video. In three days of rioting, fifty-three people were killed and more than sixteen thousand were arrested. Businesses were looted or burned in Koreatown, Hollywood, Mid-Wilshire, Watts, Westwood, Beverly Hills, Compton, Culver City, Hawthorne, Long Beach, Norwalk, and Pomona. The fire department received more than five thousand structure fire calls and responded to some five hundred fires. Total property losses were estimated as high as $1 billion—twenty-five times the amount lost in the Watts riots.

While Watts is located well within the 1992 riot zone, the event diffused itself across the region we now call "South Central," the vast, flat, once-industrialized plain that stretches from the Coliseum in the north to the docked *Queen Mary* in Long Beach in the south, and from the Los Angeles airport in the west to the hills that crumple up against downtown in the east. The effort to rebuild Watts and the surrounding areas had resulted, by 1992, in a new shopping center at Vermont and Slauson as well as a 400,000-square-foot mall named after Martin Luther King. Five thousand housing units had been built in Watts since 1965. On the other hand, a steel mill located at 109th and Central had become a Catholic high school. Major employers like General Motors, Goodyear, and Firestone had fled the area. New freeway construction continued to bisect the region. And the first new sit-down restaurant to open in Watts after the 1965 riots did not do so until November 1991.

The abundance of visual evidence in the King case produced a crisis of interpretation. To make a judgment about the event, it seemed only necessary to believe one's eyes. A prime witness was also available—Rodney King himself. "Some observers expect him to be on the stand for two weeks," wrote Richard Serrano in a *Los Angeles Times* article of January 16, 1992. In the article King gives his version of what happened after he moved to the ground in response to police commands. "They walked over to me and I felt a blow to the head. He [one of the police officers] walked over to me and, boom, he kicked me in the face. And then I heard . . . 'We're going to kill you, nigger! Run.' " The same issue of the *Times* carried another article by Serrano with the title, "Attempt to Blunt Effect of the Video Seen as Key to Trial."

Despite King's already-voiced account, the prosecution based its case on the videotape and decided against calling King to the stand. Los Angeles district attorney Ira Reiner told a television interviewer that "there isn't any way Rodney King with all those blows raining down on him could have told the story as clearly and as coherently as that video tape." The prosecution's tactic backfired. Yet the belief that a videotape somehow speaks for itself persisted. In another Los Angeles trial vexed by race, in which closing arguments were given in September 1995, defense attorney Johnnie Cochran pointed to a videotape of his "smiling" client, one taken on the day he was alleged to have committed a double murder. "Thank God for videotapes," Cochran said. "We know in this city how important videotapes can be."

Rodney King did testify in the April 1993 federal civil rights trial, in which officers Powell and Koon were found guilty. In the two-part civil trial that began in March 1994, King was awarded $3.8 million in damages for medical bills and pain and suffering after he gave graphic testimony describing his beating and asserted that he had heard racial epithets as he lay on the ground. He was not, however, awarded punitive damages.

In the first trial the videotape turned out to be "something other than it was seen to be." Anna Deavere Smith quotes these words by Homi Bhabha in *Twilight* (1994), the published version of her one-woman performance piece about the Los Angeles riots. The metaphor of "twilight" pervades Smith's work as a kind of promise, a reminder of "an in-between moment" where the "hard outlines" between black and white give way to enabling intersections. "We have to interpret more in twilight," Bhabha continues, "we have to make ourselves part of the act, we have to interpret, we have to project more. But also the thing itself in twilight challenges us to be aware of how we are projecting onto the event itself." If, as Bhabha argues, "we are part of producing the event" called "Rodney King" and the event called "riot," then Smith's piece, an assemblage of voices, stands as the most comprehensive and sublime rendition of how Americans attending to the event have produced what they have heard.

Smith is above all a performer who requires disciplined response. Before performing pieces from *Twilight* at the University of Maryland in April 1996, she encouraged her audience "to listen to silence." Her work is done, she maintained, "in praise of the unfinished sentence"; much of its meaning can be gathered in the pauses and things unsaid between the spoken words of her interviewees. She enjoined us, that night, "not to listen to beginnings, middles, and ends." As in *Twilight* itself, in this performance there would be no attempt to provide "a unifying voice." Instead of seeking to gratify the narrative desire for closure and spectacle, her performance invited us to participate in reconstructing a series of broken testimonies, an act that offered intense but fleeting moments of empathy.

ANY ACCOUNT OF THE INCIDENTS surrounding Rodney King will be an interpretation of them. My own references to King as a "motorist," for instance, may be judged by some commentators to be a racist or at best a dismissive epithet. I adopt the term because it has become received usage and because the debate over what to call King seems, to me, a quibble. I refer to the events that followed the verdict as a "riot," while others choose to call it an "uprising" or a "rebellion." In *Why Men Rebel* (1970), Ted Gurr gives "relatively spontaneous, unorganized political violence" the name "turmoil," a form of rebellion he distinguishes from the more highly organized acts of "conspiracy" and "internal war." I prefer the word "riot" because of the status given the term by Congresswoman Maxine Waters, who maintains that "riot is the voice of the unheard," modifying Martin Luther King's sentence, "A riot is the language of the unheard." By calling what happened in South Central a riot, I retain King's sense that such an event *expresses* as well as Waters's claim that this specific riot entailed a speaking out or act of voicing by those who otherwise went unlistened-to. My point is not to defend word choices but to suggest that no event in recent American history has so clearly fore-grounded the fact that description is interpretation and that even in taking in the riot we help to produce it.

In the year he served as president of the Modern Language Associa-tion, the professional organization of college and university teachers of English and foreign languages, Houston Baker, Jr., wrote an article on the Rodney King case called "Scene . . . Not Heard" that carefully analyzes the dynamics of the trial and the antecedents to the treatment of King. Baker's professional position would seem to identify him as an authority on English style and usage, yet when he describes the night of the arrest, not even he can escape writing from a standpoint. Here is Baker on that balmy California night in the spring of 1991:

It is 3rd March 1991. A speeding car occupied by three black men drives through red lights on California Highway 210. In pursuit . . . not Mr. Gore . . . but a husband-and-wife team of the California Highway Patrol. When the lead vehicle finally pulls over, out jumps a 6'3", 200-pound black man, who, according to witnesses, danced about, grabbed his behind, and laughed crazily. Was this Nehemiah in the face of David Wharton? The police were not amused. Twenty-one Los Angeles city police officers had arrived at the scene along with two Unified School District officers by the time Rodney G. King jumped out of his car. The newly arrived told the husband-and-wife Highway Patrol team that they would handle matters. Fifty-six crushing blows, several stun-gun blasts, and random savage kicks and pushes later, these bold white officers had indeed succeeded in "handling" matters.

These are clearly the words of a man appalled by the event. The irony in phrases like "not amused" and the quotation marks around "handling" bespeak a controlled rage. The references to Mr. Gore, Nehemiah, and David Wharton refer back to Baker's earlier comparison of the event to incidents in the *Narrative of the Life of Frederick Douglass* (1845), asserting a historical continuity. Even the numbers he cites constitute an interpretation; while Baker counts fifty-six blows, Sergeant Stacey Koon, in his book *Presumed Guilty* (1992), counted only thirty-three. Baker's summary of that balmy California night expresses his feelings about it, and that is as it should be.

Presumed Guilty takes control of "The Tragedy of the Rodney King Affair"—the book's subtitle—by translating it into professional and legal jargon. It amplifies the threat presented by King while it converts the police behavior into a complex act of rule-following. Thus Rodney King's leg was not bent; it was "cocked." King did not flail about but indulged in the threatening "Folsom Roll," a maneuver for which the book's index even provides an entry. The police officers attempting to subdue and arrest him do not inflict pain: "There is no evidence that Rodney King experienced any pain until I ordered the baton power strokes to his joints," Koon maintains. Instead, they "escalate and de-escalate the violence."

Koon represents this act of translation as a mere shift in perspective. At the beginning of his book he tells his reader that "you will not be asked to forget what you saw on the video tape" but then asks "you" to "look at the evidence from a different angle," the angle of a police officer on the scene. Yet the shift Koon asks us to make is from a visual field—the videotape—to a verbal field, which he can better control. Any written account of the videotape, the trial, or the riots will ask us to do this, and the specific challenge Koon's book sets a reader is to retain the sense of what was felt at what was seen while merely reading about it. Still, Koon's selective and abstract rendition of the "affair" makes it temporarily possible for us to enter into the logic of the actions of the police.

Koon freely admits that the major strategy of the defense was "to prove that Rodney King was always in control of the situation, not the officers." The defense labeled King's actions as continually threatening and assaultive. Koon walks us through the steps of what he calls "The Stop." As the ranking LAPD officer, he commands Melanie Singer and the other officers who have drawn on King to holster their guns. He then orders the four LAPD officers nearest King to swarm the suspect. King throws the officers off. "Now I *know* that the suspect is under the influence of PCP"; despite the absence of blood-test evidence in support of this point, Koon remains fully committed to this surmise. Koon then tells King to get down or he will Tase him. The Taser is an electronic stun-gun that fires cassette cartridges, each of which carries fifty thousand volts. King keeps moving, so Koon Tases him. King falls, then rises, and Koon Tases him a second time. King is now lying on the ground. At this point George Holliday begins videotaping, thus producing a record that also includes the "crucial first two seconds usually edited out by the media," seconds which show King, in Koon's words, "rising from a fully prone position to launch a full-charge attack on Officer Powell."

Despite Koon's careful notation of the events leading up to the moment when the tape begins, the images recorded by Holliday's newly purchased camcorder appeared unambiguous to most viewers. After the trial Mayor Tom Bradley of Los Angeles declared that "the jury's verdict will never blind us to what we saw on that videotape," while President Bush said that "viewed from the outside, it was hard to understand how the verdict could possibly square with the video." The prosecution made the Holliday tape its primary piece of evidence. A neighbor of Holliday who witnessed the beating firsthand is quoted in *Twilight* on this point: Josie Morales tells Smith that prosecutor Terry White decided against calling her to the stand because "he was dead set on that video and that the video would tell all."

But of course a video cannot tell, it can only show, and the defense controlled the prosecutor's show-and-tell by subjecting the videotape to a carefully orchestrated formalist reading, so that it also became the defense's primary exhibit. Defense lawyers interrupted the dynamic of the sequence and isolated moment from moment so that what had looked obvious became ambiguous. They took the stills that they wanted to isolate to a photo shop and had them blown up, cropped, and backed with foam board. These stills then became the basis of the defense as the jury was led through the videotape almost frame by frame. "Viewed continuously," Koon writes, "you couldn't make out precisely what Rodney King was doing all the time. But when you isolated each frame, he could clearly be seen trying to rise to his feet." Instead of being read in a historical context or being given a living voice, the videotape was chopped up into unconnected bytes of information. "The attorney's new critical reading," Baker writes, "is like all new critical readings. That is to say, it is a misreading, a misprision—taking the 'scene' and controlling it. It is a policing of images by dissection and tends always to preserve the tale of violence and control in its primal form."

It might be as accurate to say that the defense supplied the tape with its controlling context, and hence a way of reading it. Koon makes this point at the end of his narrative. "The Rodney King video tape is true. But it is not the truth. The truth can only be found by viewing the video tape in the context of everything else that happened when Rodney King finally stopped his car in Foothill Division of Los Angeles on March 3, 1991."

In fact, both sides attempted to provide a context for understanding the tape by submitting isolated frames to formalist analysis. Sergeant Charles Duke did this for the defense, while he was testifying on the LAPD standards for use of force. He also did it at the request of the prosecution; it is in response to Terry White's questioning about the content of one stopped frame that Duke locates King on a "spectrum of aggression." Commander Michael Bostic, the head of the LAPD's Use of Force Review Board and the major police witness for the prosecution, also agreed, at White's request, to stop the tape and to comment on it. In doing so, Bostic contradicted Duke in open court and testified that the use of force against Rodney King was "excessive." Yet Bostic's vocabulary proves indistinguishable from Koon's. He too talks about "escalation and de-escalation of force," and his own willingness to "dissect the tape," as Court TV reporter Fred Graham puts it, also freezes the violence in a distanced and abstract form.

Koon makes no mention of Bostic in his book. His patient, step-by-step account of the arrest and trial suddenly speeds up on page 181 and condenses the last sixteen days of the trial into four pages. It was during this interval that Bostic gave his testimony, testimony that was recorded by and is available from the Court TV network.

Like Koon's book, the Court TV videotape is an edited account, condensing over 150 hours of testimony during eight weeks into one hour and fifty-six minutes. It shares with *Presumed Guilty* an uncanny power to make at least temporary sense of the verdict. The last significant witness that it shows testifying, before the judge issues instructions to the jury, is Sergeant Charles Duke. Duke reiterates his view that the officers pictured on the tape did not use excessive force, and he dismisses Commander Bostic as "a use of force expert by appointment only." Court TV does not then interview Bostic or allow him a rebuttal. The viewer is left with Duke's word as the last word.

Court TV broadcast most of the trial proceedings live, without editing them. After the trial a part owner of the network said that "those who watched the [whole] trial were not nearly as surprised at the verdicts as those who had only seen the much-broadcasted portion of the video," Koon reports. Koon would like to believe that this response was the result of a well-made and truthful defense case. Judith Butler has argued, on the other hand, that the jury was operating under "racial constraints on what it means to see" and was therefore predisposed to see Rodney King as a threat rather than as a victim. Certainly these jurors were selected from and operated within a local context favorable to the defense; in 1992 two thousand of the 8,300 officers of the LAPD lived in Simi Valley, the Ventura County town to which the trial venue was shifted in order to avoid excessive publicity. While it is possible to explain the verdict by adducing everything from the ineptitude of the prosecution to the unconscious racism of the jury, the Court TV video of the trial reveals that the decorum and ideology of the courtroom also contributed to the outcome.

"Rodney King" is a synecdoche for a series of events that can best be taken in not through a trial but through a play. This is why Anna Deavere Smith's work of "documentary theater" will remain, I believe, the most adequate calling-up of the event. The Court TV video reveals the limits of legal as opposed to dramatic truth. The "drama" it captures—the American criminal trial—is biased in favor of a certain kind of player and a certain kind of audience response, where the audience is understood to be the jury. A courtroom is most obviously a venue for uniforms, from the judge's to the bailiff's, and it is therefore an unlikely place in which to pass judgment on officers of the law. Everything about the courtroom atmosphere lends a police officer sitting in it an air of probity and authority; he is the logical extension of the bench. This detail of atmosphere, however, pales in importance next to the audience-effect of legal procedure. There is a clear continuity between the formalist strategy adopted by the defense and the evidentiary process in a criminal trial. Both processes abstract a happening from its physical and temporal context and therefore from passionate response. Courtroom procedure is by nature decontextualizing and antinarrative; while *L.A. Law* may reduce a case to a one-hour television drama, the 150 hours of testimony to which the Simi Valley jurors were exposed made it difficult to see the events of March 3, 1991, steadily and to see them whole. All this took place in the service of the noble ideal of dispassionate judgment, but the judgment rendered supports the view that the law is about not truth but advocacy.

Both the Holliday videotape and the case of *California v. Powell* enforce a decision, a judgment. To many onlookers, the tape showed the officers to be as guilty as the trial found them not guilty. Neither the videotape nor the trial succeeded, however, in providing a satisfactory context for understanding. What was needed was an interpretation grounded in California history and in the testimony of the Californians who lived through this period of twilight. Anna Deavere Smith's *Twilight* gives that history a living voice.

IT IS VOICE out of which Smith constructs her performance, just as it was voice that went unheard at the first trial. "I'm just trying to create possibilities for dialogue," Smith said in a 1993 interview with the *Los Angeles Times*, "to decentralize the race discussion, to try to bring more voices to it that don't get heard. I believe we haven't found the language for discussing difference yet, and the only way we find that language is by talking in it—not about it—and talking in it in these moments of crisis, when our anxieties are so big that we can barely speak." Out of interviews she conducted with more than two hundred Angelenos, Smith selected twenty-five to reenact for the May 1993 premiere of *Twilight* at the Mark Taper Forum. For the 1994 publication of the play she added some twenty more interviews. Each interview is given a title and a paragraph that describes and situates the speaker. (Smith elects to arrange the typed words of her speakers in free-verse lines; I quote them as ordinary prose.) In the introduction to *Twilight* she affirms that the piece "is not really an attempt to find causes." Free of analytical language, her text instead presents a drama to be staged.

In her debut performance Smith preceded her one-woman show with a fifteen-minute video produced by Jon Stolzberg. The video replayed familiar images of the beating of Rodney King and the riots of April 1992, reminding the viewer that the media created as well as recorded the entire "Rodney King" event. But they also revealed all that the camera could not show or tell.

Through her performance Smith brings together the arguments of this book, as if the history of California converged to produce her work. California attracts her as the site of arresting catastrophe. The catastrophe is one of race. Smith gains access to the story, in part, by way of her status as a woman, a culturally designated "listener." Her gender allows her to operate as a kind of spy within the category of color. As a black woman, Smith partakes of—even suffers, a little—the ordeal she explores. Yet her coloring and her physical aspect—she is slender, with a café-au-lait complexion, over five foot nine—undermines any easy designation of her standing. The lightness of her skin, regularity of her features, and the boyishness of her figure all work against received categories of identity. Smith capitalizes on this ambiguity in order to play up the ways in which bodies can and do escape the projections of race and gender. *Twilight* liberates the viewer into a realm where all borders are at play, confounding the very categories that Smith evokes and embodies.

By taking on the voices of so many different people and so many different cultures, Smith challenges the belief that our born form traps us in a certain perspective. She solicits her material through an act of reception; she interviews and tapes her subjects. Actively giving back what she has heard by way of her own voice, she conflates the roles of watcher and doer—and thereby converts overwhelming spectacle into assimilable event. By virtue of her willingness to play with her natural endowments and her cultural surroundings, she creates an experience adequate to the ongoing catastrophe of California life.

"When I was in my teens running around as a zoot-suiter," Rudy Salas says in *Twilight,* "one night the cop really tore me up bad." Kicks to the head fracture his eardrum, "and, uh, I couldn't hear on both ears. I was deaf, worse than I am now." Smith begins with a speaker who has lost his hearing. She does this, in part, to emphasize the importance to her project of the auditory imagination. As she writes in her introduction, "This book is first and foremost a document of what an *actress heard* in Los Angeles." The story of Rodney King is one in which images fail to make a case and in which, for a certain kind of audience, spectacle misleads. Smith reports that Rodney King's aunt, Angela, bursts into tears on seeing the televised beating and "hearing him holler." She hears King's screams the first time she sees the tape. "Yet a juror in the federal civil rights trial against the officers who also heard King's reaction to the police blows told me," Smith continues, "that the rest of the jury had difficulty hearing what she and King's aunt had heard. But when, during deliberations, they focused on the audio rather than the video image, their perspective changed. The physical image of Rodney King had to be taken away for them to agree that he was in pain and responding to the beating."

Twilight answers this failed act of showing with some fifty individual acts of speaking. The result is that the riot becomes the sum of voices heard. But Smith does not merely play the voices back. By carefully selecting the voices and ordering their presentation, Smith converts her virtually unmediated material into an arousing work of art, one in which casual asides create telling patterns and where offhand figures of speech acquire the status of complex arguments.

Anna Deavere Smith as Angela King in a 1996 performance of Twilight *at the Berkeley Repertory Theatre. Smith interviewed more than two hundred Angelenos about their experience of the 1992 riots. The one-woman performance that resulted premiered in May 1993 at the Mark Taper Forum. Courtesy of Steven Rivers and the Berkeley Repertory Theatre.*

The first Chicano speaker we hear has lost his hearing; the first black speaker has lost his sight. Maced while trying to protest the arrest of a "brother," Michael Zinzun "finally got my vision" and attempts to flee the police. A flashlight catches him in the right eye. "I couldn't see no more since then." He wins his trial for damages, and the "city on an eye had to cough up one point two million dollars." Zinzun's fate connects him with Jason Sanford, a white actor who lives in a world controlled by looking: "Because of what I look like I don't know if I'd been beaten." In his numerous arrests, Sanford has been told by police that "you look like an all-American white boy." Sanford's "look" protects him from abuse, while Rodney King's "look" is literally altered by it. "It's a hell of a look," Angela King muses about her nephew. "I, I mean you wouldn't have known him to look at him now." Life in Los Angeles for its citizens involves a threat not only to the organs of perception but to a body's very aspect.

Smith positions Reginald Denny at the center of her chorus even though he remains curiously distant from the voices that surround him. Denny admits that "I didn't usually pay too much attention of what was going on in California." The trip to Inglewood was one he made "every single day." He had a curiosity about the nearly fatal street: "we, lot of guys looked forward to going down that street 'cause there was always something going on." Then the window of his truck is bashed in, and he remembers nothing until five or six days later. Arsenio Hall pokes his head into Denny's hospital room doorway. "And then, about then I started to, uh, started to get it." He begins to watch "it" on TV. "It" becomes Denny's word both for what happened to him and for the riot. *It* veils the pain. The word expresses his desire to look away or withdraw into a safe haven: "Someday when I, uh, get a house, I'm gonna have one of the rooms and it's just gonna be of all the riot stuff and it won't be a blood-and-guts memorial, it's not gonna be a sad, it's gonna be a happy room." "There won't be a color problem in this room." Another voice responds to the fantasy of a safe room by arguing that "our own house" is "burning" and that "we all live in the same house." "And shutting the door in your room, it doesn't matter. Fact is, you have a stronger sense of getting incinerated."

Smith precedes Denny's monologue with that of black ex-gang member Allen Cooper. Cooper maintains that the events in Los Angeles have been converted into a melodrama about two individuals. "But we're not basin' our life on Reginald Denny; neither are we basin' our lives on Rodney King." The press and the courts have "handled" the affair "like a soap opera." But "it's not Rotney King," Cooper protests. "It's the ghetto." More than thirty people were assaulted at the intersection of Florence and Normandie, "and their sufferings," as George Sanchez tells us, "were duly videotaped." "Denny was one of only two white people attacked at that intersection . . . the rest of the victims were Asian or Latino." Denny, like King, was recognizable as a symbol in a black / white dichotomy. Cooper argues for a generic rather than an exceptionalist vision, for the kind of thinking halfway envisioned by the anonymous white man who asks the anguished question: "Did I deserve this, do I, do I deserve it? I thought me, personally—no, me, generically, maybe so." In such juxtapositions, Smith invites readers to think antithetically, to look at themselves as if they stood on another side of the color line.

Smith also interviewed Coroner Dean Gilmour, the man responsible

"Eye on L.A." The photograph shows the intersection of Florence and Normandie, where Reginald Denny was beaten during the 1992 riot. "Eye on L.A." © *James Jeffrey, from* Life in a Day of Black L.A.: The Way We See It, *published by the UCLA Center for African American Studies, 1993. Reprinted by permission.*

for identifying "riot-related" deaths. In *Twilight,* while talking to Smith, Gilmour flips through some stapled pages and finds the "numbers." "Oh, here we go. Forty-one gunshot wounds. These are the races. Okay, but these are not official. Some of these are not. Twenty-six black, Eighteen Hispanic, Ten Caucasian, Two Asian. Uh, types of death. Gunshot wounds were forty. Uh, traffics were six. Four assaults, Four arsons and four other." Alive to the pathos of statistics, Gilmour speaks haltingly, his voice trailing off into the silence of ellipses. His broken speech contrasts with the burden of his professional calling, which is to search out connections from very partial evidence and to establish, where possible, the fact of human remains.

Gilmour tells Smith that he has been working with an attorney trying to have a young woman declared dead. She had been trapped in a New Guys appliance store when the place caught fire. "There may be human remains in there. We searched that place four times. And the fire was so hot that the ruff [sic, meaning "roof"] had totally collapsed.... We couldn't find any human remains. . . . We couldn't find a tooth or a finger or anything." Gilmour comprehends the importance of his work for the living. "The family doesn't have . . . They can't really get on with their life until they have some resolution to it. . . . And that's the thing about our society is *until,* um, until there's some type of a *service,* whatever it is, whether there's a cremation or there's a burial, uh, most people just can't let go with their lives and then pick up the pieces and start from there. There has to be some resolution." The woman was so badly burned that she cannot be found, yet some kind of resolution to her story—a burial or a cremation—is needed. The redundancy of burning what has already been burned would be absurd, did it not terrifyingly illuminate the actions of those in Los Angeles who have set fire to their "own house." In a place inexorably filling up with the "living dead," as one speaker calls them, the fire that displaced forty thousand people takes on the aspect not only of an outcry or a protest but of a continuing act of cremation that can "burst out," in the words of Korean liquor-store owner Mrs. Young-Soon Han, "anytime."

In talking about the pain felt by the survivors of the riot, Coroner Gilmour is prompted to remember his own losses: "I've lost . . . My first

Anna Deavere Smith as Mrs. Young-Soon Han in Twilight. *Courtesy of Steven Rivers and the Berkeley Repertory Theatre.*

child was a full-term stillborn. My brother was murdered up in Big Bear and the guy got four years' probation. Um, my sister was killed by a drunk driver, leaving three kids and a husband behind. So I can empathize with these families as far as what they've gone through." Empathy is the rare emotion to which Gilmour finally lays claim: not sympathy *for,* but feeling *with*. In this supreme moment, one punctuated by a deep inarticulateness and all of Gilmour's awkward love, a speaker in the play merges with a watcher of the play, if that watcher has accepted *Twilight's* invitation to imagine a way into the feel of other people's lives.

Smith's work has as its deepest ambition a renovation of the social usefulness of empathy. She accomplishes this through a style of performance in which her unique gifts for mimicry place her subjects fully before us: "The most sublime act," as Blake says, "is to set another before you." Sublimity is a matter of transgressing boundaries, and by electing to speak and to hear these different voices, Smith and her audience enter into a realm where the most intransigent border—that between self and other—can be momentarily breached.

Coroner Gilmour's job is to put a limit on the number of "riot-related" deaths, to contain the dimensions of the catastrophe. There is therefore something moving about a voice so committed to the precise notation of public loss breaching decorum by talking about its private story. Gilmour attempts to connect himself with the victims of the riot, even as his deeply personal aside reveals the limits of empathy. Smith's job is to expand the number of voices that go into producing the event. The resonance among her selected voices implies an infinity of reach and argues that when it comes to the search for the riot-related, relations stop nowhere.

It is important that these voices do not speak to each other: they are overheard by the reader and it is in that mind that a dialogue between them can be constructed. Such a mind is free to hear the unwitting echoes among these voices as participating in a realm of concern that ranges across boundaries of race and gender. We—the audience—must do this work, and the extent to which we enter into it measures our capacity and willingness to deal with a world that is many-voiced.

Much was done to convert the Los Angeles riots into a spectacle that would divert viewers from its human dimensions and costs. It was ever thus in California. By choosing neither to amplify nor to glamorize the experience she explores, Smith discovers a form in which California hurts can be felt without being transformed into spectacle. Her work is a work of writing and of imagining, and, as such, it does its part in changing the world. Insofar as the catastrophes that have shaped California's history are made possible by collective and continuing acts of repression or distanced spectatorship, Smith then joins that company of watchers and listeners who, in the diligence and shapeliness and immediacy of their efforts at memorial, encourages Californians to return upon and understand their past without, perhaps, repeating it.

SMITH BEGINS *TWILIGHT* with the voice of Rudy Salas, Sr., a man of Mexican descent who takes us back in memory to the Zoot Suit Riots of 1943. He also calls up a century of struggle between Anglo and Mexican immigrants; as early as 1856 a Yankee described a Los Angeles gunfight between a Ruiz and a Jenkins as a "war of the races." By beginning with Salas's voice, Smith reminds a reader of the multiplicity of racial borders in California and that "the story of race in America is much larger and more complex than a story of black and white."

Smith's book in fact has a precedent, in both theme and structure, in the 1948 volume *American Me*. *American Me* collates the "anonymous" voices of Mexican-American children as they register the pain of the Zoot Suit Riots. Beatrice Griffith, who compiled the volume, is perhaps too willing to create composite voices out of the testimony of "real girls and boys." She divides the book into three parts: The Smoke; The Fire; The Phoenix. *American Me* thus organizes itself around the metaphor of a fire that brings not only death but hope. The last story, "Let Life Happen," deals with a fire in Watts, or Mudtown. "Not even water could stop this fire," the child's voice says. It burns the neighborhood cornfields. "And like that corn crop, when you plowed under the burned land, plowed it deep, turned it over and dug it up, the next crop was strong— richer and taller." In the years since the publication of *American Me,* the truly unstoppable crop has been not a plant but a people, the original colonizers not only of Watts but of all of Alta California. The metaphor of fire works not only to figure a remnant recovered from ashes but summons the passion that has driven the post-1848 migrations of Mexicans to their lost colony of California, the inevitable and enriching return of the repressed.

Mike Davis asserts that the 1992 Los Angeles riots were "as much a Latino as a Black rebellion." Of the first five thousand people arrested, 52 percent were Latino and only 39 percent Black. The 1990 census revealed a Los Angeles in which Latinos had become the most numerous group: 39.9 percent out of a total city population of 3,485,398. Whites comprised 37.3 percent; Blacks 14 percent; Asians 9.8 percent. The 1990 population ratios were much the same for Los Angeles County. For decades, the Latino population in the basin had been concentrated in the eastern part of the city, beyond the Los Angeles River. During the 1970s and 1980s, this population had begun to shift to places like Anaheim, Inglewood, and the San Fernando Valley. By 1990, 45 percent of South Central was Latino.

In 1965 the Immigration and Naturalization Act attempted to limit further national population growth by imposing a quota of 120,000 annual immigrants from Canada and Latin America. The result was a politics of exclusion that brought at least a million "illegal" Latino immigrants to California in the 1970s. In *The Fourth Wave* Thomas Muller points out that "no other area of the state experienced greater migration from Mexico between 1970 and 1980 than Los Angeles County."

In the 1980s this movement persisted, bringing more than 866,000 Mexican immigrants to the Los Angeles area. "In general," *The New York Times* reported, "the Mexicans who came to the United States between 1980 and 1990 had less education, a weaker command of English, more children, and less money than those in earlier waves of immigrants who arrived before 1980." The impact of the Mexican workers who entered the California economy during these decades was significant. Muller calculates that the "economic benefits" of their influx—especially the low wages that kept down the local cost of living—well outweighed the "fiscal deficits."

Despite this growing interdependence, 59 percent of Californians voted for Proposition 187 in 1994. In San Diego, 67.4 percent of voters favored the initiative. The measure, later curtailed by the courts, banned public services like schooling and nonemergency medical care to illegal immigrants. The vote reflected a belief that immigrants from Mexico could somehow be eliminated without cost to the local economy. In a 1996 *New York Times* article, the director of the Center for U.S.–Mexican Studies at the University of California at San Diego pointed out the irony. "Every sector of the economy here is heavily dependent on immigrants," he said. "They all draw heavily on this labor pool, and most of it is illegal. It underwrites an affluent lifestyle. But the anti-immigrant line is very popular because of all the anger. People really want to have it both ways."

ONE OF THE MOST POWERFUL testimonies to adaptation and resistance made during these years comes from Luis J. Rodriguez. His 1993 *Always Running—La Vida Loca: Gang Days in L.A.* is the story of a Mexican immigrant trying to write his way out of *la vida loca,* the crazy life of gang warfare in East Los Angeles. At the end of his narrative, Rodriguez finds himself watching an embittered gang enemy "hobble away, two confused teenagers at his side, and as he vanishes into a flicker of neon, I hear the final tempo of the crazy life leave my body, the last song before the dying, lapsing forever out of mind as Chava disappears, enveloped in flames breaking through the asphalt, wrested into the black heart of night." The closing metaphor of flames reminds the reader that the crazy life consumes its adherents, promising identity but delivering only immolation in the irresistible imperatives of the gang.

In the closing pages of his book, Luis Rodriguez writes that "fire for me has been a constant motif." The motif pervades Chicano and Mexican-American writing about life in California. It surfaces in the first chapter of a book as benign as Gary Soto's memoir of a Fresno childhood, *Living Up the Street* (1985): "Perhaps the most enjoyable summer day was when Rick, Debra, and I decided to burn down our house." When Soto writes that "a small flame lit my brain," he is describing a meanness—one generated in part by growing up brown—that his memoir works to overcome.

For Richard Rodriguez, the trope of burning focuses the issue of complexion. "My skin is brown. More exactly, terra-cotta in sunlight, tawny in shade. I do not redden in sunlight. Instead, my skin becomes progressively dark; the sun singes the flesh." Stay out of the sun, his mother urges: "With *los gringos* looks are all that they judge on. . . . You won't be satisfied till you end up looking like *los pobres* who work in the fields, *los braceros*." The sun that darkens also highlights the narrator's struggle with issues of race and class and especially with sexual life. Judging himself "dark" and therefore "ugly," Richard grows "divorced from my body." The argument he began in the 1982 *Hunger of Memory* is not resolved but continued, as the title suggests, in the 1992 *Days of*

Obligation: An Argument with My Mexican Father. There he begins to
recover and accept the colors implicit in the brown: "I used to stare at the
Indian in the mirror." In such autobiographies fire serves as a complex
metaphor for the self-destructive anger that a writer can convert into
creative assertion and even, perhaps, into what Rodriguez calls "The
Achievement of Desire."

Luis Rodriguez's deliverance from the life and from the motif of fire
is hard-won. "I was 11 years old when the 1965 Watts Rebellion tore
through my former neighborhood. At age 16, I participated in the Chicano Moratorium against the Vietnam War—the so-called East L.A.
Riot." The book begins in 1991 with another rebellion, in which Luis
chases his fifteen-year-old son down an icy Chicago street. "As I watched
his escape, it was like looking back into a distant time, back to my own
youth, when I ran and ran, when I jumped over peeling fences, fleeing
vatos locos, the police or my own shadow in some drug-induced hysteria."
Ramiro disappears, like Chava, into the night. But he has given his father
back his own story, and also his title—a poem Ramiro reads at a poetry
festival in 1992, called "Running Away."

At the age of two Luis was brought by his parents from Chihuahua to
Los Angeles. They settled in La Colonia, the oldest and the Mexican
section of Watts. After an abortive move to Reseda, the family resettled in
an unincorporated part of the county. "I hated school. And I loved
fighting," he writes. At thirteen he began banging with the Tribe, one of
the two gangs that ran South San Gabriel. He started sniffing glue, paint,
and gasoline. He shot heroin after being dumped by a prostitute and, at
the command of his gang leader, stabbed a rival with a screwdriver. He
tried to straighten out by joining the Neighborhood Youth Corps; he
worked hard and did well at boxing. In 1970 he ended up in a jail cell next
to Charles Manson after being arrested during the Chicano Moratorium
Against the War.

"You can't be in a fire and not get burned": This is his father's response
when he learns of Luis's trouble in junior high. Throughout his narrative,
Rodriguez works toward the recognition that while the condition of his
people may be fire, they can learn to channel its energies. "The Watts
Rebellion of 1965 changed forever the civil rights struggle in this country," he writes. "The fires that swept through my old neighborhood that
summer swept through me, cutting deep lines, as it swept through
America, turning it toward its greatest fears and hardest questions."

"My family (minus my mother, who was taking the picture) in Watts, 1960." Luis Rodriguez is the boy in the middle. Eleven years old when the Watts Riots destroyed his former neighborhood, Rodriguez joined a Chicano gang two years later. In 1970 he found himself in a jail cell next to Charles Manson after being arrested during the Chicano Moratorium Against the War. Captions and photographs courtesy of Luis Rodriguez.

"Me at age 16—after my release from jail following the ELA 'Riot.' "

"My son Ramiro, age 1, in Watts on top of my 1954 Chevy—1976."

"Me in East L.A. with my two children—1987."

Writing his memoir is Rodriguez's primary act of self-kindling, but the process began with his many acts of artistic and political assertion, from playwriting and Aztec dancing to mural painting to organizing a student walkout that resulted in the adoption of a course on Chicano history and culture. "Swept through me," he writes, as if the fires burning in his world raged beyond his control. Yet his book itself attests to the possible marriage of comprehending spectatorship with voluntary participation. It is precisely in its deployment and mastery of the complex metaphor of fire that *Always Running* demonstrates the capacity of the responsive and responsible individual to meet the violence from without by a salutary and transforming violence from within.

By taking up the metaphor of fire, Luis Rodriguez signals that a collective as well as an individual motion is being repeated—and completed. The first Spanish-speaking explorers to arrive on California's shores described Los Angeles as Bahia de los Fumos, Bay of Smokes. Even as early as 1542 the inversion layer over the Los Angeles basin had begun trapping the heat, heat generated in part by Indian cooking fires. Cabrillo first landed at San Diego, then sailed north to visit San Pedro, Santa Monica, and the Channel Islands. He fell and broke his arm on the island later called San Miguel, voyaged north to a point near Fort Ross, and returned to San Miguel where, in 1543, he died, perhaps from an infection in his injured arm. The Spanish would take two more centuries to complete the conquest he began, bringing with them something we call "history." Their language, customs, diseases, and accidentally imported seeds swept like a fire through California, inaugurating the cycles of catastrophic change that have been the subject of this book.

To live with this history can be like living with the hot Santa Ana winds, which may be "to accept," as Joan Didion argues, "a deeply mechanistic view of human behavior." To structure that history as a sequence of five fires may seem to suggest, as Rodriguez writes, that such history sweeps through us as a force beyond our control. Rodriguez knows that his people have lost their original colony, and he knows how often they live as aliens within it. Yet he finds a way to write his way out of the determinism that would see the history of his people, or any history, as merely fated. "There's a small but intense fire burning in Ramiro," Rodriguez concludes about his son. The word *in* is the hopeful one, a token of the power of language and imagination to alter the terms and conditions of our lives. *In* is the simple preposition that argues that individuals, like the communities that sustain them, can educate themselves toward an understanding of their place in history and of the political dimensions of rebellion, thereby externalizing its power as they internalize the fire.

EPILOGUE

On a warm December night in 1995, my wife and I went to hear Bruce Springsteen sing at Constitution Hall. He was on tour solo with a few guitars, doing songs from a new album called *The Ghost of Tom Joad*. I hadn't heard the album, but I hold Springsteen and Steinbeck in high regard, so the evening held, for me, considerable promise. It turned out to be a transforming emotional and intellectual event, one that confirmed and also redirected the argument of this book.

After Ann and I found our seats near the top and the back of the auditorium, we watched the crowd file in. Most of the people looked middle aged, like us, with a scattering of groups in their thirties and twenties. Most took their seats quietly, but near us, sitting on the stairs, a pumped-up guy in tight jeans talked loudly with his friends. "I'm a Boss Man," I heard him say, and I knew he had come for the Loud Noise, that wall of sound that has poured out over standing, cheering crowds, like a blessing, from the drums and the guitars of the E Street Band and its successors for over twenty years. From what I'd heard, that wasn't the kind of music, on this evening, he was likely to get.

Cries of "BROO-CE, BROO-CE" began to go up. They sounded strangely like boos. The hall has great sight lines—it's an uninterrupted rectangle with a curved ceiling—and superb acoustics, so the noise swelled and carried. Given his stadium concerts of the mid-eighties, the three-thousand-seat hall was, for Springsteen, an almost intimate space. It was also a space that the DAR had refused to make available, in 1939, for a concert by Marian Anderson because she was black. 1939 was also the year in which Tom Joad first made his way from Oklahoma to California, on the pages of Steinbeck's book.

The lights went down. When they came back up, I saw a man about my size standing in a funnel of light. He picked up a harp rack and a six-string acoustic guitar. He began singing a song that opened with the words "Men walkin' long the railroad tracks." The place he sang about sounded strangely familiar. It was made up of underpasses and highway patrol choppers and nights warm enough for just a campfire and a sleeping bag. When he got to bathing in the city aqueduct, I was home, knew where I stood, and remembered that a few years back Springsteen had settled down in Los Angeles. By the end of the song, Springsteen had positioned himself around one of those campfires, a fire burning not in 1939 but in 1995, sittin' down here in the campfire light, waitin' on the ghost of old Tom Joad. The song ended by quoting the words from Tom's farewell speech to Ma, where he promises her that wherever people are hungry or beaten or looking for a place to stand, "I'll be there."

Springsteen sang the lyrics in a deep, haunted voice, and I heard every word. Most of the Springsteen songs I knew rode down their lyrics with an overwhelming beat—they were less about reception than transport. He had chosen to make the words of this song *audible*. In order for this strategy to work, the crowd had to stay quiet. During the second, down-beat song, the crowd began to get restless, and my friend on the stairs again began yelling "BROO-CE!" When the song ended, Springsteen paused, then said that tonight he had to ask the crowd's unique coopera-tion. "These songs were mostly written in silence," he told us, and that's what he asked for—and received—for the rest of the night. Even the Boss Man quieted down.

I honestly can't remember the order in which he sang his new songs; I wasn't paying that kind of attention. I do know that he sang about Sinaloa cowboys who come up from Mexico to cook methamphetamine in a shack on a Fresno chicken ranch. There was a song about a border agent along the San Diego line who allows Louisa to slip through one night and then quits the line to search for her in the bars of the Central Valley. In "Balboa Park," the border boys came out from under the freeways in the cool of the evening to offer their services to the men in their Mercedes. A man looking for work in another song hoes sugar beets outside Firebaugh and picks peaches from the Marysville trees.

Border and line; these were the words I kept hearing, and they argued that Springsteen's imagination had migrated to a new place. While he also sang about the abandoned steel mills in Youngstown and the Vietnamese fishermen in Galveston Bay, it was clear that this place was a tormented and magnetic new True West, a California increasingly defined not by the people it was letting in but, as had been true for the Joads, by the people it was trying to keep out. The need to patrol the "line," to cross or define or manage a "border," bespoke another dark chapter in the history of a state where a mystique of invitation has traditionally operated, as Springsteen had so recently discovered, to mask a stubbornly recurring politics of exclusion.

This is why the most heartbreakingly beautiful song he sang that night—the one most able to satisfy the romantic longing for solace and communion and transcendence that the Boss Man and most of the rest of the crowd had brought with them into the hall that night—was called "Across the Border." A man dreams of meeting his love "on the other side," somewhere across the border. They will drink from the Bravo's muddy water. It is not clear whether they plan to head north or south; they just want to cross over. And not to El Norte, the land of money and power, or down to Mexico, the land of origins and warmth. Here Springsteen imagines a crossing over to a land without limits, a realm like Mary Austin's Inyo of the mind, the land of Lost Borders, a place where politics and need and race and gender and difference itself—where all those hard facts Springsteen sings so well about—fall away.

The song that follows "Across the Border" on the album is called "My Best Was Never Good Enough." In it, Springsteen repeats, and by repeating rejects, the self-pitying and delusional clichés on which so much of our public and private life, in the United States, is founded. He even repeats the line of recent movie fame, "Life's like a box of chocolates." In the withering irony of this closing song, Springsteen distances himself from the Forrest Gumpism that doles out American history in sugar-coated vignettes. *Forrest Gump* disdains analysis and consequence and gives back an image of the past fifty years as best negotiated by an idiot. To the burning question, How did we get from there to here? the movie answers, By magic and goodwill!

As a native rather than a transplanted Californian, this is the question I set out to address in the writing of *Five Fires*. Springsteen's performance that night reinforced my sense of the urgency of the task. What looked like diverging paths had carried us both to a similar place. Born in 1949, in Freehold, New Jersey, Springsteen had eventually moved West to settle in Los Angeles in the early 1990s. Born in South Central Los Angeles in 1948, I had gone east, to Virginia, to seek my fortune in the university. At middle age we found ourselves arrested by the same sense of conflict and breakdown that had compelled another migrant between East and West, Joan Didion, into the Haight-Ashbury of the late 1960s. Hers were the strategies I had long admired and that inspired my first book on California. But they were the strategies of a spectator, a critic, someone who, with immense intelligence and an almost unlawful verbal gift, stands back to let it all be. What I liked about Springsteen's performance was that he took it all on, that he identified and entered in, and that he had the courage to sing in the voices of people or about the lives of people whom he could never become, but whom he struggled to care about and to understand.

Springsteen also refused to reduce his material to spectacle. The vast, ear-splitting concerts are terrific fun, and I am as content as the next fan to shake my fist in the air along with thirty thousand others during the chorus of "Born to Run." The power of such moments is in creating an illusion of community through synchronized motion and a volume of sound. But at forty-seven a little triumph of the will goes a long way. The power of the Constitution Hall concert lay in its silence. Springsteen appeared alone onstage, sang with minimal amplification, displayed a commitment to the craft of guitar-playing. He provided a model of one person alone with his thoughts, with the means of giving them expressive form. The performance enjoined a model of community not gained through the ecstatic merging of a roaring crowd but in the simultaneous but silent inwardness of citizens thinking and feeling about the borders that connect and separate them.

Springsteen also provided an example of how culture gets passed down, especially in a place like California, so dedicated to forgetting. In talking about the Tom Joad song, Springsteen allowed that he had come across the story of the immigrants from Oklahoma through the 1940 John Ford movie. From the way he quoted Tom's speech, one Tom delivers in the Central Valley and before leaving Ma perhaps forever, it was not clear that Springsteen had ever read the novel on which the movie is based.

Instead of disturbing the English professor in me, this cheered me up. In 1939 Steinbeck brought out a "slow but sure" book, as he called it, and in the year following its publication John Ford made of it an Academy Award–winning film. Twenty or thirty years later, a singer-songwriter from New Jersey saw the movie, remembered it, and when he needed it, made of the movie a song. The song not only gives new life to the Ford masterpiece but takes its place within a larger work of art (the album) entirely in sympathy with the anger and sorrow of a novel that the songwriter may never have read. However the transmission occurred, Steinbeck's Tom Joad lives. And he lives in 1995, and can kindle Springsteen's imagination, because the California to which he has so recently moved continues to sow the grapes of wrath.

"Welcome to the new world order," Springsteen sings, in the sixth line of the first song. It is the most knowing line on the album. Just as the 1982 album *Nebraska* marked one of the decade's most eloquent protests against the greed and unconcern of the Reagan years, so *The Ghost of Tom Joad* does essential cultural work in the mid-1990s. It locates the threats to "order" firmly in California, and it does so not only because the state happens to be the artist's immediate home but because California is the place in which, by virtue of the history of the past two hundred years, the greatest number of borders meet.

Springsteen's ongoing performance renews a contract between artist and audience that descends from so many California natives, settlers, and sojourners, from Pablo Tac, sailing away forever on his ship to Rome, to Jade Snow Wong, working her way through Mills and into a writing career, to Luis Rodriguez, chasing his son down an icy Chicago street. It is the promise that a voice will arise that listens to and helps us to hear California's many voices. "Pay attention," a speaker says in *Twilight*. That is what we are asked to do. If we do so, if we enter into the offered dialogue, see beyond the catastrophes and through the spectacles, try to hear this place steadily and hear it whole, imagine its many communities and its many lives, perhaps we can, in the quiet of the silences, negotiate a future.

NOTES

PROLOGUE

1 "not to stay": *Praise,* 29.

1 "The city burning": *Slouching Towards Bethlehem,* 220.

2 "the entire catastrophe": Clappe, 147.

3 "I found that": Dana, 503.

3 "His style": Lawrence, 123.

3 *"melange":* Dana, 222.

4 "fine specimen": Ibid., 134.

4 "The Spanish": Ibid., 221–22.

5 "Every Kanaka": Ibid., 207.

5 "such as I": Ibid., 357.

5 "positively alone": Ibid., 197.

5 "The single body": Ibid., 158.

5 "hated coast": Ibid., 362.

6 "face burnt": Ibid., 458.

6 "that there are": *History of California,* Vol. I, 14.

7 "It's all falling": Snyder, 46.

7 "Every China Man": *China Men,* 150.

THE WILD OAT *The Spanish and American Conquests*

11 "delicious monotony": Harte, 107.

12 "You stay": Theodora Kroeber, 238.

13 "received one hundred": Hastings, 89.

13 "the Brobdignag": *New Pictures from California,* 8.

14 "Upon one table": Ibid., 9.

14 "perhaps grown": Burbank, 262.

14 "it becomes": Ibid., 372.

15 "human plant": Ibid., 349.

18 "invasion . . . catastrophe": Bakker, 149.

18 "When mother nature": Anderson, 15.

19 "entire Central Valley": Preston, 56.

19 "the wild oat": Hittell, 104.

19 "over-advertised": Bolton, xviii.

20 "city of one": Dana, 499.

20 "Some five": Ibid., 498.

20 "Now I will": Bolton, 22–23.

21 "I am greatly": Ibid., 19.

22 "deep chasms": Leonard, 129.

22 "incredibly large": Ibid., 136.

22 "if the ships": Bolton, 30.

23 "humane tenderheartedness": Royce, *California,* 26.

23 "Civilized warfare": Ibid., 25.

24 "The condition": Ibid., 39.

25 "we must understand": Ibid., 40.

25 "character": Ibid., 3.

25 "mystery": Ibid., 67.

25 "It is a curious": Ibid., 106.

26 "The whole interview": Ibid., 96.

26 "I was bearer": Ibid., 103.

27 "brought a dispatch": Ibid., 91.

27 "substance . . . of letters": Ibid., 92.

27 "How fate pursues": Frémont, vol. 2, 107.

28 "Your letter": Royce, *California,* 104–5.

28 "sister republic": Ibid., 107.

28 "brethren": Ibid., 108.

28 "exasperate beyond": Ibid., 110.

28 "no reader": Ibid., 111.

28 "afterthought": Ibid., 115.

28 "Thomas O. Larkin, Esq": Ibid., 113–14.

29 "I have meanwhile": Ibid., 117.

31 "split voice": Rosaura Sanchez, 8.

31 "he and California": Padilla, 85.

31 "was known to favor": Beck and Williams, 118.

31 "a legend grew": *Americans and the California Dream,* 29.

32 "a soldier who": *Heath Anthology of American Literature,* vol. 1, 1955.

32 "to regain a loss": Padilla, 9.

32 "The recent arrivals": *Heath Anthology,* 1955.

33 "the common rights": Royce, *California,* 60.

33 "we are robbers": Ibid., 57.

33 "a jar filled": *Heath Anthology,* 1959.

33 "The flag was": Ibid., 1957.

34 "If the men": Ibid., 1960.

34 "queer flag": Ibid., 1957.

34 "true character": Ibid., 1960.

34 "had filled us": Ibid., 1960.

34 "Ill-advisedly": Ibid., 1960–61.

35 "change of flags": Machado, 200.

35 "catch an Indian": Serra, vol. 1, 363.

35 "This lady is A": Machado, 195.

36 "All the weddings": Ibid., 207.

36 "When I was": Ibid., 199.

36 "hated": Ibid., 212.

38 "The Jamul episode": Sanchez, 144.

38 "When he went": Machado, 204.

38 "He said that": Ibid., 205.

39 "A great multitude": Englehardt, 4.

39 "fearful creatures": Monroy, 41.

40 "final outcome": Royce, *California,* 14.

41 "any inclination": Geiger, 479.

41 "We notice": Ibid., 487.

42 "the first writing": Tac, 87.

42 "Always there was war": Ibid., 93.

42 "What is it": Ibid., 94.

43 "place where *posole*": Ibid., 96.

43 "none of the neophytes": Ibid., 97.

43 "Once a neophyte": Ibid., 97–98.

45 "In the annals": *Days of Obligation,* 22.

45 "The Sanjuaneños": Tac, 106.

46 "A few days before": Machado, 217.

47 "My brother succeeded": Ibid., 218.

48 "change of flag in 1822": Ibid., 200.

48 "Since then": Ibid., 217.

48 "oppositional": Padilla, 211.

48 "During the twilight": Bryant, 364–65.

49 "The hills": Ibid., 364.

THE GOLD RUSH: *Men Without Women*

51 "commotion": Harte, 7.

51 "Nature": Ibid., 69.

51 "Ages will not": *El Dorado,* 69.

52 "there was as much": Ibid., 78.

52 "He saw, for instance": *California,* 239.

52 "quarters in the loft": *New Pictures from California,* 1.

52 "There was nothing": Ibid., 5.

52 "grandeur": Ibid., 81.

52 "enough material": McPhee, 66.

52 "the earth seemed": *New Pictures,* 113.

52 "a land where": Ibid., 133.

53 "It is a question": Bidwell, 111.

53 "Gold miners": Harte, 290.

54 "sociology of good luck": *The Great Exception,* 61.

54 "Do you know": Delano, 48.

54 "in the afternoon": Borthwick, 286.

54 "California can": Helper, 68.

55 "invested upwards": Ibid., 158.

55 "lives lost": Ibid., 27.

55 "country of unparalleled": Ibid., 38.

55 "A California conflagration": Ibid., 144.

55 "sundry fires": Ibid., 27.

55 "One of the most beautiful": Ibid., 144.

56 "a national tragedy": Holliday, 495.

56 "a society of lonely men": Ibid., 454.

56 "It was difficult, Burnett, 301.

56 "unlike any other country": Holliday, 369.

56 "You see no women here": Ibid., 308.

56 "Got nearer": Ibid., 355.

56 "may have constituted": Jeffrey, 120.

56 "At that period": Farnham, 22–23.

57 "company of females": Ibid., 24.

57 "privations": Ibid., 25.

57 "the third is": Ibid., 27.

57 "a female friend": Ibid., 41.

57 "There is little": Ibid., 155.

57 "will feel herself": Ibid., 156.

57 "theatre of unrest": Ibid., 330.

57 "a woman of genius": Ibid., 158.

57 "theory and practice": Ibid., 170.

57 "a universal sense": Ibid., 292.

58 "The true worth": Ibid., 383.

58 "the family circle": Holliday, 443.

59 "I have written": Ibid., 348.

60 "I should ever": Ibid., 361.

60 "There was some talk": Ibid., 319.

60 "We cannot realize": Ibid., 173.

60 "It wasn't getting here". *The Long Valley,* 225.

61 "I have always": Holliday, 98.

61 "crucifixion of feeling": Ibid., 258.

61 "I want very much": Ibid., 80.

61 "O! William": Ibid., 223.

61 "I often dream": Ibid., 224.

62 "My anxieties": Ibid., 85.

62 "Not only my back": Ibid., 138–39.

62 "Never, until your absence": Ibid., 294.

62 "My feelings are such": Ibid., 139.

62 "Poor pa": Ibid., 387.

63 "I was attacked": Ibid., 443.

63 "He looked": Ibid., 444.

63 "I have been": Ibid., 445.

63 "To my '49er": Ibid., 450.

63 *"mineress"*: Clappe, 74.

63 "California herself": Ibid., 19.

64 "innocent of a floor": Ibid., 176.

64 "are so very uneven": Ibid., 20.

64 "Guiltless of glass": Ibid., 52.

64 "carpentering as a child": Ibid., 21.

64 "no place for a lady": Ibid., 50.

64 "by the sound": Ibid., 39.

64 "I find it difficult": Ibid., 116.

64 "as all men cannot": Ibid., 39.

64 "those unfortunates": Ibid., 21.

64 "excessive egotism": Ibid., 18.

65 "formations": Ibid., 25.

65 "He sings": Ibid., 80.

65 "home-sickness": Ibid., 81.

65 "beloved solitude": Ibid., 82.

65 "power of language": Ibid., 47.

65 "How oddly": Ibid., 34.

65 "we have had murders": Ibid., 145.

65 "dish of horrors": Ibid., 156.

65 "majestic-looking Spaniard": Ibid., 146.

65 "Down with the Spaniards": Ibid., 147.

66 "To many foreign miners": Burns, 45.

66 "the arm": Clappe, 146.

66 "The first act": Ibid., 150.

66 *"wife"*: Ibid., 79.

66 "stained": Ibid., 18.

67 "invalid": Ibid., 198.

67 "the use of Anglo-Saxon": Horsman, 208–9.

68 "the lawless and desperate men": Ridge, 9.

68 "before his eyes": Ibid., 10.

68 "Then it was": Ibid., 12–13.

68 "There were two": Ibid., 7.

68 "I can't help it": Ibid., 64.

68 "mild and peaceable": Ibid., 8.

68 "the soul": Ibid., 10.

68 "His soul swelled": Ibid., 12.

69 "a war of the races": Pitt, 166.

69 "equalize": Ibid., 160.

69 "a deep-seated principle": Walker, 48.

69 *"wiped out* the most": Ridge, 13.

70 "thirty-six men": Walker, 48.

70 "Only his wiry": Ibid., 49.

70 "long, glossy black hair": Ridge, 9.

70 "He caused the head": Ibid., 156.

71 "The jar with the head": *Days of Obligation,* 144–45.

71 "He has found": Ibid., 145.

71 "I look away": Ibid., 147.

71 " 'Es bastante' ": Burns, 275.

71 "Don't shoot any more": Ridge, 153.

72 "We are of the opinion": Foner, 18.

72 "no encouragement": Harte, 15.

73 "There were so few women": Brooks, 201.

73 "Imperialist nostalgia": Rosaldo, 68.

74 "It was that glorious": Harte, 107.

74 "used sex for sentiment": Henry Adams, 1071.

75 "last 'Greaser' ": Harte, 139.

75 "vulgar clamor": Ibid., 144.

75 "set upon and killed": Ibid., 208.

75 "available memory": Ibid., 278.

75 "get even": Ibid., 281.

76 "dissolute, abandoned": Ibid., 7.

76 "Nature." Ibid., 12.

76 "the d—d little cuss": Ibid., 10.

76 "The tall red-woods": Ibid., 15.

76 "With the prosperity": Ibid., 16.

77 "evasion of emotion": Ibid., 251.

EXCLUSION, THE CHINESE, AND THE DAUGHTER'S ARRIVAL

78 "He did not know": *China Men,* 59.

79 "Only males were brought": *East of Eden,* 358.

79 "A little boulder": Ibid., 360.

80 "Family development": Tong, xvii.

80 "filthy": Foner, 210–11.

81 "China rampant": London, vol. 2, 1237.

81 "a vast and happy": Ibid., 1245.

81 "The local prejudice": Dooner, 17.

82 "a corps of observation": Ibid., 20.

82 "I have not been": Ibid., 21.

82 "a scheme of immigration": Ibid., 28.

82 "she saw that": Ibid., 190.

82 "The very name": Ibid., 256–57.

82 "peculiarity": Ibid., 122–23.

84 "We have read": Speer, 578.

84 "Now, the natives of China": Foner, 76–77.

84 "the people of the Flowery land": Ibid., 77.

85 "abandoned women": Speer, 600.

85 "Almost all Chinese prostitutes": Tong, 54.

86 "four loathsome diseases": Takaki, 121.

87 "Innocent men ruined": *Chinese Immigration,* v.

87 "great deal of gold": Park, 31.

87 "shield her mother": Ibid., 32.

88 "I have left you": Ibid., 34.

88 "A son is a human": Ibid., 34–35.

90 "Let us now look": Sucheng Chan, 104.

92 "The dynamite added": *China Men,* 136.

92 "what a man was": Ibid., 144.

92 " 'What's the catch?' ": Ibid., 139.

92 " 'Eight hours a day' ": Ibid., 140.

92 "The Central Pacific announced": Ibid., 144.

92 "untold hordes": Coolidge, 65.

93 "a dispute concerning": Dorney, 231.

93 "It is obvious": Foner, 84.

93 "bade the man": Coolidge, 115.

93 "They work": Speer, 526.

93 "I must employ": Takaki, 28.

94 "The Central Pacific people": Takaki, 87.

94 "too much fire": Tan, 19.

94 "you have fire": *Fifth Chinese Daughter,* 225.

94 "element of Fire": Eaton, 95.

95 *"perfect American English"*: Tan, 3.

95 "heroine": Ling, 120.

95 "when Mrs. Spring Fragrance": Eaton, 10.

96 "the common uses of women": Ibid., 65.

96 "the secret talk of women": Ibid., 3.

96 "May the bamboo": Ibid., 7.

97 "It was there between us": Ibid., 139.

98 "the Mother of Chinese": Ling, 120.

98 "Although a 'first person singular' ": Wong, vii.

98 "I tell the story": Ibid., 2.

98 "centered around Jade Snow's": Ibid., 90–91.

98 "Today we recognize": Ibid., 125.

99 "full meaning": Ibid., 127.

99 "Sons must have priority": Ibid., 108–9.

100 "unfilial theory": Ibid., 128.

100 "I am an individual": Ibid., 125.

100 "You can't compete": Ibid., 234.

100 "The answer which came": Ibid., 235.

100 "Chinese did not": Ibid., 244.

100 "You do not realize": Ibid., 246.

101 "immodest": Ibid., vii.

101 "They wrote to me": Ling, 137.

101 "My father has asked": Tan, 5.

102 "I have a story": Ibid., 24.

103 "the Kweilin story": Ibid., 12.

103 "told me a completely": Ibid., 13.

103 "We have something important": Ibid., 29.

103 "So your aunties": Ibid., 29–30.

103 "What can I tell them": Ibid., 31.

104 "Suyuan didn't tell me": Ibid., 321.

104 "good leftover stuff": Ibid., 323.

104 "they have died": Ibid., 328.

104 "eyes, her same mouth": Ibid., 332.

105 "Why do you think": Ibid., 13.

105 "to despair": Ibid., 11–12.

THE SAN FRANCISCO EARTHQUAKE AND FIRE:
The Culture of Spectacle

107 "I hope they'll treat": *The Letters of William James,* 248.

108 "Sitting up involuntarily": James, *Memories and Studies,* 210.

108 "earthquake is simply": Ibid., 213.

109 "consciously or unconsciously": *Slouching Towards Bethlehem,* 217.

109 "gleeful recognition": *Memories and Studies,* 210.

109 "sensation and emotion": Ibid., 210–11.

109 "the rapidity": Ibid., 221.

109 "universal equanimity": Ibid., 224.

110 "casual when you knew": Hulme, 79.

110 "possible to visit": Himmelwright, 7.

111 "subjected to normal fire": Ibid., 63.

111 "Avoid Locations": Ibid., 268.

112 " 'Ell of a place!": Genthe, 89.

112 "decided to try": Ibid., 33.

112 "Every paper a China Man": *China Men,* 150.

116 "There are two islands": Shawn Wong, 95.

116 "one Chinese woman": Yung, 62.

117 "The sea-scape resembles": Lai, 34.

118 "If the land": Ibid., 92.

118 "Perhaps, I thought": Genthe, 41.

118 "terrifying sound": Ibid., 87.

118 "that the most suitable": Ibid., 88.

119 "For several weeks": Ibid., 94.

121 "I'm a California photographer": Adams, *An Autobiography,* 124.

121 "top man": Adams, *Letters and Images,* 125.

122 " 'Why didn't I print' ": *An Autobiography,* 204.

122 "At five-fifteen the next morning": Ibid., 7.

123 "I tumbled against": Ibid., 7–8.

123 "I have heard an estimate": Ibid., 9.

123 "America is a land": *Letters and Images,* 109.

123 "The promise of the world": Ibid., 258.

124 "Perhaps we must go": Ibid., 198.

124 "happier than almost anyone": Ibid., 153.

125 "tender": Muir, *The Mountains of California,* 16.

125 "Glaciers work apart": Muir, *To Yosemite and Beyond,* 80.

125 "terrible ice-engines": *Mountaineering in the Sierra Nevada,* 37.

125 "was distinctly catastrophic": King, "Catastrophism and the Evolution of Environment," 16.

126 "I will always remember": *Letters and Images,* 59.

126 "neat, clean, clear-cut technique": Ibid., 30.

126 "There was light everywhere": *An Autobiography,* 53.

126 "From that time on": *Letters and Images,* 151.

126 "crystal days": Ibid., 170.

126 "No pain here": Muir, *The Yosemite,* 131.

127 "Transcendental": *Letters and Images,* 233.

127 "crytalization of perception": Ibid., 38.

127 "crystal incisiveness": *An Autobiography,* 4.

127 "I remain the same": *Letters and Images,* 348.

127 "There are always": Adams, *Yosemite and the Range of Light,* 15.

127 "What is lonely": A. C. Bradley, 142.

127 "Even in portraying": *Letters and Images,* 6.

127 "Elevation": Ibid., 291.

128 "I wonder if I am": Ibid., 296.

128 "The subject is": Ibid., 285.

128 "One bright Yosemite day": *An Autobiography,* 73.

128 "my first true visualization": Ibid., 76.

129 *"How it felt to me"*: *Slouching Towards Bethlehem,* 134.

129 "Public presentation": *Letters and Images,* 33.

131 "the whole problem": Ibid., 206.

131 "To me the essence": Ibid., 207.

131 "a *regime* which is": Ibid., 172.

131 "the price of things": *Slouching Towards Bethlehem,* 145.

132 "Few American cities": *Days of Obligation,* 27–28.

THE POLITICS OF WATER: *The Shift South*

135 "cleared the way": *Washington Post,* Jan. 27, 1994.

137 "greatest unnatural disaster": Kahrl, 313.

138 "The failure was due": Margaret Leslie Davis, 231.

138 "no more reason": Ibid., 192.

139 "the one universally acknowledged": *Material Dreams,* 50.

140 "long brown land": Mary Austin, *The Land of Little Rain,* 11.

140 "Strange things": *Earth Horizon,* 307–8.

140 "the history of California": Kahrl, 1.

141 "straight history": Herr, 51.

141 "The Los Angeles River": Kahrl, 20.

142 "public owned": Ibid., 54.

142 "the possible sources": Ibid., 59.

145 "Perhaps more than": Lotchin, 68–69.

145 "the Mulholland political": Nordskog, 28.

145 *"The Federal Government"*: Mayo, 246.

146 "the government held": Chalfant (1922 edition), 329.

146 "great creators": Ostrom, 78.

146 "far more complex": Hoffman, xv.

146 "unwitting victim": Ibid., 273.

146 "Probably no character": Kahrl, 439.

146 "sincere in his belief": Ibid., 58.

146 "comically ineffectual": Ibid., 439.

146 "never conceived": Ibid., 48.

146 "somewhat less than": Ibid., 440.

146 "tragedy": Ibid., 441.

147 "I didn't base": Brady, 414.

147 "grainy but unmistakably": Robert Towne, *Chinatown* (Third Draft), 1.

148 "No script ever drove": McGilligan, 249.

148 "reading Chandler": Brady, 416–17.

148 "I was in L.A.": *Roman, By Polanski,* 347.

148 "Evelyn had to die": Ibid., 348.

151 "EVELYN (*continuing*)": Towne, *Chinatown* (Third Draft), 128.

152 "about the thirties": Roman, 349.

WORLD WAR II: *Los Angeles and the Production of Anger*

156 "too often come": *California,* 394.

157 "federal captivity": Limerick, 46.

158 "in its extremes": Robert Murray Davis, 21.

158 "the distress in which": Didion, "The Golden Land." 93.

160 "There are no countries": McShane, 21.

161 "I never slept": Ibid., 59.

161 "A long time ago": *The Little Sister,* 202.

162 "the bright gardens": *The Big Sleep,* 215.

162 "everything is like": Ibid., 176.

162 "the most of everything": *The Little Sister,* 170.

163 "most of the aircraft": Gerald Nash, *World War II and the West,* 76.

163 "At the detective": Lundquist, 1.

163 "Los Angeles hurt": *The Quality of Hurt,* 73.

163 "All of a sudden": *If He Hollers Let Him Go,* 9.

163 "I felt better": Ibid., 110.

164 "I noticed": Ibid., 177.

164 "The pressure": Ibid., 169.

164 "I didn't feel": Ibid., 182.

165 "To me it was racial": Ibid., 14.

165 "race was a handicap": Ibid., 3.

165 "in any incident": Ibid., 168.

165 "two Mexican youths": Ibid., 203.

165 "you were the first": Ibid., 202.

165 "Looks like this man": Ibid., 203.

166 "Your war is on": *Zoot Suit,* 30.

167 "white men": Meier, 26.

167 "top picker": Ibid., 110.

169 "In the souls": *The Grapes of Wrath,* 477.

169 "Grapes must remain": Moquin, 365.

169 "defense plants": Meier, 127.

169 "The Zoot suits they wore": Thomas Sanchez, 3.

170 "biological": Meier, 130.

170 "hoodlums": *Los Angeles Times,* August 3, 1942.

171 "youngsters of Mexican descent": McWilliams, *North From Mexico,* 244.

171 "the police had worked out": Ibid., 247.

171 "The zoot suit is": *Gravity's Rainbow,* 289.

172 *"Panzer*-division": *Time,* June 21, 1943, 18.

172 "disregard for human life": Meier, 129.

172 "desire is to kill": Ibid., 131.

174 "weird sexual activity": Griffith, 321.

174 "little tornadoes": Ibid., 47.

174 "The Mexican *pachuquitas"*: Servin, 152.

174 "Those kids were getting it": Griffith, 8.

175 "as though it was her husband": Jacobs, 34.

175 "The Slaves We Rent": Meier, 161.

175 "a roundedness": Horsman, 234.

176 "The women have but": Dana, 236.

176 "with grace and spirit": Ibid., 317.

176 "loose . . . bare": Ibid., 126.

176 "mockery of the patriarchy": Rosaldo, 149.

176 "The Mexicans": Cisneros, 12.

177 "rigid sex role expectations": Alarcón, 172.

177 *"eight-hundred years"*: López-Medina, 162.

177 "who do we choose": Alarcón, 48.

177 "señorita": Ponce, 332.

177 "she reached the very edge": Alma Luz Villanueva, 259.

178 "essentially of the forties": Morris, 85.

178 "somewhere near the heart": Ibid., 88.

178 "These Second World War": "Trouble in Lakewood," 47.

180 "Males are encouraged": Ibid., 64.

180 "The sad, bad times": Ibid., 60.

180 "artificial": Ibid., 48.

180 "There are a lot": Ibid., 64.

180 "the number of workers": *Washington Post,* May 19, 1996.

181 "In April": "Trouble in Lakewood," 62.

RELOCATION, THE JAPANESE, AND THE TWICE DIVORCED

182 "it is nowhere": Isamu Noguchi, *A Sculptor's World,* 170.

184 "all resident Japanese": Heizer, 170.

184 "Once a Japanese": *California and the Oriental,* 198.

185 "If Japan and the United States": Heizer, 186.

185 "My first sensation": Yone Noguchi, *The Story of Yone Noguchi,* 1.

187 "A sudden turning": Ibid., 8.

187 "requires no fewer": Marberry, 56.

188 "the most natural man": *The Story of Yone Noguchi,* 59.

188 "fully lived": Ibid., 71.

188 "Tomb of the Unknown Singers": *American Diary of a Japanese Girl,* 184.

188 "high seasoning": Ibid., 75.

189 "I felt in my heart": *The Story of Yone Noguchi,* 167.

189 "Maybe he didn't": Yone Noguchi, *Selected Writings,* vol. 1, 43.

189 "a language of silence": *The Story of Yone Noguchi,* 232.

189 "the real heart": Ibid., 222.

189 "the full urge": Ibid., 239.

189 "by the duality": Ashton, 11.

189 "More than any other immigrant": Heizer, 180.

190 "This 'interview' ": *California and the Oriental,* 155.

191 "the people of California": Ibid., 9.

191 "sudden removal": Ibid., 118.

191 "out of nothing": Pagus, 81.

193 "Edgar Hoover's special report": Sone, 157–58.

193 "the very *absence*": Klein, 78.

194 "In our isolated world": *Farewell to Manzanar,* 131–32.

194 "My memories": Ibid., 162.

194 "Now, having seen it": Ibid., 169–70.

195 "I have been accused": Ansel Adams, *An Autobiography,* 260.

196 "sadness": Mori, 125.

196 "walled in": Ibid., 117.

197 "This thing fills me": *The Long Valley,* 61.

197 "taste the silence": Mori, 25.

197 "it is her day": Ibid., 166.

197 "She is still alive": Ibid., 25.

197 "Long ago": Ibid., 15.

198 "Turn back?": Ibid., 16.

198 "If there were no war": Ibid., 21.

199 "Come back": Ibid., 20.

199 "Today I would": Uchida, 148.

199 "Why did you": Ibid., 147.

199 "It was *before camp*": Yamauchi, *Songs My Mother Taught Me,* 3.

200 "Promise me": Yamamoto, *Seventeen Syllables and Other Stories,* 19.

200 "Do you know": Ibid., 18.

201 "our possibilities must": Mirikitani, 150.

202 "there was a subtle": Yamauchi, 34.

202 "I know now": Ibid., 38.

203 "my mother's malaise": Ibid., 36.

FROM WATTS TO SOUTH CENTRAL: *Internalizing the Fire*

204 "the friendly Caucasian city": Horne, 27.

207 "if the white man": Elman, 27.

207 "minority group": Ibid., 27.

208 "It's racial *déjà vu*": *Washington Post,* August 24, 1994.

208 "Blacks structure space": Marchand, 209.

210 " 'melting pot' area": Lipsitz, 373.

210 "residential expansion": Marchand, 209.

211 "The search for causes": Robert M. Fogelson, *The Los Angeles Riots of 1965,*
    26.

211 "while the Negro districts": Ibid., 3.

211 "when the rioting came": Ibid., 4–5.

212 "riff-raff theory": Ibid., 118.

212 "many Negroes": Ibid., 27.

212 "extreme statements": Ibid., 93.

212 "a full share": Ibid., 94.

212 "I do not believe": Ibid., 95–96.

212 "conviction that": Ibid., 120.

212 "dealing with forces": Norris, 1037.

212 "manifestations": Fogelson, 143.

212 "moralistic": Ibid., 152.

213 "disjuncture": Cohen, 141.

213 "the one thread which ran": Ibid., 247–50.

214 "Mistreatment or exploitation": Ibid., 250.

214 "Los Angeles could have": Horne, 184.

214 "in order for a revolution": Millikin, 294.

215 "the culture industry": Horkheimer and Adorno, 139.

215 "Los Angeles, more than": "A Journey into the Heart of Watts," 78.

215 "If the riots": Cohen, 720.

216 "Some observers expect": *Los Angeles Times,* January 16, 1992.

216 "there isn't any way": "The 'Rodney King' Case," Court TV Video.

216 "smiling": *Washington Post,* September 28, 1995.

217 "something other than": Anna Deavere Smith, 232.

217 "hard outlines": Ibid., 233.

217 "a unifying voice": Ibid., xxv.

218 "relatively spontaneous": Gurr, 11.

218 "riot is the voice": Smith, 162.

218 "It is 3rd March 1991": Robert Gooding-Williams, *Reading Rodney King / Reading Urban Uprising,* 42.

219 "cocked": Koon, 247.

219 "Folsom Roll": Ibid., 42.

219 "There is no evidence": Ibid., 238.

219 "escalate and de-escalate": Ibid., 62.

219 "you will not be asked": Ibid., 12.

219 "to prove that Rodney King": Ibid., 182.

220 "Now I *know*": Ibid., 37.

220 "crucial first two seconds": Ibid., 131.

220 "the jury's verdict": Ibid., 192.

220 "he was dead set": Smith, 68.

220 "Viewed continuously": Koon, 131.

221 "The attorney's new critical": Gooding-Williams, 44.

221 "The Rodney King video tape": Koon, 235.

221 "spectrum of aggression": "The 'Rodney King' Case," Court TV Video.

222 "those who watched": Koon, 161.

222 "racial constraints": Gooding-Williams, 16.

223 "I'm just trying to create": *Los Angeles Times,* "Calendar," April 25, 1993.

223 "is not really": Smith, xxi.

224 "When I was": Ibid., 2.

224 "This book is first": Ibid., xxiv.

224 "hearing him holler": Ibid., xx.

225 "finally got": Ibid., 17.

225 "I couldn't see": Ibid., 19.

225 "city on an eye": Ibid., 20.

225 "Because of what I": Ibid., 22.

225 "It's a hell of a look": Ibid., 54.

226 "I didn't": Ibid., 104.

226 "every single day": Ibid., 103.

226 "we, lot of guys": Ibid., 105.

226 "And then": Ibid., 107.

226 "Someday when I": Ibid., 110.

226 "There won't": Ibid., 111.

226 "our own house": Ibid., 200.

226 "But we're not": Ibid., 100.

226 "it's not Rotney": Ibid., 101.

226 "and their sufferings": George Sanchez, "Reading Reginald Denny," 388.

226 "Did I deserve": Smith, 139.

227 "riot-related": Ibid., 192.

227 "numbers": Ibid., 194.

227 "Oh, here we go": Ibid., 195.

227 "There may be": Ibid., 189–90.

228 "The family": Ibid., 190.

228 "living dead": Ibid., 256.

228 "burst out": Ibid., 249.

228 "I've lost": Ibid., 195.

230 "war of the races": Pitt, 166.

230 "the story of race": Smith, xxi.

230 "anonymous": Griffith, vi.

230 "Not even water": Ibid., 306.

230 "And like that corn": Ibid., 309.

231 "as much a Latino": Gooding-Williams, 144.

231 "no other area": Muller, 53.

231 "In general": *New York Times,* October 30, 1994.

231 "economic benefits": Muller, 157.

231 "Every sector": *New York Times,* March 23, 1996.

232 "hobble away": Luis Rodriguez, 245–46.

232 "fire for me": Ibid., 247.

232 "Perhaps the most": Soto, *Living Up the Street,* 12.

232 "a small flame": Ibid., 11.

232 "My skin is brown": Richard Rodriguez, *Hunger of Memory,* 113.

232 "With *los gringos*": Ibid., 113.

232 "dark . . . ugly": Ibid., 125.

233 "I used to stare": *Days of Obligation,* 1.

233 "The Achievement of Desire": *Hunger of Memory,* 41.

233 "I was 11 years": Luis Rodriguez, 247.

233 "As I watched": Ibid., 6.

233 "I hated school": Ibid., 100.

233 "You can't be": Ibid., 47.

233 "The Watts Rebellion": Ibid., 164.

234 "There's a small": Ibid., 251.

EPILOGUE

241 "slow but sure": *Working Days,* 25.

BIBLIOGRAPHY

Abelmann, Nancy, and John Lie. *Blue Dreams: Korean Americans and the Los Angeles Riots*. Cambridge: Harvard University Press, 1995.

Acuna, Rodolfo. *A Community Under Siege: A Chronicle of Chicanos East of the Los Angeles River, 1945–1975*. Los Angeles: Chicano Studies Research Center, 1984.

Adams, Ansel. *An Autobiography*. Boston: Little, Brown, 1985.

———. *Ansel Adams: Letters and Images, 1916–1984*. Boston: Little, Brown, 1988.

———. *Born Free and Equal*. New York: U.S. Camera, 1944.

———. *Yosemite and the Range of Light*. Boston: New York Graphic Society, 1979.

Adams, Henry. *Novels, Mont Saint Michel, and the Education*. New York: Library of America, 1983.

Alarcón, Norma, et al. *Chicana Critical Issues*. Berkeley: Third Woman Press, 1993.

———. *Sexuality of Latinas*. Berkeley: Third Woman Press, 1993.

Allen, Jennifer. "Boys: Hanging with the Spur Posse." *Rolling Stone,* July 8–22, 1993.

American Me (film). Universal, 1992.

Anderson, Edgar. *Plants, Man, and Life*. Berkeley: University of California Press, 1952.

Anzaldúa, Gloria. *Borderlands/La Frontera: The New Mestiza*. San Francisco: Spinsters/Aunt Lute, 1982.

Armor, John, and Peter Wright. *Manzanar*. Commentary by John Hersey and photographs by Ansel Adams. New York: Times Books, 1988.

Arnold, Mary Elliott, and Mabel Reed. *In the Land of the Grasshopper Song: Two Women in the Klamath River Indian Country in 1908–09*. 1957; rpt. Lincoln: University of Nebraska Press, 1980.

Ashton, Dore. *Noguchi: East and West*. New York: Knopf, 1991.

Atherton, Gertrude. *California: An Intimate History*. New York: Harper Bros., 1914.

Austin, Mary. *Earth Horizon*. Boston: Houghton Mifflin, 1932.

————. *The Ford*. Boston: Houghton Mifflin, 1917.

————. *Stories from the Country of Lost Borders*. 1903 and 1909; rpt. New Brunswick: Rutgers University Press, 1987. Contains *The Land of Little Rain* and *Lost Borders*.

Bailey, Paul. *City in the Sun: The Japanese Concentration Camp at Poston, Arizona*. Los Angeles: Western Lore Press, 1971.

Baker, Houston A., Jr., ed. *Three American Literatures: Essays in Chicano, Native American, and Asian-American Literature for Teachers of American Literature*. New York: Modern Language Association, 1982.

Bakker, Elna S. *An Island Called California*. Berkeley: University of California Press, 1971.

Bancroft, Hubert Howe. *History of California*. 7 vols. San Francisco: History Co., 1884–89.

————. *Literary Industries*. San Francisco: History Co., 1890.

————. *Pastoral California*. San Francisco: History Co., 1888.

————. *Retrospection*. New York: Bancroft Co., 1913.

————. *Some Cities and San Francisco Resurgam*. New York: Bancroft Co., 1907.

Banham, Reyner. *Los Angeles: The Architecture of Four Ecologies*. New York: Harper & Row, 1971.

Barrio, Raymond. *The Plum Plum Pickers*. New York: Harper & Row, 1969.

Bean, Walton. *California: An Interpretive History*. New York: McGraw-Hill, 1968.

Beasley, Delilah. *The Negro Trail Blazers of California*. 1919; rpt. San Francisco: R and E Research Associates, 1968.

Beck, Warren A., and David A. Williams. *California: A History of the Golden State*. Garden City, N.Y.: Doubleday, 1972.

Bidwell, John. *Echoes of the Past*. 1890; rpt. Chicago: Lakeside Press, 1928.

Bierce, Ambrose. "The Haunted Valley" (1871). In *The Collected Works of Ambrose Bierce,* vol. 3. Neale Publishing Co., 1910.

Boggs, Mae. *My Playhouse Was a Concord Coach: An Anthology of Newspaper Clippings and Documents Relating to Those Who Made California History During the Years 1822–1888*. Oakland, Calif.: Howell-North Press, 1942.

Bolton, Herbert Eugene. *Fray Juan Crespi: Missionary Explorer of the Pacific Coast, 1769–1774*. Berkeley: University of California Press, 1927.

Borthwick, J. D. *Three Years in California*. 1857; rpt. Oakland, Calif.: Biobooks, 1948.

Bradley, A. C. *Oxford Lectures in Poetry*. London: Macmillan, 1907.

Brady, John. *The Craft of the Screenwriter: Interviews with Six Celebrated Screenwriters*. New York: Simon & Schuster, 1981.

Brooks, Van Wyck. *The Ordeal of Mark Twain*. New York: Dutton, 1920.

Browne, J. Ross. *Crusoe's Island*. New York: Harper Bros., 1864.

Bruff, J. Goldsborough. *Gold Rush*. (originally published 1849–51); rpt. New York: Columbia University Press, 1944.

Bryant, Edwin. *What I Saw in California*. 1848; rpt. Minneapolis: Ross & Haines, 1967.

Bulosan, Carlos. *America Is in the Heart*. New York: Harcourt Brace, 1946.

Burbank, Luther. *Luther Burbank*, vol. 8. New York: P. F. Collier & Son, 1921.

Burnett, Peter H. *Recollections and Opinions of an Old Pioneer*. 1880; rpt. New York: Da Capo Press, 1969.

Burns, Walter Noble. *The Robin Hood of El Dorado: The Saga of Joaquin Murietta, Famous Outlaw of California's Age of Gold*. New York: Coward-McCann, 1932.

Butler, Anne M. *Daughters of Joy, Sisters of Misery: Prostitutes in the American West, 1865–90*. Chicago: University of Illinois Press, 1985.

Cain, James M. *The Postman Always Rings Twice*. New York: Knopf, 1934.

California and the Oriental: Japanese, Chinese, and Hindu. 1922; rpt. San Francisco: R and E Research Associates, 1970.

Campbell, Bebe Moore. *Brothers and Sisters*. New York: G. P. Putnam's Sons, 1994.

Carghill, Oscar. *The Big Four: The Story of Huntington, Stanford, Hopkins, and Crocker*. New York: Knopf, 1941.

Carver, Raymond. *What We Talk About When We Talk About Love*. New York: Knopf, 1981.

Cervantes, Lorna Dee. *Emplumada*. Pittsburgh: University of Pittsburgh Press, 1981.

Chalfant, Willie Arthur. *The Story of Inyo*. Bishop, Calif.: privately printed, 1922; rev. ed., 1933.

Chan, Jeffrey Paul, Frank Chin, Lawson Fusao Inada, and Shawn Wong. *The Big AIIIEEEEE! An Anthology of Chinese American and Japanese American Literature*. New York: Meridian, 1991.

Chan, Sucheng. *This Bittersweet Soil: The Chinese in California Agriculture, 1860–1910*. Berkeley: University of California Press, 1986.

Chandler, Raymond. *The Big Sleep*. 1939; rpt. New York: Random House, 1976.

———. *The Little Sister*. 1949; rpt. New York: Ballantine, 1971.

Chang, Edward T., and Russell C. Leong. *Los Angeles—Struggles Toward Multiethnic Community: Asian American, African American, and Latino Perspectives*. Seattle: University of Washington Press, 1994.

Chartkoff, Joseph L., and Kerry Kona Chartkoff. *The Archaeology of California*. Stanford, Calif.: Stanford University Press, 1984.

Cheung, King-Kok, and Stan Yogi, eds. *Asian American Literature: An Annotated Bibliography*. New York: Modern Language Association, 1988.

Chinatown (film). Paramount, 1974.

Chinese Immigration. Sacramento: California State Printing Office, 1876; rpt. San Francisco: R and E Research Associates, 1970.

Chu, Louis. *Eat a Bowl of Tea*. New York: Lyle Stuart, 1961.

Cisneros, Sandra. *The House on Mango Street*. New York: Vintage, 1991.

Clappe, Louise. *The Shirley Letters*, 1854–55; rpt. Salt Lake City: Peregrine Smith, 1970.

Cleland, Robert Glass. *From Wilderness to Empire: A History of California*. Glen S. Dunke, ed. New York: Knopf, 1967.

Cohen, Nathan. *The Los Angeles Riots: A Socio-Psychological Study*. New York: Praeger, 1970.

Colton, Walter. *Three Years in California*. New York: A. S. Barnes, 1850.

Coolidge, Mary Roberts. *Chinese Immigration*. New York: Henry Holt, 1909.

Cook, S. F. *The Conflict Between the California Indian and White Civilization*. Ibero-American, nos. 21, 22, and 23. Berkeley: University of California Press, 1943.

Dana, Richard Henry. *Two Years Before the Mast* and "Twenty-Four Years After." 1840 and 1869; rpt. New York: Penguin, 1981.

Daniels, Roger. *Coming to America: A History of Immigration and Ethnicity in American Life*. New York: HarperCollins, 1990.

Davidson, Michael. *The San Francisco Renaissance: Poetics and Community at Mid-Century*. Cambridge: Cambridge University Press, 1989.

Davis, Margaret Leslie. *Rivers in the Desert: William Mulholland and the Inventing of Los Angeles*. New York: HarperCollins, 1993.

Davis, Mike. *City of Quartz: Excavating the Future in Los Angeles*. 1990; rpt. New York: Viking, 1992.

Davis, Robert Murray. *Steinbeck: A Collection of Critical Essays*. Englewood Cliffs, N.J.: Prentice-Hall, 1972.

De La Guerra (Ord), Maria de las Angustias. *Occurrences in Hispanic California*. 1878. Translated and edited by Francis Price and William H. Ellison. Washington, D.C.: Academy of American Franciscan History, 1956.

De La Torre, Adela, and Beatriz M. Pesquera. *Building with Our Hands: New Directions in Chicana Studies*. Berkeley: University of California Press, 1993.

Delano, Alonzo. *Old Block's Sketch-Book; or, Tales of California Life*. 1856; rpt. Santa Ana, Calif.: Fine Arts Press, 1947.

Didion, Joan. *After Henry*. New York: Simon & Schuster, 1992.

————. "The Golden Land." *New York Review of Books*. October 21, 1993.

————. *Slouching Towards Bethlehem*. 1968; rpt. New York: Farrar, Straus and Giroux, 1990.

————. "Trouble in Lakewood." *New Yorker*. June 26, 1993.

————. *The White Album*. New York: Simon & Schuster, 1979.

Dobie, Charles Caldwell. *San Francisco: A Pageant*. New York: Appleton-Century, 1933.

Dooner, Pierton W. *Last Days of the Republic*. 1880; rpt. New York: Arno Press, 1978.

Dorney, P. S. "A Prophecy Partly Verified." *Overland Monthly,* vol. 7 (March 1886), 1231–34.

Double Indemnity (film). Paramount, 1944.

Eaton, Edith Maud. *Mrs. Spring Fragrance*. Chicago: A. C. McClurg & Co., 1912.

Egli, Ida Rae. *No Rooms of Their Own: Women Writers of Early California*. Berkeley, Calif.: Heydey Books, 1992.

Ellroy, James. *The Big Nowhere*. New York: Mysterious Press, 1988.

Elman, Richard. *Ill-At-Ease in Compton*. New York: Pantheon, 1967.

Englehardt, Fr. Zephyrin. *San Gabriel Mission and the Beginnings of Los Angeles*. Chicago: Franciscan Herald Press, 1927.

Fages, Pedro. *A Historical, Political, and Natural Description of California by Pedro Fages, Soldier of Spain*. 1775; rpt. Herbert Ingram Priestley, ed. Berkeley: University of California Press, 1937.

Falling Down (film). Warner Bros., 1993.

Farnham, Eliza. *California In-doors and Out*. New York: Dix, Edwards, 1856.

Fitzgerald, F. Scott. *The Last Tycoon*. New York: Scribners, 1941.

Fogelson, Robert M. *The Fragmented Metropolis: Los Angeles, 1880–1930*. Cambridge: Harvard University Press, 1967.

————. *The Los Angeles Riots of 1965*. New York: Arno Press, 1969.

Foner, Philip S., and Daniel Rosenberg, eds. *Racism, Dissent, and Asian Americans from 1850 to the Present*. Westport, Conn.: Greenwood Press, 1993.

Frémont, John Charles. *The Expeditions of John Charles Frémont*. Vol. 1, *Travels from 1838 to 1844*. Donald Jackson and Mary Lee Spence, ed. Urbana, Ill.: University of Illinois Press, 1970; vol. 2, *The Bear Flag Revolt and the Court-Martial*. Urbana, Ill.: Jackson and Spence, 1973.

Frost, Robert. *The Poetry of Robert Frost*. Edward Connery Lathem, ed. New York: Holt Rinehart, 1969.

Galarza, Ernesto. *Barrio Boy*. Notre Dame, Ind.: University of Notre Dame Press, 1971.

Geiger, Maynard, ed. and trans. "Questionnaire of the Spanish Government in 1812 Concerning the Native Culture of the California Mission Indians," from *Preguntas y Respuetas*. *The Americas,* vol 5. (April 1949), 474–90.

Genthe, Arnold. *As I Remember*. New York: Reynal & Hitchcock, 1936.

———. *Pictures of Old Chinatown*. 1908; rpt. New York: Dover, 1984.

George, Henry. *Progress and Poverty; An Inquiry into the Cause of Industrial Depressions, and of Increase of Want with Increase of Wealth—The Remedy*. San Francisco: W. M. Hinton & Co., 1879.

Goode, Kenneth G. *California's Black Pioneers*. Santa Barbara, Calif.: McNally & Loftin, 1974.

Gooding-Williams, Robert. *Reading Rodney King / Reading Urban Uprising*. New York: Routledge, 1993.

Griffith, Beatrice. *American Me*. 1948; rpt. Westport, Conn.: Greenwood Press, 1973.

Grove, Nancy, and Diane Botwick. *The Sculpture of Isamu Noguchi, 1924–1979*. New York: Garland, 1980.

Gurr, Ted Robert. *Why Men Rebel*. Princeton, N.J.: Princeton University Press, 1971.

Haas, Lisbeth. *Conquest and Historical Identities in California, 1769–1936*. Berkeley: University of California Press, 1995.

Hagedorn, Jessica, ed. *Charlie Chan Is Dead: An Anthology of Contemporary Asian American Fiction*. New York: Penguin, 1993.

Hammett, Dashiell. *The Continental Op*. New York: Random House, 1974.

———. *The Big Knockover*. New York: Random House, 1966.

Haraszthy, Agoston. *Grape Culture, Wines, and Wine-Making*. In *Father of California Wine: Agoston Haraszthy*. New York: Harper & Bros., 1862; rpt. Theodore Schoenman, ed. Santa Barbara, Calif.: Capra Press, 1979.

Harlow, Neal. *California Conquered*. Berkeley: University of California Press, 1982.

Hart, James D. *A Companion to California*. New York: Oxford University Press, 1978.

Harte, Bret. *Selected Stories and Sketches*. David Wyatt, ed. Oxford: Oxford University Press, 1995.

Hass, Robert. *Field Guide*. New Haven, Conn.: Yale University Press, 1973.

———. *Praise*. New York: Ecco, 1979.

Hastings, Lansford. *Emigrant's Guide to Oregon and California*. Cincinnati: George Conclin, 1845.

Heizer, Robert F., and Alan J. Almquist. *The Other Californians: Prejudice and Discrimination Under Spain, Mexico, and the United States to 1920*. Berkeley: University of California Press, 1971.

Helper, Hinton Rowland. *The Land of Gold: Reality Versus Fiction*. Baltimore: Henry Taylor, 1855.

Herr, Michael. *Dispatches*. New York: Knopf, 1977.

Herrera, Juan Felipe. *Love After the Riots*. Willimantic, Conn.: Curbstone Press, 1996.

Herrera-Sobek, Marío, ed. *Reconstructing a Chicano/a Literary Heritage*. Tucson: University of Arizona Press, 1993.

Himes, Chester. *If He Hollers Let Him Go*. 1945; rpt. New York: Thunder's Mouth Press, 1986.

———. *The Quality of Hurt: The Autobiography of Chester Himes*. vol. 1. New York: Doubleday, 1972.

Himmelwright, A.L.A. *The San Francisco Earthquake and Fire*. New York: Roebling Construction Co., 1906.

Hittell, John. *The Resources of California*. San Francisco: A. Roman & Co., 1863.

Hoffman, Abraham. *Vision or Villainy: Origins of the Owens Valley Water Controversy*. College Station: Texas A & M University Press, 1981.

Holliday, J. S. *The World Rushed In: The California Gold Rush Experience*. New York: Simon & Schuster, 1981.

Holt, Hamilton, ed. *The Life Stories of Undistinguished Americans as Told by Themselves*. 1906; 2d ed., New York: Routledge, 1990.

Horkheimer, Max, and Theodor W. Adorno. *Dialectic of Enlightenment*. 1944. Translated by John Cumming. New York: Herder and Herder, 1977.

Horne, Gerald. *Fire This Time: The Watts Uprising and the 1960s*. Charlottesville: University of Virginia Press, 1995.

Horsman, Reginald. *Race and Manifest Destiny: The Origins of American Racial Anglo-Saxonism*. Cambridge, Mass.: Harvard University Press, 1981.

Houston, Jeanne Wakatsuki, and James D. Houston. *Farewell to Manzanar*. Boston: Houghton Mifflin, 1973.

Houston, Velina Haso. *The Politics of Life: Four Plays by Asian American Women*. Philadelphia: Temple University Press, 1993.

Huerta, Jorge A. *Chicano Theater: Themes and Forms*. Ypsilanti, Mich.: Bilingual Press, 1988.

Hulme, Kathryn. *We Lived As Children*. New York: Knopf, 1938.

Jackson, Helen Hunt. *A Century of Dishonor*. 1881; new ed. Boston: Little, Brown, 1903.

———. *Ramona*. Boston: Roberts Bros., 1884.

Jacobs, Harriet. *Incidents in the Life of a Slave Girl*. 1861; rpt. Cambridge, Mass.: Harvard University Press, 1987.

James, William. *The Letters of William James,* vol. 11. Henry James, ed. Boston: Atlantic Monthly Press, 1920.

———. *Memories and Studies*. New York: Longmans, Green, & Co., 1911.

Jeffrey, Julie Ray. *Frontier Women: The Trans-Mississippi West, 1840–1880*. New York: Hill and Wang, 1979.

Johnson, Marilynn S. *The Second Gold Rush: Oakland and the East Bay in World War II*. Berkeley: University of California Press, 1993.

Kadohata, Cynthia. *The Floating World*. New York: Penguin, 1989.

Kahrl, William L. *Water and Power: The Conflict Over Los Angeles' Water Supply in the Owens Valley*. Berkeley: University of California Press, 1982.

Kim, Elaine. *Asian American Literature: An Introduction to the Writings and Their Social Contexts*. Philadelphia: Temple University Press, 1982.

King, Clarence. "Catastrophism and the Evolution of Environment." Printed in *American Naturalist* 9 (1877) as "Catastrophism and Evolution."

————. *Mountaineering in the Sierra Nevada*. 1872 and 1874; rpt. Lincoln: University of Nebraska Press, 1970.

Kingston, Maxine Hong. *China Men*. New York: Knopf, 1980.

————. *The Woman Warrior*. New York: Vintage, 1977.

Kirsch, Robert, and William S. Murphy. *West of the West: The Story of California from the Conquistadores to the Great Earthquake, as Described by the Men and Women Who Were There*. New York: Dutton, 1967.

Klein, Norman M., and Martin J. Schiesl, eds. *20th Century Los Angeles: Power, Promotion, and Social Conflict*. Claremont, Calif.: Regina Books, 1990.

Koon, Sgt. Stacey C., LAPD. *Presumed Guilty: The Tragedy of the Rodney King Affair*. Washington, D.C.: Regnery Gateway, 1992.

Kroeber, A. C. *Handbook of the Indians of California*. 1925; rpt. St. Clair Shores, Mich.: Scholarly Press, 1972.

Kroeber, Theodora. *Ishi in Two Worlds: A Biography of the Last Wild Indian in North America*. Berkeley: University of California Press, 1967.

Lai Chun-Chuen. *Remarks of the Chinese Merchants of San Francisco, Upon Governor Bigler's Message*. San Francisco: Office of the Oriental, 1855.

Lai, H. Mark, Genny Lim, and Judy Young. *Island: Poetry and History of Chinese Immigrants on Angel Island, 1910–1940*. San Francisco: San Francisco Study Center, 1980.

Lamar, Howard. "Rites of Passage: Young Men and Their Families in the Overland Trails Experience, 1843–69." In *"Soul Butter and Hog Wash" and Other Essays on the American West*. Thomas G. Alexander, ed. Provo, Utah: Brigham Young University Press, 1978.

Langum, David J. *Law and Community on the Mexican California Frontier*. Norman: University of Oklahoma Press, 1987.

Latta, Frank. *Joaquín Murietta and His Horse Gangs*. Santa Cruz, Calif.: Bear State Books, 1980.

Lawrence, D. H. *Studies in Classic American Literature*. 1923; rpt. New York: Albert and Charles Boni, 1930.

Lee, Gus. *China Boy*. New York: Dutton, 1991.

Leonard, Zenas. *Narrative of the Adventures of Zenas Leonard*. 1839; rpt. Lincoln: University of Nebraska Press, 1978.

Limerick, Patricia Nelson. *The Legacy of Conquest: The Unbroken Past of the American West*. New York: Norton, 1987.

Ling, Amy. *Between Worlds: Women Writers of Chinese Ancestry*. New York: Pergamon Press, 1990.

Lipsitz, George. "The Possessive Investment in Whiteness: Radicalized Social Democracy and the 'White' Problem in American Studies. *American Quarterly,* vol 47 (September 1995), 369–87.

London, Jack. *The Complete Stories of Jack London*. Vols. 1, 2, and 3. Earle Labor, Robert C. Leitz III, and I. Milo Shepard, eds. Stanford: Stanford University Press, 1993.

Lopez, Tiffany. *Growing Up Chicana/o*. New York: William Morrow, 1993.

Lopez-Medina, Sylvia. *Cantora*. New York: Ballantine, 1992.

Los Angeles Times. "Attempt to Blunt Video Seen as Key to Trial." January 16, 1992.

——. "Four Suspects Seized in Attacks on Women." June 2, 1943.

——. "Gangs Warned 'Kid Gloves Off!' " August 4, 1942.

——. "Jury Delves into Boy Gang Terror Wave." August 4, 1942.

——. "King Tells of Beating, Racial Taunts by Police." January 16, 1992.

——. "One Killed and 10 Hurt in Boy 'Wars.' " August 3, 1942.

——. "One Slain and 10 Beaten by Boy Gang Terrorists." August 3, 1942.

——. "Three Teen-Age Girls Held in Boy-Gang Slaying Inquiry." August 5, 1942.

——. "The Voices of the City." *Calendar*. April 25, 1993.

——. "Youth Gangs Leading Cause of Delinquencies." June 2, 1942.

——. "Zoot Suiters Learn Lesson in Fights with Servicemen." June 7, 1943.

Lotchin, Roger W. *Fortress California, 1910–1961. From Warfare to Welfare*. New York: Oxford, 1992.

Lundquist, James. *Chester Himes*. New York: Unger, 1976.

McCunn, Ruthanne Lum. *Thousand Pieces of Gold: A Biographical Novel*. Boston: Beacon Press, 1988.

McGilligan, Patrick. *Jack's Life: A Biography of Jack Nicholson*. New York: Norton, 1994.

McPhee, John. *Assembling California*. New York: Farrar, Straus and Giroux, 1993.

McShane, Frank. *The Life of Raymond Chandler*. New York: Columbia University Press, 1981.

McWilliams, Carey. *California: The Great Exception*. 1949; rpt. Westport, Conn.: Greenwood, 1971.

————. *North from Mexico*. New York: Greenwood Press, 1968.

————. *Southern California: An Island on the Land*. 1946; rpt. Santa Barbara, Calif.: Peregrine Smith, 1973.

Machado, Juana (de Ridington). *Times Gone By in Alta California*. 1878. Translated by Raymond S. Brandes. *The Historical Society of Southern California Quarterly,* vol. 16 (September 1959), 195–240.

Madhubuti, Haki R. *Why L.A. Happened: Implications of the '92 Los Angeles Rebellion*. Chicago: Third World Press, 1993.

The Man Who Shot Liberty Valance (film). Paramount, 1962.

Marberry, M. M. *Splendid Poseur: Joaquin Miller—American Poet*. New York: Thomas Y. Crowell, 1953.

Marchand, B. *The Emergence of Los Angeles: Population and Housing in the City of Dreams, 1940–1970*. London: Pion, 1986.

Marchetti, Gina. *Romance and the "Yellow Peril": Race, Sex, and Discourse Strategies in Hollywood Fiction*. Berkeley: University of California Press, 1993.

Maryatt, Frank. *Mountains and Molehills*. 1855; rpt. Philadelphia: Lippincott, 1962.

Mayo, Morrow. *Los Angeles*. New York: Knopf, 1933.

Mazon, Mauricio. *The Zoot-Suit Riots: The Psychology of Symbolic Annihilation*. Austin: University of Texas Press, 1984.

Meier, Matt S., and Feliciano Rivera. *The Chicanos: A History of Mexican Americans*. New York: Hill and Wang, 1972.

————. *Readings on La Raza: The Twentieth Century*. New York: Hill and Wang, 1974.

Memorial, Six Chinese Companies: An Address to the Senate and House of Representatives of the United States. 1877; rpt. San Francisco: R and E Research Associates, 1970.

Miller, Joaquin. *Complete Poetical Works of Joaquin Miller*. New York: Arno Press, 1972.

————. *Life Amongst the Modocs: Unwritten History*. London: Michael Bentley, 1873.

————. *Songs of the Sierras*. London: Longmans, Green, Reader, and Dyer, 1871.

Miller, Stuart C. *The Unwelcome Immigrant: The American Image of the Chinese, 1785–1882*. Berkeley: University of California Press, 1969.

Milliken, Stephen F. *Chester Himes: A Critical Appraisal*. Columbia: University of Missouri Press, 1976.

Mirikitani, Janice. *We the Dangerous: New and Selected Poems*. London: Virago, 1995.

Monroy, Douglas. *Thrown Among Strangers: The Making of Mexican Culture in Frontier California*. Berkeley: University of California Press, 1990.

Montalvo, Garci Rodriguez de. *Las Sergas de Esplandían*. 1510. See *The Labors of the Very Brave Knight Esplandían.* Translated by William Thomas Little. Binghamton, N.Y.: Medieval and Renaissance Texts and Studies, 1992.

Moquin, Wayne, ed. *A Documentary History of Mexican Americans.* New York: Praeger, 1971.

Mora, Pat. *Nepantla: Essays from the Land in the Middle.* Albuquerque: University of New Mexico Press, 1993.

Moraga, Cherríe. *Heroes and Saints & Other Plays.* Albuquerque: West End Press, 1994.

————. *Loving in the War Years.* Boston: South End Press, 1983.

Moraga, Cherríe, and Gloria Anzaldúa, eds. *This Bridge Called My Back: Writings by Radical Women of Color.* Watertown, Mass.: Persephone Press, 1981.

Mori, Toshio. *Yokohama, California.* 1949; rpt. Seattle: University of Washington Press, 1985.

Morris, Jan. *Destinations.* New York: Oxford University Press, 1980.

Mosley, Walter. *Devil in a Blue Dress.* New York: Norton, 1990.

Muir, John. *The Mountains of California.* 1894 and 1911; rpt. New York: Penguin, 1985.

————. *To Yosemite and Beyond.* Robert Engberg and Donald Wesling, eds. Madison: University of Wisconsin Press, 1980.

————. *The Yosemite.* 1912; rpt. Garden City, N.Y.: Natural History Press, 1976.

Muller, Thomas, and Thomas J. Espenshade. *The Fourth Wave: California's Newest Immigrants.* Washington, D.C.: Urban Institute Press, 1985.

Munz, Philip A., in collaboration with David D. Keck. *A California Flora.* 1959; rpt. Berkeley: University of California Press, 1973.

Muybridge, Eadweard. *Animal Locomotion.* Philadelphia: Lippincott, 1888.

Nabokov, Peter. *Native American Testimony: Chronicle of Indian-White Relations from Prophecy to the Present, 1492–1992.* New York: Viking, 1991.

Nadeau, Remi. *The Water Seekers.* Garden City, N.Y.: Doubleday, 1950.

Nash, Gerald D. *The American West Transformed: The Impact of the Second World War.* Bloomington: Indiana University Press, 1985.

————. *World War II and the West: Reshaping the Economy.* Lincoln: University of Nebraska Press, 1990.

Nee, Victor G., and Brett de Bary. *Longtime Californ': A Documentary Study of an American Chinatown.* 1972; rpt. Stanford: Stanford University Press, 1986.

Nevins, Allan. *Frémont: Pathmarker of the West.* New York: D. Appleton-Century, 1939.

Newhall, Nancy. *Ansel Adams: The Eloquent Light.* New York: Harper & Row, 1980.

New York Times. "In California, the Numbers Add Up to Anxiety." October 30, 1994.

———. "Parallel Immigration Debates Plague G.O.P. and San Diego." March 23, 1996.

Ng, Fae Myenne. *Bone.* New York: Harper, 1993.

Niiya, Brian, ed. *Japanese American History.* New York: Facts on File, 1993.

Noguchi, Isamu. *A Sculptor's World.* New York: Harper & Row, 1968.

———. "Trouble Among Japanese Americans." *New Republic,* vol. 108 (1943), 142–43.

Noguchi, Yone. *American Diary of a Japanese Girl.* New York: Frederick A. Stokes Co., 1902.

———. *Selected Writings of Yone Noguchi,* vols. 1 and 2. Yoshinobu Hakutani, ed. Rutherford, N.J.: Farleigh Dickinson University Press, 1990.

———. *The Story of Yone Noguchi.* Philadelphia: George W. Jacobs & Co., 1915.

Nordskog, Andrae B. *Communication to the California Legislature Relating to the Owens Valley Situation.* Sacramento: State Printing Office, 1931.

Norris, Frank. *Novels and Essays.* New York: Library of America, 1986.

———. *The Third Circle and a Deal in Wheat.* Garden City, N.Y.: Doubleday, Doran & Co., 1928.

Okada, John. *No-No Boy.* 1957; rpt. Seattle: Combined Asia Resources Project, 1976.

Ostrom, Vincent. *Water and Politics: A Study of Water Policies and Administration in the Development of Los Angeles.* Los Angeles: Haynes Foundation, 1953.

Padilla, Genaro M. *My History, Not Yours: The Formation of Mexican American Autobiography.* Madison: University of Wisconsin Press, 1993.

Pagus, Jean. *The Real Japanese California.* 1937; rpt. San Francisco: R and E Research Associates, 1971.

Park, Robert E. *Orientals and Their Cultural Adjustment.* Social Science Institute, Fisk University. Nashville, 1946.

Pascoe, Peggy. *Relations of Rescue: The Search for Moral Authority in the American West, 1874–1934.* New York: Oxford University Press, 1990.

Pattie, James Ohio. *The Personal Narrative.* 1831; rpt. Philadelphia: Lippincott, 1962.

Paz, Octavio. *The Labyrinth of Solitude: Life and Thought in Mexico.* 1950; rpt. New York: Grove Press, 1961.

Perez, Eulalia. "An Old Woman and Her Recollections." 1877. In *Three Memoirs of Mexican California.* Vivian C. Fisher, ed. Berkeley: University of California Press, 1988.

Pitt, Leonard. *The Decline of the Californios: A Social History of the Spanish-*

Speaking Californians, 1846–1890. Berkeley: University of California Press, 1966.

Polanski, Roman. *Roman, By Polanski.* New York: William Morrow, 1984.

Ponce, Mary Helen. *Hoyt Street: An Autobiography.* Albuquerque: University of New Mexico Press, 1993.

Powell, Lawrence Clark. *California Classics.* Santa Barbara, Calif.: Capra Press, 1971.

Preston, William C. *Vanishing Landscapes: Land and Life in the Tulare Lake Basin.* Berkeley: University of California Press, 1981.

Pynchon, Thomas. *The Crying of Lot 49.* New York: Lippincott, 1966.

———. *Gravity's Rainbow.* New York: Viking, 1973.

———. "A Journey into the Heart of Watts." *New York Times Magazine.* June 12, 1966.

———. *Vineland.* Boston: Little, Brown, 1990.

Rebolledo, Tey Diana, and Eliana S. Rivero, eds. *Infinite Divisions: An Anthology of Chicana Literature.* Tucson: University of Arizona Press, 1993.

Reed, Ishmael. *Calafia: The California Poetry.* Berkeley: Y' Bird Books, 1979.

Reisner, Mark. *Cadillac Desert: The American West and Its Disappearing Water.* New York: Viking, 1986.

Ridge, John Rollin. *The Life and Adventures of Joaquín Murieta.* Joseph Henry Jackson, ed. Norman: University of Oklahoma Press, 1955.

Rios, Isabella. *Victuum.* Ventura, Calif.: Diana-Etna, 1976.

Robinson, Alfred. *Life in California.* 1846; rpt. New York: Da Capo, 1969.

Robinson, Marilynne. *Housekeeping.* New York: Bantam, 1980.

"The 'Rodney King' Case: What the Jury Saw in *California v. Powell.*" Produced by Jamie Adler. Courtroom Television Network, 1992.

Rodriguez, Joe. *Oddsplayer.* Houston: Arte Publico, 1989.

Rodriguez, Luis. *Always Running: La Vida Loca—Gang Days in L.A.* New York: Penguin, 1993.

Rodriguez, Richard. *Days of Obligation: An Argument with My Mexican Father.* New York: Knopf, 1992.

———. *Hunger of Memory: The Education of Richard Rodriguez.* New York: Knopf, 1982.

Rosaldo, Renato. *Culture and Truth: The Remaking of Social Analysis.* Stanford, Calif.: Stanford University Press, 1989.

Royce, Josiah. *California; from the Conquest in 1846 to the Second Vigilance Committee in San Francisco.* 1886; rpt. New York: Knopf, 1948.

———. *The Feud of Oakfield Creek.* Boston: Houghton Mifflin, 1887.

———. *The Philosophy of Loyalty.* New York: Macmillan, 1908.

———. *Race Questions, Provincialism, and Other American Problems.* New York: Macmillan, 1908.

Royce, Sarah. *A Frontier Lady: Recollections of the Gold Rush and Early California*. Ralph Henry Gabriel, ed. New Haven: Yale University Press, 1932.

Ruiz, Vicki. *Cannery Women, Cannery Lives: Mexican Women, Unionization, and the California Food Processing Industry, 1930–1950*. Albuquerque: University of New Mexico Press, 1987.

Salvidar, Ramon. *Chicano Narrative: The Dialectics of Difference*. Madison: University of Wisconsin Press, 1990.

San Francisco (film). Metro-Goldwyn-Mayer, 1936.

Sanchez, George J. *Becoming Mexican American: Ethnicity, Culture, and Identity in Chicano Los Angeles, 1900–1945*. New York: Oxford, 1993.

———. "Reading Reginald Denny: The Politics of Whiteness in the Late Twentieth Century." *American Quarterly*, vol. 47 (September 1995), 388–94.

Sanchez, Rosaura. *Telling Identities: The Californio Testimonios*. Minneapolis: University of Minnesota Press, 1995.

Sanchez, Thomas. *Angels Burning: Native Notes from the Land of Earthquake and Fire*. Santa Barbara, Calif.: Capra Press, 1987.

———. *Rabbit Boss*. New York: Knopf, 1973.

———. *Zoot Suit Murders*. New York: Dutton, 1978.

Sarris, Andrew. "Chinatown & Polanski-Towne Tilting Toward Tragedy." *Village Voice*. November 7, 1974.

Savage, William. *Blacks in the West*. Westport, Conn.: Greenwood Press, 1976.

Saxton, Alexander. *The Indispensable Enemy: Labor and the Anti-Chinese Movement in California*. Berkeley: University of California Press, 1971.

See, Carolyn. *Dreaming: Hard Luck and Good Times in America*. New York: Random House, 1995.

———. *Golden Days*. New York: McGraw-Hill, 1987.

———. *Making History*. Boston: Houghton Mifflin, 1991.

Serra, Junípero. *Writings of Junípero Serra*. 4 vols. Antonine Tibesar. Washington, D.C.: Academy of American Franciscan History, 1955.

Servin, Manuel P. *An Awakened Minority: Mexican-Americans*. New York: Macmillan, 1993.

Shakur, Sanyika. *Monster: The Autobiography of an L.A. Gang Member*. New York: Penguin, 1993.

Short Cuts (film). Warner Bros., 1992.

Sinclair, Upton. *Oil!* New York: Albert and Charles Boni, 1927.

Skerry, Peter. *Mexican Americans: The Ambivalent Minority*. New York: Macmillan, 1993.

Smith, Anna Deavere. *Twilight: Los Angeles, 1992*. New York: Doubleday, 1994.

Smith, Richard Candida. *Utopia and Dissent: Art, Poetry, and Politics in California*. Berkeley: University of California Press, 1995.

Snyder, Gary. *Myths & Texts*. New York: Totem Press, 1960.

Soja, Edward. W. *Postmodern Geographies: The Reassertion of Space in Critical Theory*. London: Verso, 1989.

Sommers, Joseph, and Tomas Ybarra-Fausto. *Modern Chicano Writers: A Collection of Critical Essays*. Englewood Cliffs, N.J.: Prentice-Hall, 1979.

Sone, Monica. *Nisei Daughter*. Boston: Little, Brown, 1953.

Song, Cathy. *Picture Bride*. New York: Yale University Press, 1983.

Soto, Gary. *California Childhood: Recollections and Stories of the Golden State*. Berkeley, Calif.: Creative Arts Book Co., 1988.

———. *Living Up the Street: Narrative Recollections*. San Francisco: Strawberry Hill Press, 1985.

———. *Pieces of the Heart: New Chicano Fiction*. San Francisco: Chronicle Books, 1993.

Speer, William. *The Oldest and the Newest Empire: China and the United States*. Chicago: National Publishing Co., 1870.

Springsteen, Bruce. *The Ghost of Tom Joad* (album). Columbia, 1995.

Starr, Kevin. *Americans and the California Dream: 1850–1915*. New York: Oxford University Press, 1973.

———. *Endangered Dreams: The Great Depression in California*. New York: Oxford University Press, 1996.

———. *Inventing the Dream: California through the Progressive Era*. New York: Oxford University Press, 1985.

———. *Material Dreams: Southern California through the 1920s*. New York: Oxford University Press, 1990.

Starr, M. B. *The Coming Struggle, or What the People of the Pacific Coast Think of the Coolie Invasion*. San Francisco: Bacon & Co., 1873.

Steinbeck, John. *East of Eden*. 1952; rpt. New York: Penguin Twentieth-Century Classics, 1992.

———. *The Grapes of Wrath*. 1939; rpt. New York: Penguin Twentieth-Century Classics, 1992.

———. *The Long Valley*. 1938; rpt. New York: Penguin Twentieth-Century Classics, 1995.

———. *Working Days: The Journals of The Grapes of Wrath*, ed. Robert DeMott. New York: Viking, 1989.

Stewart, George. *Fire*. New York: Random House, 1948.

———. *Ordeal by Hunger*. 1936; rpt. New York: Simon & Schuster, 1971.

———. *Storm*. New York: Random House, 1941.

Stillman, J.D.B. *The Horse in Motion*. Boston: James R. Osgood & Co., 1882.

Strong, Edward. K. *Japanese in California*. Stanford, Calif.: Stanford University Press, 1933.

Tac, Pablo. "Conversion de Los San Luiseños de la Alta California." *The Americas: A Quarterly Review of Inter-American History,* vol. 9 (July 1952), 87–106.

Takaki, Ronald. *Strangers from a Different Shore: A History of Asian Americans.* New York: Penguin, 1989.

Tan, Amy. *The Joy Luck Club.* New York: Putnam, 1989.

Taylor, Bayard. *El Dorado.* 1850; rpt. New York: Knopf, 1949.

———. *New Pictures from California.* 1862; rpt. Oakland, Calif.: Biobooks, 1941.

Time. "Zoot-Suit War." June 21, 1943.

Tong, Benson. *Unsubmissive Women: Chinese Prostitutes in Nineteenth-Century San Francisco.* Norman: University of Oklahoma Press, 1994.

Towne, Robert. "Chinatown." Third Draft: October 9, 1973. UCLA Extension.

Tuck, Ruth. *Not with the Fist: Mexican-Americans in a Southwest City.* New York: Harcourt Brace, 1946.

The Two Jakes (film). Paramount, 1990.

Tygiel, Jules. *The Great Los Angeles Swindle: Oil, Stocks, and Scandal During the Roaring Twenties.* New York: Oxford University Press, 1994.

Uchida, Yoshiko. *Desert Exile: The Uprooting of a Japanese American Family.* Seattle: University of Washington Press, 1982.

Unruh, John D., Jr. *The Plains Across: The Overland Emigrants and the Trans-Mississippi West, 1840–1860.* Urbana: University of Illinois Press, 1979.

Valdez, Luis. *Actos y El Theatro Campesino.* 1971; rpt. San Juan Bautista, Calif.: Menyah Productions, 1978.

———. *Zoot Suit and Other Plays.* Houston: Arte Publico Press, 1992.

Valdez, Luis, and Stan Steiner. *Aztlan: An Anthology of Mexican American Literature.* New York: Knopf, 1972.

Vallejo, Mariano. *Recuerdos historicos y personales tocante a la alta California.* Selections in *The Heath Anthology of American Literature,* vol. 1. Paul Lauter, ed. Lexington, Mass.: D.C. Heath & Co., 1990.

Villanueva, Alma Luz. *Naked Ladies.* Tempe, Ariz.: Bilingual Press, 1994.

Villanueva, Tino. *Scene from the Movie Giant.* Willimantic, Conn.: Curbstone Press, 1993.

Villarreal, José Antonio. *Pocho.* Garden City, N.Y.: Doubleday, 1970.

Waldie, D. J. *Holy Land.* New York: Norton, 1996.

Walker, Franklin. *San Francisco's Literary Frontier.* New York: Knopf, 1939.

Washington Post. "L.A.'s Unspoken Rule: Positively No Pessimists Allowed." January 27, 1994.

———. "King Is Awarded $3.8 Million in Los Angeles Police Beating." April 20, 1994.

———. "Lights! Camera! Action! Entertainment Revives Southern California." May 19, 1996.

———. "New Amateur Video Agitates L.A. Area." August 24, 1994.

———. "Redirecting of California's Water Proposed." December 16, 1993.

———. "Remembering Its Strengths, California Starts to Recover." June 22, 1994.

———. "Simpson Defense Decries 'Rush to Judgment.'" September 28, 1995.

Webber, Herbert John, and Leon Dexter Batchelor. *The Citrus Industry,* vol. 1. Berkeley, Calif.: University of California Press, 1943.

Weber, David J. *The Spanish Frontier in North America*. New Haven, Conn.: Yale University Press, 1993.

West, Nathaniel. *The Day of the Locust*. New York: Random House, 1939.

Weston, Edward. *California and the West*. New York: Duell, Sloan, & Pearce, 1940.

White, Richard. *"It's Your Misfortune and None of My Own": A History of the American West*. Norman: University of Oklahoma Press, 1991.

Williams, Stanley T. *The Spanish Background of American Literature*. New Haven, Conn.: Yale University Press, 1955.

Wong, Jade Snow. *Fifth Chinese Daughter*. New York: Harper & Brothers, 1950.

———. *No Chinese Stranger*. New York: Harper & Row, 1975.

Wong, Shawn. *Homebase*. New York: I. Reed, 1979.

Wu, William F. *The Yellow Peril: Chinese Americans in American Fiction, 1850–1940*. Hamden, Conn.: Archon Books, 1982.

Wyatt, David. *The Fall into Eden: Landscape and Imagination in California*. New York: Cambridge University Press, 1986.

Yamamoto, Hisaye. *"Seventeen Syllables."* King-Kok Cheung, ed. New Brunswick, N.J.: Rutgers University Press, 1994.

———. *Seventeen Syllables and Other Stories*. Latham, N.Y.: Kitchen Table: Women of Color Press, 1988.

Yamauchi, Wakako. *Songs My Mother Taught Me*. New York: Feminist Press at the City University of New York, 1994.

Yung, Judy. *Unbound Feet: A Social History of Chinese Women in San Francisco*. Berkeley: University of California Press, 1995.

INDEX

Italic page numbers indicate illustrations.

281